CANADA-

AN EVOLVING VISION

Samy Appadurai

authorHOUSE®

AuthorHouse™
1663 Liberty Drive
Bloomington, IN 47403
www.authorhouse.com
Phone: 1 (800) 839-8640

Published by AuthorHouse 08/11/2016

ISBN: 978-1-5246-1862-9 (sc)
ISBN: 978-1-5246-1860-5 (hc)
ISBN: 978-1-5246-1861-2 (e)

Library of Congress Control Number: 2016911414

Print information available on the last page.

CONTENTS

Tribute

On the 150th birthday

to

Canada

my beloved nation,
a miniature world,
with love, compassion, tolerance, acceptance and
caring in nature
and built on freedom and democracy

Samy Appadurai

FOREWORD

by
Mitch Engel, Barrister and Solicitor

It is my very great honour and privilege to call to your attention to Mr. Samy Appadurai, a man I have personally admired for many years. Mr. Samy Appadurai is a scholar, educator, community worker and activist, policy advocate and journalist. Samy Appadurai wears many hats in response to the many calls from those who are trying to determine the future course of this great nation.

It is imperative that we listen to someone who views matters both as an immigrant and as a patriotic Canadian who is grateful to and loves the land which gave him and many others like him refuge as it had with the waves of Scottish, Irish, and British immigrants which followed the French and those who continue to arrive to a land so beautifully described in Samy Appadurai's first book about Canada entitled "Canada—the Meat of the World Sandwich" (2009).

The supreme value of this book is the author's deep love and concern for the future of this country which gave him and continues to give him and many others abundant opportunities to fully participate in our society and contribute to its future. It is delightful to see how Samy repeats the oath of Canadian citizenship in this book and highlights how much this oath means to him in his critical analysis of immigration policies and demographic changes.

Samy moves so gracefully in this work from the history of Canadian immigration policies to deep thought about the reconciliation process with the First Nations peoples of this country, and comes to a beautiful analysis about the Canadian economy and gives intelligent and valuable advice to policy makers and concerned citizens. Samy comes from a civilization with a very long history and is learning to be patient with this young giant of a nation, Canada.

Canadians have taken great pride in accepting the large numbers of refugees from Syria in recent months and Samy Appadurai while also very proud of this accomplishment outlines very carefully in "Canada—An Evolving Vision" that our immigration policies were not always so generous. Samy describes that in the early days of this nation, immigration was directed to those born to the British culture and many were deemed "undesirable". Samy outlines quite extensively the exact immigration policies that led to would be immigrants from other European countries, Asians and South Asians either getting barred entirely from entering Canada or drastically limiting the number of immigrants from these groups that would be received. Samy in his analysis does not condemn Canada; rather he is reminding us of the importance of remembering our mistakes so that we can move forward in creating an even better future.

Radicalization and the threat posed by terrorism has been a regular feature on newscasts all over the world. Canada is not immune to such threats and our government has faced criticism from the international community in regards to its response. In "Canada—An Evolving Vision" Samy Appadurai outlines the Canadian approach very effectively and accurately. It is true, we Canadians do not march to the same tune as everyone else; rather we prefer to do things in our own unique way without undue pressure. While Canada is known as a peace keeping nation, Samy makes it clear that Canada does indeed have a history of going to war and the First and Second World Wars are prime examples. However, Samy also points out that Canada's participation in armed conflicts is not always a guarantee and he believes that despite the criticism, the way our government handles this issue has earned us some respect.

As a scholar, Samy Appadurai substantiates his facts with data and this is displayed excellently in his chapter on demographics. One need only turn on their radio or read on social media that the population of Baby Boomers is aging and the birth rate is lowering, not only in Canada but around the world. Samy keenly observes that Canada like many other nations is going to need more immigrants to fill the population gap to replace the aging population. Samy cleverly outlines the values held by the boomer, bust and echo generations and states that each generation has made positive contributions to our society. But he also says that the current generation, our youth should not be perceived as lazy and that as a society we need to be more accommodating and that we can learn from our youth; these are very wise words indeed.

My favourite chapter in this wonderful work deals with the actualization of our vision as a nation. I particularly like the opening statement in the first paragraph which states that even though Canada is not a super power it is not dancing to the music of another one. Samy points out the many things that make Canada the envy of the world such as our commitment to multiculturalism, our stable government, our balanced foreign policy and the very fact that if any of us should fall sick we do not need our credit card with us when we go to the hospital. It is true, the vision of our nation is not like stagnant water—it needs to flow in order to survive; Samy points out that how the future of Canada will be shaped depends on many factors. He asks what will be altered and what will have to change and what things must be left behind if this nation is to not only survive, but thrive.

Many issues have not been fully addressed as Samy thoughtfully points out and there are new challenges presenting themselves. For example the inclusion of the First Nations, Metis and Inuit needs to be given priority in order to foster true reconciliation and address long standing grievances such as land claims and the legacy of the residential schools. As a new Canadian Heritage Minute points out, our relationship with the First Nations peoples of this country was not always positive.

Samy also mentions Quebec sovereignty and how it is important that the people of Quebec need to look at the bigger picture and that Quebec and its people and distinctive culture are valuable to all Canadians. The issue of Senate reform is also covered in this chapter and Samy clearly explains how vital the Senate is when it comes to providing sober second thought before any bill is passed into law. Our relationship with the United States is also crucial and Samy is correct in saying that our relationship is indeed unique and that Canada is not viewed as another foreign nation.

"Canada—An Evolving Vision" is a book that should be studied by all of our policy makers, who far too often neglect the perspective of those who are not politicians or political pundits. Samy Appadurai's perspective is that of a proud Canadian who so accurately describes what makes Canada unique and what we will need to do as citizens of this nation to keep it that way. It is true, we Canadians do not like to make changes for the sake of change itself; rather we make adjustments when they are needed as the author says.

I personally look forward to future work by this author for he grasps so beautifully the nature of this country, what makes it the envy of many and what the future may hold.

INTRODUCTION
TO THE AUTHOR

When asked if I would write an introduction to this book, I asked myself "What could I possibly write?" I say this because I have known the author Samy Appadurai for eight years and because he has such impressive credentials and experience I wondered how my humble words could draw you the readers in when the author's résumé would be enough to draw your interest.

Samy Appadurai is an award winning journalist, a well-respected television and radio commentator, columnist, consultant and community worker with a deep love for his country. In his previous two books "Canada: the Meat of the World Sandwich" and "Canada: a Nation in Motion" Samy's knowledge of Canadian history and politics feature very prominently and I was impressed with the incredible amount of detail and Samy's courage to take on issues that we Canadians hold dear.

"Canada an Evolving Vision" continues in this vein. Samy Appadurai dives deep into Canada's past and he is not afraid to bring up certain aspects of our history that are less than flattering. For example, I knew about the Komogata Maru, the Japanese freighter full of would be immigrants from India that was docked at Vancouver's Burrard Inlet for two months in the early 20th century. I knew that the passengers were deprived of food and water and were finally forced to leave. Samy Appadurai's extensive research into this incident points out the immigration policy that allowed this tragedy to take place. He also points out how this policy was deliberately used to discriminate against so called "undesirable "immigrants. I must admit, that though I was quite disturbed when I read about this, I was glad that Samy pointed these details out because he further explains that this policy has had an influence in recent years. Samy also explains quite beautifully that not all immigrants from Europe were considered equal. We are familiar with how the Scots and the Irish were treated, but people from Southern Europe were also considered an ill fit for this country and again deliberate attempts were made to stop these people from coming. After reading these chapters, I thought "Thank goodness things have changed". The situation is not perfect, but positive changes have occurred and Samy displays great optimism in this regard.

Samy's incredible wit also comes out on the cover of this book. There is an image of a Rubik's Cube on the cover of this book and at first I wondered why he chose it. I then realized that it was a great way to explain Canadian identity; the more you twist and turn a Rubik's Cube, the more mixed up the colours become. In Canada, the more we are twisted and turned; the situation becomes more difficult for us hence we tend to favour policies and legislation that do not rock the boat too much. Samy is not saying that we as Canadians are resistant to change; rather we always ask ourselves "what kind of country do we want to be?" when it comes to making major policy decisions.

I truly enjoyed reading this book because Samy Appadurai writes with such confidence but what also strikes me is how he can shift between topics so easily and explain the variety of subjects he covers in this book in such a way that anyone can understand. Economics for example is one subject that I personally find rather dry, but Samy makes it quite interesting because he connects it to other issues such as immigration.

Samy is very fair, balanced and forgiving in his views not to mention quite self-effacing. When you read this book, it is easy to forget that Samy Appadurai came to this country as an immigrant himself and there are very few books written about Canada by people of Sri Lankan and South Asian heritage. Even though Samy is very proud of his culture, his perspective is that of a patriotic Canadian.

So I would encourage you to read this book for it is insightful, thought provoking and entertaining. Samy's optimistic outlook for this country is truly encouraging and it would benefit us all to read it.

Jessica Smith

B.A Philosophy

INTRODUCTION

By
The Author

The motivation, encouragement and support extended by the readers, researchers, post secondary students, politicians and academics around the world for my other two books entitled "Canada a Nation in Motion" and "Canada the Meat of the World Sandwich" prompted me to write this book "Canada An Evolving Vision".

Canada like any other developed nation around the globe has been undergoing some fundamental changes from the patterns and structure of family life, the rising demand for overhauling and maintaining traditional values while accommodating new ones, changes in the economic sector, politics, immigration and emigration, demographics, national peace and security, and our place on the world stage. Instead of having a compartmentalized approach I prefer to have an integrated and balanced overall vision for Canada. This integrated approach is highly required for the future planners, nation builders, politicians, educators and last but not least the people of this great nation.

There are leaders and academics who have shared their vision for Canada and some are similar to each other and others differ but the bottom line is all those who have thought about this country and where it is going have one thing in common and that is there concern for the best interests of this nation. They also agree that the First Nations peoples with their amazing diversity amongst themselves, still fundamentally have a similar approach and structure in their objectives, desires, and the goals for their lives. When it comes to the European settlers in North America particularly the British and French descendants, there has been a large difference between Canada and the United States of America. Canada never aimed to reach the position of a super power and dominating or unduly interfering in international affairs, however it does not mean that Canada keeps to itself and is not a participating member internationally. Canada as a nation has been built with unique, solid and strong crystalline stones. Although Canada has a close relationship with the United States of America, it keeps its own identity and maintains it without any undue influence.

While writing this book, the image of the Rubik's cube came to mind and prompted me into portraying the multi dimensional structure of the Canadian fabric as such. Canada, is like a Rubik's cube with all of its colours and dimensions but when twisted can be hard to restore back to normal. It is not that we as Canadians do not like or appreciate change, but we seem to prefer a slow and steady approach and change for the sake of enrichment rather than change for its own sake.

ACKNOWLEDGEMENTS

I would like to extend my special thanks to certain government departments, mass medias and also some individuals who have made tremendous contributions. I give my sincere thanks to Statistics Canada and Citizenship and Immigration Canada in that I was able to obtain certain statistics for my analysis.

There are also some national and international organizations and no –profit corporations who entertained my requests and spared their valuable time in conducting important discussions on certain issues that supplemented my ideas in this book and I am grateful for their contributions. I also thank SV media for their constant encouragement for writing this book with my very busy schedule.

I would also like to thank Mitch Engel for his wonderful foreword to this book and to Jessica Smith for writing an introduction that outlines the true nature of who I am and my perspective. I would also like to thank my family, in particular my spouse Gnanam for their support. Special thanks also go to Mr. Surendran Sornalingam who has always been supportive of my writing.

Last, but not least I thank Author House for not only publishing "Canada: the Meat of The World Sandwich" and "Canada: A Nation in Motion" but also this current book "Canada: An Evolving Vision" and helped promote and bring them to international readers.

CHAPTER 1

Canada Unique in its Nature

Canada is an enviable young nation of only one and a half century's worth of history among many other nations that are enriched with glorious ancient civilizations that are highly advanced economically and are politically stable in terms of democratic rule when compared with the former colonial rulers, the former USSR, the USA and the emerging super powers of China, India and Brazil. When comparing Canada with these nations, Canada has certain unique qualities. I do not mean to undervalue the strength, outstanding achievements, progress and richness of these other nations, but allow me to cite some examples for how those nations cannot reach the unique position that Canada has attained and maintained in a short period of time. For example, China is progressing rapidly in its economy, strengthening its military power, entering into space research, and has a steady government. But still, it is lacking in terms of respect for the fundamental freedoms of expression, press, and basic economic freedoms under its so-called proletarian dictatorship proclaimed as another form of democracy. The Amnesty International annual report in 2013 on China has documented widespread human rights violations in the country.

"An estimated 500,000 people are currently enduring punitive detention without charge or trial, and millions are unable to access the legal system to seek redress for their grievances. Harassment, surveillance, house arrest, and imprisonment of human rights defenders are on the rise, and censorship of the interment and other media has grown. Repression of minority groups, including Tibetans, Uighurs and Mongolians, and of Falun Gong practitioners and Christians who practise their religion outside state-sanctioned churches continues. While the recent reinstatement of the Supreme People's Court review of the death penalty may result in lower numbers of executions, China remains the leading executioner in the world."

The United States of America our friendly neighbouring border nation in the South and North West, in spite of having the unshakable position as a superpower, and claims to be exercising true democracy with the sons and daughters of liberty has earned more enmity than any other nation in the world. Whatever the reasons may be, their position on the world's stage is very controversial and most of the recent terrorist activities although generally targeted against the western world, are primarily focused on the USA. Its economic supremacy as the number one nation in the economy will be overtaken by China sooner rather than later.

When it comes to the glorious ancient civilizations of the world, instantaneous we are all remained of the Greeks, the Romans, the Egyptians, the Babylonians, the Indus, the Chinese, the Mohenjo-Daro Harappa civilization and Lemuria. Of course the locations of these civilizations were not necessarily bound by the modern political boundaries which define these countries today. Most of these nations would not be able to have the continuation of glory and maintain their precious positions. Today, countries such as Greece and Italy are on the verge of economic collapse. The prolonged global recession of 2008 became worse and almost reached the level of depression, as it was in 1929 around the world, the banks were closed for a few weeks with a short interval period of time and the unemployment rate reached above one quarter of the workable and committed man power in 2016. Once upon a time, those nations led the world but today many of them have been led and supported by other nations with the exception of India and China, which have been able to maintain the continuity of their age old traditions and their religion in spite of cruel oppressive colonial rulers from Europe over five centuries. Although India is the most populous nation practising the democratic system of government, it is still lacking in certain areas such as the eradication of corruption, caste discrimination, and the deprivation of women's rights. When U.S President Barack Obama attended and graced the occasion of the celebration of Indian Independence on the 27th of January 2015 he delivered an elegant speech and touched on these aspects by saying:

"Your constitution begins with a pledge to uphold 'the dignity of the individual'. And our declaration of independence proclaims that 'all men are created equal 'in both our countries, generations have worked to live up to these ideals. When he came to India, Martin Luther King, Jr. was introduced to some school children as "fellow untouchables".

The portrayed positive image of the former colonial rulers over the colonized nations has earned mixed reactions from these former colonies. These are views based on the opinions of many radical intellectuals. Within these nations however, there are more negative opinions about their colonial rulers than positive comments. A few examples follow:

The colonial rulers particularly the British used various techniques, one of the most commonly used was the technique of divide and rule by favouring a certain group. In most cases the minority was favoured against the majority and that eroded the peace and harmony that had existed between those groups and created an unpleasant environment which in turn divided them and they were made to fight due to a series of mischievous and manipulative moves. The people would engage themselves in fighting each other, which weakened their strength and distracted their focus from fighting against the common enemy, the colonizer. They used many tactics and some of them were very ugly and cheap in nature. For an example in India though the Muslims and Hindus fought each other at times, still they had some kind of mutual understandings and shared common values. It was said that the colonial rulers quietly and secretly slaughtered some cows, considered sacred by most of the Hindus and then slaughtered some pigs which are considered unclean by Muslims and then placed them respectively in the front yards of the Hindu temples and mosques. Innocent people, when coming upon this scene, would make the hasty conclusion that it was deliberately done by the other community in order to insult their beliefs. It resulted in unwanted fights and destruction.

Even after these nations gained independence from their colonial rulers the remains of the divide and rule policy created other problems such as the over or unduly privileged minorities not being able to keep their status due to the majority ethnic group obtaining the same rights and privileges and this led to civil disturbance and in some cases civil war.

The deliberate demarcation of the boundaries of colonies by splitting up some ethnic groups into more than one nation and creating a new nation that had people from many different ethnicities gave birth to unpleasant circumstances and created more problems, misunderstandings and unwanted conflict and wars. I have personally heard about this from East African elites from the former East African colonies of Uganda, Tanzania, and Kenya when I was working in Africa for almost a decade

The British, the French, and the Spanish introduced cash crops such as sugar, tobacco, coffee, tea, and coconut palm trees into their colonies and these became important sources for generating export income. Later on the mining of minerals joined the rest after the introduction of the Industrial Revolution in England. There are two controversial schools of thought and many of the scholars are convinced that the introduction of the plantation sector and mining remain as the best source of generating national income. Whereas the rest strongly believe that this exploited their natural resources and exporting these goods to their respective colonial ruling countries ruined their self-sufficiency in terms of their local economy. Furthermore, it is claimed that the former colonial powers still have control of the economy of the former colonies directly or indirectly thus making political independence meaningless without economic independence.

We should also remember that before the colonial rule of these countries, they never united as a nation; rather they were scattered as many small kingdoms and fought among themselves and destroyed each other. The good thing that colonial rulers brought for them was that it brought them together as nations as sovereign states today.

The comparison of these nations with Canada might seem a little strange to the untrained observer. But the point of my comparison is to show that these former colonies have a long history of evolutionary and revolutionary change whereas Canada is a young nation that has not yet celebrated its bicentennial even though the evolution of this nation goes back almost five hundred years with the exception of the history of the First Nations. Though Canada is young in its chronological age it has reached maturity with its constructive ideas, innovations, values and perceptions which are greater than many nations who are enriched with ancient civilizations.

When we travel with Canadian passports, the customs and immigration officers open their eyes wide with special respect and a broad smile of enthusiasm in the busy and crowded environment. It reminds us that there is something unique when it comes to having a Canadian passport but once we move on and become engaged in carrying out our work this thought moves from our mind like passing clouds. Though it is only a symbolic gesture, it somehow reflects the core values of Canada.

The main sources which make up the Canadian mosaic are the First Nations, the French and the British. Whatever has been said and done, we owe a certain amount of respect to the native peoples. The amazing thing is that the increase in the natural net birth rate of the First Nations people is rapid and comparatively high. Though their values are confined mostly within themselves in designated regions, they are part and parcel of the Canadian family. They only account for 1.4 million people (4.3%) among the population of 35 million Canadians. Approximately half of them have migrated from their reserves to other parts of this nation and have intermingled with the rest of Canada. In spite of this however the growing number of youth in the First Nations communities has motivated them into direct action against the prevailing policies of the government. They helped in the birth of the "Idle No More" movement with four women who began it in Alberta and quickly grew to over forty five thousand participants.

The contribution made by mobilizing the various Chiefs in terms of addressing, resolving and finding solutions for their immediate and age old grievances is only the beginning.

The arrival of the Europeans in general and the French and British in particular in the fifteenth century is a new era in the Canadian mosaic. Although the Spanish came to North America by accident while aiming to reach the western part of India and landed in Central America and became the first European settlers when they touched the Canadian portion of the Atlantic ocean they never made any significant impact by building settlements. The first settlers were the French who gradually settled into the hinterland of the St. Lawrence River. The French were the dominating Europeans and they were the majority among the European settlers. The French would have been the dominant European ethnic community if not for the arrival of the British who made settlements in broader areas in the east and central eastern parts of this nation.

The French had made a remarkable contribution in developing Canadian values both in maintaining the French traditions, language and culture as an entity inland of itself and as part of the greater Canadian culture.

The descendants of the British exclusive of the Irish, Scots and Welsh are the core contributors to the Canadian mosaic and they have been instrumental in modeling this nation's identity by establishing the very foundational values that this country holds dear to this day.

Unlike the French-Canadians who belonged to a single ethnic group from France, the British were descendants from the Welsh, the Irish, the Scots and the English who came from the British Isles. All of them were not treated in the same manner; rather they were treated differently and in some cases unequally for the English speaking British wanted to secure their monopoly. After discovering the possibility of utilizing the abundant potential and they became somewhat more flexible, relaxed their self centered attitudes and became more accommodating.

The gate for the next wave of immigrants was opened slightly wider than ever before and the restrictions relaxed during and after the construction of the Canadian Pacific Railway where the government invited and accepted the so-called unflavoured Europeans from the Southern and Eastern parts of Europe. Still the gate was closed to other parts of the world with the exception of restricted entry for Chinese and Indians for discharging manual labour in the construction of the railway line and that too because of the decline or the unwillingness to accept the offer given to the Europeans and the Canadians.

The Canadian process of becoming an independent nation from the British Empire laid the foundation for Canadian values that are different from the Americans. Although they both left Britain with the similar purpose under the prevailing circumstances, gradually the British loyalists did not want to go to war against their colonial rulers. Until recently Canada had stronger ties with Britain than the United States of America and these days after the terrorist attacks in the U.S.A of America on September 11th, 2001 the relationship with the United States and Britain got closer than ever before in collaboration in the fight against terrorism. However the fight against terrorism has brought Canada's values into the spotlight which has set us apart from other nations when it comes to this issue.

With all of its abundant natural resources, technical advancement and richness in economy stable government, the trend in the increasing number of the baby boomers and the echo generation, the declining of the natural birth rate, less interest in migrating to Canada by Europeans and the fast increase in the active population and surplus for the labour market has opened the immigration gate wider for the Asians. There is a lingering concern of how to maintain Canadian values without losing its nature by these new comers. Though this is not openly discussed or expressed, it is in the heart of some of Canadians.

The comprehensive vision for Canada in moving forward in its traditional path is very much secured but there are some pending unsolved internal issue and we may have to leave it as it is and time will resolve it or make use of the time and have mutual dialogue, and negotiation and finding the solution or react instead of act on those issues. More than internal challenges which is somewhat within our jurisdiction, the western world in particular and the most parts of the globe in general are being challenged and directly or indirectly targeted by radicalized forces from other continents.

It has to be critically analyzed the uniqueness of this country and how through the evolutionary process Canada as a nation has grown and changed. The challenge some of the deeply held values and beliefs that we as Canadians have for it is through analysis that we can fully define the mission and the vision for this country.

CHAPTER 2

Mission and Vision

The identity of this young nation began with the inherited heritage values of the immigrants who came from the colonial super powers of England and France. These values laid the foundation on which the values and ideas brought by so called new comers from southern and Eastern Europe flourished and in due course with the subsequent addition of new immigrants has led to the notion of Canada as a unique nation on the world stage.

The national identity of Canada is very complex compared with other the G-20 Nations or with the nations who have deep rooted ancient civilizations which eventually declined or have survived in an ornamental sense. Although the original European settlers of the United States of America arrived from Britain with their culture and traditions and established the thirteen colonies in the new continent; later on they treated Britain as a colonial ruler and no matter what the common language, culture and traditions they once shared were, they fought in a revolution and established their own traditions. They do not have a government such as Canada which maintains the Queen as Head of State. In fact America is one of the pioneer nations that developed modern democracy in terms of the presidential system of federal government. The members of the three organs of the federal government are duly elected by the people and none of them are appointed unlike the Governor General of Canada and Canadian Senators. Their mission and vision is very clear in that no matter where and when citizens and potential citizens arrived in the United States, they are considered Americans regardless of ethnicity, race and religion. The establishment of this idea was not a difficult task because the old British Americans themselves were brought up in a similar manner and were cited as examples for new immigrants. Although in some parts of the United States black Americans are addressed as Afro Americans, it has not been blessed by the core of society. America had another advantage in terms of their economic state for the glorious golden age in England began to decline after the rule of Queen Victoria. But the United States had overtaken not only Britain but also all of the other powerful nations and had reached the top of the ladder as a world super power. China has been making every possible effort in overtaking the economic superiority status of America; still the influences of it in the world nations are unbeatable. It then competed with Soviet Union that was confederated in 1917 in a political structure based on the theory of scientific socialism by Karl Marx which in turn lead the Soviet Union to become another super world power and a potential challenge for three quarters of a century and then collapsed in the 1990's. Socialism should have survived, if it would been established in a system of capitalistic economy that exploited at the optimum level of the labour force. Once they revolt against the system of such government, it would not turn back to Capitalism, because they had seen the evil side of it. But in the case of Soviet Union it jumped from feudalism, by passing capitalism.

The vision of the United States of America also has its significant elements and its evolution has been shaped by accommodating global changes and local pressures. America is a new nation among the developed nations in such that its nationhood with its own identity has a history of only four centuries and does not have much to claim in terms of achievements by their ancestors over many centuries like the Scandinavians, British, French, Russians, Ukrainians, Spanish, Japanese, Chinese, and Indians have in their own lands. In fact the American continent as a whole has similar characteristics in their demographic patterns. In the south the Spanish with the exception of the British, French and Portuguese, colonized other countries almost in the same period of time and then controlled the natives by various means and established their rule.

The vision of Canada by former Prime Minister Jean Chrétien was based on the idea that Canada could speak for itself without due influence from the United States. This vision contrasted strongly with that of Brian Mulroney who forged a rather strong relationship with the United States. But Jean Chrétien's vision of Canada really came into play after the September 11, 2001 terrorist attacks in New York and Washington.

He mentioned in his book entitled "My Years as Prime Minister"

"Wait a minute, I thought to myself –Saddam isn't the Taliban or Al Qaeda, so what does he have to do with the attacks on New York and Washington? The first President Bush ought to have gotten rid of him. Helms went on, support for extending the war into Baghdad, and his own generals had opposed the idea for strategic reasons. And hadn't the Americans once used Saddam against the Iranians, just as they had also used the Taliban against the Russians? So I began by being sceptical about an invasion of Iraq and I remained sceptical"

Furthermore he did mention that President Bush said Iraq was part of the "axis of evil" and then he wrote that:

"I would have told Bush that the key issue for Canada was whether such an invasion would obtain the blessing of the United Nations. At the time of the Gulf War against Iraq in 1991, Mulroney had insisted on getting the UN's approval, and he was right"

Jean Chrétien had a vision for Canada and he did not want to accept that every decision that the American President made was always right nor were we obliged to accept them just because they were our cousins or shared elements of our culture or have economic dependency intrude. I don't mean to say that I totally accept this entire concept of his foreign polices but he was bold enough to say that President Bush invaded Iraq at a time when Americans were very furious and highly worried about their national security.

The interesting part about Mr. Jean Chrétien was that he did not realize that he had a vision for Canada. He once said that:

'Formed, 'vision' is perhaps the emptiest and most ill-used word in politics. It's easy for someone to wake up in the middle of the night and say he or she has a 'vision'. But what does that mean nothing"

Similarly, I don't accept the vision for America related by U.S President Obama. I do admire him for his vision in bridging the gap between the low income, the middle class and the rich and have fair distribution of the wealth of the nation. But when it comes to his foreign policies he rejected the direct and offensive war against Al- Qaeda but he should have presented an alternative measure or policy. Al -Qaeda and the ISIS and ISIL have a very clear vision in that they want to create a powerful Islamic world in accordance with their interpretation of the Holy Quran and remove all obstacles at any cost. Their primary target is America and its western and other allies and Islamic nations who extend support to them.

Let us now have a look at a vision for Canada by another Canadian Prime Minister John Diefenbaker whose vision extended both internally and externally. His regime was on the peak of the cold war between the Soviet Union and our southern border nation America. The Cuban Missile Crisis of 1962 made for a panicky situation in the United States of America and it was portrayed as a threat to national security for not only the U.S but all of North America. America was targeted by the Soviet Union and had sent missiles to Cuba a nation located only three hundred miles away from the U.S. Cuba's system of government had changed due to the overthrow of Dictator Fulgencio Batista by Fidel Castro who was an ally of the Soviet Union. President Nikita Khrushchev decided to target the U.S by sending missiles and not giving any respect for the warnings made by U.S President John F Kennedy. Canada was approached by America for help and Diefenbaker extended his full level of support. Although he was aware that the U.S was trying to dominate Canadian foreign policies and other affairs by somehow getting a copy of a document called the "Rostov memo' which outlined how Canada could be pushed to their side. In spite of it this however he extended timely and full levels of cooperation and both moral and material support like other western nations while China extended its instant support for Cuba. I wonder what would have happened if he had been in power during the war on terrorism in Iraq and Afghanistan by America in collaboration with major parts of the NATO nations, just after the September 11, 2001 attacks.

Diefenbaker expressed in a statement on October 28, 1962 that:

"Mankind will breathe more hopefully now that there is an early prospect that the threat to the Western Hemisphere from long-range Soviet missiles in Cuba will be removed. This prospect has resulted from the high degree of unity, understanding and cooperation among the Western allies.

In this the Canadian Government has played its full part. Indeed Canada was the first nation to stop over flights of Soviet aircraft so as to prevent war material being carried to Cuba and as well to that end instituted a full search of all Cuban and Czech planes which are entitled under international agreement to use Canadian airport facilities. The introduction of missiles into the Western Hemisphere has brought the world too close to disaster for anyone to indulge -in either self-congratulations or complacency at this time. I know there will be universal relief that in the last two days the outlook for the peaceful solution of the Cuban problem has greatly improved but there is a continuing need for negotiation on this and other potential sources of threats to world peace."

He further expressed more on the new vision for Canada at the Civic Auditorium in Winnipeg on February 12, 1958:

"This national development policy will create a new sense of national purpose and national destiny. One Canada: one Canada, wherein Canadians will have preserved the control of their own economic and political destiny. Sir John Alexander Macdonald gave his life to this party. He opened the West. He saw Canada from East to West. Ladies and gentlemen, we now intend to bring in legislation to encourage progressively increasing processing of our domestic raw materials in Canada, rather than shipping them out in raw material form. We will ensure that Canada's national resources are used to benefit Canadians and that Canadians have an opportunity to participate in Canada's development. We have not discouraged foreign investment, but we will encourage the partnership of the foreign investors with the Canadian people.

This party has become the party of national destiny. I hope it will be the party of vision and courage; the party of one Canada, with equal opportunities for all.

He was also highly concerned with the Canadian imagination which needed leaders with vision and dreams, coupled with the ability to take us with them in the journey along the way to a better tomorrow.

The members and supporters of the Quebec sovereignty movement has a vision that one day Quebec will be an independent nation not as a nation within united Canada, under the federal system of the government of Canada with the British monarchy as their head of state. Some may brand it as a dream or ambition or a betrayal of Canada but I consider clearly as their vision and it is in the bottom of their heart.

Former Liberal leader, author and academic, Michael Ignatief was interviewed by Glenn Campbell for the British Broadcasting Corporation said that Quebec "eventually" will become an independent country and that a victory for Scottish separatists in an expected 2014 referendum will launch a new effort by Quebec nationalists to fulfil their sovereignty dream.

He also said Quebec and the rest of Canada have little to say to each other and that the two already are "almost" separate countries. He further said to BBC Scotland that devolution of central powers, whether from London to Edinburgh or from Ottawa to Quebec City, likely will be only temporary". We also acknowledge that he also said that he couldn't imagine Canada without Quebec.

The premier Pauline Marois of the Party Quebecois met with Scottish leader Alex Salmon and was willing to offer him the documents from the Quebec referendum 1980 and that of 1995 while the Scottish Leader was on the verge of completing the preparations for the referendum for the independence of Scotland from Britain in the Fall of 2014. She also mentioned to the Herald newspaper prior to her visit to Europe that she would be glad to share some advice with him for the Scottish referendum with the experience of the referendums brought forward in Quebec by the Parti Quebecois. Though Ms. Marois said that both of them agreed that their people have the exclusive right to determine their own future, still what she wants is to encourage or support the Scottish to win the referendum and gain some kind of moral support for her own cause which could be considered differently by patriotic Canadians. Anyhow it is crystal clear that they have a clear vision that one day their dream will be realized. But if there is a second option of being part of a nation between the USA and Canada, they certainly are continuing with Canada rather than the states and it has been proven historically as well. Furthermore, Canada is the only country that is privileged to be members of the British Commonwealth and the Francophone Organization.

"I have fought the battle of confederation, the battle of union, the battle of dominion" said by the father of Canada Sir John A. MacDonald who had a broad vision for this nation and he wanted to even name Canada as " Kingdom of Canada" instead of the "Dominion of Canada". The above mentioned expression of his involvements in many battles simultaneously was the core of his activities in laying the foundation for this nation. He had to fight against multi-dimensioned forces from within and outside the territory of British North America. He was well aware of the reaction and sentimental attachment of the bulk of the population who had mainly migrated from Britain and they were proud of their heritage values and had forgotten their bitter experiences that they had before fleeing from their home country. They were highly engaged in building a brand new life, with social amenities, construction of roads, railway lines, bridges, churches, schools, hospitals and libraries in a vast, virgin land. It was in a way a blessing in disguise that many of those immigrants had been deprived of their political rights and fundamental freedoms which were given to certain classes at that time in the existing system of government and economically and socially positioned at the lower level. Though when they arrived in a strange land with uncertainty, little hope of survival and the lack of social amenities; after establishing themselves, their status elevated and they felt that they were a real class of people who could rightfully contribute to their society. Though they left their land with grievances and bitterness, still they did not want to lose their heritage values and unlike the new immigrants who migrated from Eastern and southern Europe later on from comparatively less resourceful countries whose resettlement was glorious and prosperous.

The demographic distribution of the Canadian population accounted for 60% of the people being of British origin, 30% were French and the rest were the natives, Métis and the new immigrants. The second group of the Brutish descendants were not very keen in the formation of provinces unified as a sovereign nation. They had their own agenda and they wanted to be liberated and declared as distinguished nations of their own. There was some liberation movements which existed in eastern Canada and it was one the reasons that the joining of New Brunswick into the Confederation was another battle for the pro conservationists and the father of the nation.

The external challenge came from south of the border, America the nation that became liberated in the bitter war popularly known the American Revolution in 1775. In fact, both the American and the former subjects of Britain migrated in a similar way at almost the same time and never thought of establishing two nations. They also initially would not have had any concept of the formation of a nation with thirteen colonies. The American Revolution was more than an independence war and it established a new era in human history. The deeper meaning of freedom and liberty in the modern world was brought and experimented upon successfully and it became a role model to the rest of the world.

Some members of the Irish group from America known as the Fenians crossed the border and invaded Canada on the 1st June 1866. They came with a clear vision to recruit Canadians to their cause and create an anti-British nation in North America. Their influence on the people of New Brunswick and Nova Scotia in particular backfired on them and aggravated anti American feelings and sentiments thus making it easier for the father of the nation to get New Brunswick and Nova Scotia to join the confederation.

Sir John A MacDonald was a patriotic citizen of Great Britain. He was born in Scotland and migrated at the age of five with his parents and re-established his life but still proudly maintained his relationship with Britain. Furthermore, he went back to Scotland and married his cousin and they returned as a couple to live in Canada together.

The point in mentioning this that even the Father of Confederation still had his attachments to the land of his birth not unlike many immigrants today. He was likewise angry with the Americans for they did not display such affection towards Britain and treated it like an enemy. The vision of Canada that Sir John A MacDonald had though now seems quaint and old fashioned forms the values that we in Canada hold dear to this day.

At times I don't feel comfortable in comparing the fundamental structure and nature of Canada with other leading nations with a similar stage in overall developments of the same calibre. The core of the difference is that countries like Germany, France, United Kingdom, India, China, Russia, Ukraine, Russia, Japan and Norway have their deep rooted historical identity of their own that has been the life wire of the national culture, tradition and the way of living and furthermore they are economically, socially, independent and able to freely decide and act on their own without having serious concerns over the consequences and the adverse effects of their allies that could be United States of America or France and United Kingdom from which came the founding European settlements and the back bone of this fabric. They were competing with each other during the colonial era and during in their early part of their colonial history. Although they had some similarities still the differences are significant. Although linguistic wise they had similar roots from Latin, however, there are a number of differences, both major and minor, between French and English. In the olden days both the countries had a monarchy system of government with the concept of divine right and then the feudal system of government. The difference in politics is that when the Americans fought against the British in their revolutionary process between the period of 1776 and 1783 and the French assisted the Americans against the British. The similarity is that both the Americans and French had revolutions almost at the same time for a democratic system of government, though the French did not set revolution against external forces but within themselves against the autocratic rule of the King and Nobles in 1789. Both the nations are very particular and cautious of keeping themselves away from the infiltration of the socialist system of government. The manufacturing industrial sector dominated the economy of both these nations and became the backbone of their economies. With all of these similarities along with becoming members of the North Atlantic Treaty Organization and members of the European Union they are no longer in two opposite camps and all three of them are friends and are very cordial and cooperate in many projects. The unique characteristics of the United States of America is that though they left Britain with bitter feelings and stress in search of liberty; like the Canadians and Australians they still maintained their root culture. This earned some criticism from around the world, even from those who became disappointed when the thirteen colonies antagonised Britain and joined us as patriotic Canadians.

Canada has maintained consistently cordial relations with Cuba in spite of considerable pressure from the United States. Canada-Cuba relations can be traced back to the 18th century, when Canada exported codfish and beer for rum and sugar. Cuba was the first country in the Caribbean selected by Canada for a diplomatic mission and did not get interrupted by the socialist revolution which changed the system of government radically to a dictatorship in 1959. Whereas today the US and Cuba normalized their relationship with certain conditions and Canada and Pope Francis were behind the scenes for the successful re-establishment of the relationship almost six decades after the discontinuation of their relationship,though there are some restrictions put forward by both parties.

The American invasion on the British North American territory in 1812 was the most serious breach in the relationship and was stopped by the British-Canadian forces. But later on, the military collaboration began during World War I and World War II and continued throughout the Cold War despite no direct reason for Canada to get involved because Canada never colonized or controlled certain countries, like the French, British, Germans, Italians, Soviet Union and the United States of America. As being a part of the group of western nations and a former British colony and thus having a very close relationship with Britain, allowed for Canada to make a high level of commitment in the First World War than the Second World War.

Canada has proclaimed itself a sovereign nation, in spite of her Majesty the Queen of England as the Queen of Canada and the head of State and has acted very independently on many occasions and at critical moments in international affairs. The North America Act was originally agreed to by the British and the Canadian counter parts and then Canada proposed and then amended the Act twenty times until the *Constitution Act* of 1982 was passed into law by the Government of Canada. The Governor General, who is the representative of the Queen and nominal head of state, signed and gave royal ascent for the bill to become law.

Where does Canada stand independently while and developing and maintaining its own identity? Why can't Canada be like those nations on its own? These are two questions I have heard many times. I am not anti-British, anti- French, nor anti- American but aim to determine what makes Canada unique. Today's Canada is a blend of five main groups:

a. The First Nations peoples

b. The British

c. The French

d. European minorities

e. Visible minorities.

Though outwardly the Canadian Government through the *Multiculturalism Act* encourages the preservation and promotion of the various cultural and religious traditions of those that make Canada home, still the inner motives of our government noble as they are, might not be manifesting as well as intended. I discussed this issue in my previous book "Canada a Nation in Motion"

'The end results of the implementation of multiculturalism have not been very successful in many European countries and France and Germany have reluctantly acknowledged their difficulties. regardless of how one may feel about multiculturalism, it is very clear that no matter what you try to do in terms of preserving one's own culture and traditions gradually over time they will fade away due to a number of pushing and pulling forces. The second and third generations who born and raised in Canada and have intermingled with other communities have become absorbed into the main stream culture and they do expose or inherit the symbolic gestures of their native cultures"

I do value and respect the positive effects on the lives of new immigrants by the bold steps outlined in the *Multiculturalism Act* of 1971 by Prime Minister Pierre Elliott Trudeau. But I do realize the limitations of such legislation since the government cannot legislate how one can think or behave, just like it cannot legislate morality.

One of the schools of thought on the vision of Canada on the endless evolution and the nature of Canadian history is that it does believe on any kind of revolutionary means. The core of many of the passive, conservative Canadians is to be a branch of the colonial tree and that basis is never been unshaken and never been allowed to be uprooted no matter how Britain or America keeps us in their inner circle as cousins or as the French leaders expressed on some occasions that the Quebecers are brothers and the rest are friends, Canada has a special place for them and lets it continue without any interruption. The land has been built as a strong and beautiful fabric by their ancestors and we Canadians owe a special and unique place for them.

There are some activities lingering in Canada that are either against or dissatisfied with the Canadian approach and want to dismantle and replace the existing structure. It is obvious and crystal clear with no doubt those global citizens from the grass roots level to the cream of the crop, potential resource sectors of the economies of both the developing and developed nations, prominent world organizations, at large the governments of most of the nations have a very positive image and high reputation with recognition for Canada. Apart from the expressed and exposed views, there is also a high level of silent positive opinion for Canada which may not be able to gauged scientifically but able to realize and account for with a minimum chance of error also adds more spices to the soup. In spite of Canada being a nation that has a high calibre nature, still there is an element of negativity, heritage, dislikes, betrayal, unpatriotic and anti- Canadians in existence from within and outside of Canada, although in comparison with similar nations around the developed world in general and developed nations in particular it is minimal and the credit goes mainly to the nation builders.

I would like to now explain the truth about the historical background and the structure of this nation with unspoken sensitive views and feelings of substantial proportion of the both the minority and visual minority Canadians who have migrated from over two hundred nations around the world in a variety of backgrounds in complex circumstances. The degree of detachment of the sentiments, loyalty from the roots, in order to have a full flesh commitments for the migrated nation, like the USA is not in any way encouraged or promoted by the Canadian philosophy of life, in order to cultivate those values within themselves for Canada. It is not a strange or a new phenomenon in Canadian history, in fact the foundation laid for this nation by the British and the French recognized and respected their root values and were proud of it. The first few waves of their migration was forced mainly by the pushing forces as such discrimination, oppression, deprivation of rights and privileges, though not by the constitution, but by the practice from the privileged and dignified personalities and certain prominent political leaders. They uprooted themselves from the age old traditional home land where their forefathers proudly established their settlements with sentiments to a strange land in which they had no of what it would be like. This combined with the risk of traveling for thousands of miles on ordinary ships that too with no experience in traveling on the ocean was a big challenge.

A vision for a nation is the totality of all the main aspects, such as its economy, system of education, moral values, traditions and culture, system of government and its policies, language and literature, physical features, location, and its history and the degree of influence of these factors various from nation to nation and within a nation from time to time.

For example the barrier between Canada and United States of America is nothing other than a line drawn as boundary. In fact the unmarked boundaries between northern Canada and that of south have shown two regions with significant patterns of life. The physical isolation by the range of the Rocky Mountains has made a certain impact between the west and the east. The physical isolation by the Pacific Ocean and a collection of 6852 islands is one of the primary factors that kept the Chinese and Korean influences away. But the Philippines, an archipelago having a collection of 7,207 islands, were a slightly greater influence in converting into the Spanish culture, the Catholic religion and losing many of its traditional values.

The root heritage for both the Americans and Canadians remains the same which is that of the British and their languages also the same the political boundaries between these two nations has less influence and more in common.

But the vision for the nature of the relationship between Britain and Canada and that of United States of America during the early period during the establishment of colonies and the American Revolution from the beginning was very different. That is why the British loyalists from the thirteen American colonies left for Canada the number is as high as 500,000, and accounted for 20% of Europeans in the colonies of America and 19,000 of them joined the British army and fought against Americans. The American government today has a strong relationship with the British government than that of Canada and Canada is also has such a relationship with America. Britain was once a superpower but today Canada and Britain are middle level power nations.

The contribution to the history for the Canadian vision is constant. Canada is a peace loving country and hardly engages in armed conflicts and the way it avoids it is through compromise, and encouraging dialogue. Though recently Canada joined in the war against ISIS in Syria and Iraq, still Canada is ranked the 7th peace loving nation in the world, while America and Mexico are respectively positioned as 101 and 138.

Canada cannot be beaten by any country when it comes to tolerance, which is why Canada is able to accommodate new immigrants from over 200 countries who speak over 160 languages. It is not an easy task in having people from various backgrounds live in an excellent co-existing manner. These days Canada is considered as the most tolerant country in the world. Canada's tolerance goes beyond any man and nature- made boundaries. The French and English were engaged in numerous wars for almost 800 years in Europe but in Canada after a short war they have been co-existing well and at the time of Americans engaged in a war on Canadian soil against Britain, the French Canadians resisted the American offers and remained with the Canadians. Today there are over a million Canadians in the United States and there is a similar number of Americans living in Canada.

How far Canada is advocating for its Anglo-French culture while accommodating, or resisting the cultures of the multi-ethnic immigrants is an evolving issue that has met some new challenges. The core of many cultures is not necessarily based on their ethnicity, religion, language, color, geographical regions, economic structure and political ideology. Most of the cultures somehow are very much intermingled with religions at the early stages and some of them have revived these days. For example in Quebec the provincial government recently made some so called radical moves in detaching the religious links with the public services offices or to eliminate them by Bill 60 that proposed to ban all public sector employees from wearing obvious religious clothing or symbols by former Party Quebecois Premier Pauline Maoris and it was reflection of the sentiments of their own French culture reflected by some Quebecers. It was opposed by certain Muslim and Jewish leaders and some protested that it targeted their religious practices. Some of the Muslim women said "" it is extremely discriminative and essentially targets Muslim women". Lucian Del Negro of the Centre for Israel and Jewish Affairs in Quebec said that "The Jewish community has been in Quebec for 250 years. Now, if you wear a kippah, you will have to choose between religious observance and joining the Quebec public service" But the interesting part of it is that in the Legislative assembly itself there is a crucifix. For the Muslims, their faith governs many aspects in life such as the judiciary system, marriage, dress code, economic activities and so on. For them regardless of their ethnic back ground all of them have been brought under Islamic umbrella. They want to practice their ways wherever they are and whatever their norm of their cultural practise. In the case of the Jewish community, they are united by race and somewhat in practising their culture but ridge in practising their religion within themselves.

Likewise east Europeans mainly Ukrainians in the prairie provinces, still maintained their cultural norms that they have brought with them and settle down in the non-urban areas as farmers and exclusively living as a Ukrainian community with less interaction with other communities and it was easy for them to maintain their culture. The first wave arrived between 1891 and 1914. They are over 1-2 million

Canadian citizens of Ukrainian descent and their second and other generations and are the ninth largest ethnic group in Canada.

The second wave of workers and professionals came and settled in Canada in 1923-1939. They emigrated mainly from Poland and, Romania and settled down in the suburban areas as well. They too maintained up to a certain degree their heritage values, but not up to the extent of their first wave of their immigrants, due to the reason that they were not confined in a closed or intensively migrated in some areas as the predominant ethnic community. One of the reasons for their high degree in the inclination in preserving their heritage value is that their forefathers established a life with a highly cultivated culture, tradition and arts of their own. Ukraine was well developed and in the 10th and 11th century reached the stage of one of the largest and most powerful states in Europe. It has been blessed with rich soil with potential minerals and was once the bread basket of the world. The richness of this nation both when its economy was predominantly agrarian and currently based on manufacturing was able to support the maintaining of its societal norms both in and outside of Ukraine when they migrated to Canada.

The current state of Ukraine was disintegrated from the Soviet Union on 16th July 1990 and adopted the declaration of Ukraine with the principles of self-rule by law without the direct or indirect influence, from other powers such as Russia, the key partner of the Soviet Union with democracy, independence.

The Ukrainian internal crisis of November 2013 that cropped up by its president Viktor Yanukovych rejected the deal for greater integration with the European Union and mass protest and the Russian undue involvement somewhat paved a way for Canada for getting sympathy by supporting the government of Ukraine against Russia. Anyhow it is an example for keeping heritage values in their life and somehow it preventing the Canadian culture in penetrating into it up to its own level.

The reviving of the traditional Canadian values by Prime Minister Justin Trudeau would certainly have a smooth and relaxed relationship with the rest of the world particularly in the sectors of immigration and migration, foreign policy and with the natives.

CHAPTER 3

Politics with Expectations

The Canadian political spectrum and its mechanisms have been smooth and the political process of Canada has its own path and the independence of Canada was granted without any labour pain. From infancy until adulthood had been nursed and raised by the British government and even at the beginning itself the Constitution of Canada was drafted and also periodically guided by Britain. Just imagine Canadian citizenship came into effect only on January 1st, 1947 which is 187 years after gaining independence while also being subjects of Britain but as fully independent nation.

The participation in the First World War by Canada with substantial man power and weapons was mainly due to the influence of Britain and we lost sixty six thousand soldiers. Canada began to realize during the post war time that it had to act differently and coupled with the effects of the Great Depression, Canada kept a short distance in its participation in the Second World War and lost almost half the number of solders. In fact Canadian politics came more into its own after the end of the Second World War. Of course the better and extensive medical treatments during the time of the Second World War compared with that of the First World War also brought down the death rate low.

Sir John A MacDonald, the father of the nation and the first Prime Minister, the second longest serving Prime Minister serving 18 years and 359 days in four full term majority governments, was Scottish born and migrated to Canada had two dimensions in that he was loyal to the land and Britain simultaneously

His foundation of having a Canadian values based on the French and British traditions and cultures at a time when the British influence was dominating Canadian affairs. On the international level the British Empire was at its peak and overtook that of the French. This was a bold step and fostered unity between the founding ethnicities. He was the one who planted the seeds of tolerance into Canadian cultural norms we must give thanks to the following leaders in maintaining such sense and even today no country in the would be able to reach such a calibre of religious, ethnic, social, linguistic, and racial tolerance.

Although he was a British born naturalized Canadian and also had a special corner in his heart for his ancestor's country Britain and its head of State the her Majesty the Queen still, he did not want to antagonize nor risk another invasion by the United States. Every step he made was calculated and careful. Although Sir John A. MacDonald is the father of confederation, but the man behind this move Sir George Etienne Cartier initially pushed the idea of confederation forward for the reason that the French Canadians would prefer confederation over British rule because some of the French Canadians had the opinion of identifying as a conquered nation and oppressed people. In fact Sir A John MacDonald acknowledged this. In his first biography Joseph Pope wrote that "Cartier was as bold as a lion. He was just the man I wanted.

But for him Confederation could not have been carried." Although Sir John A MacDonald is the father of confederation, the circumstance was such that his position could be compared with George Washington of the United States of America.

Canadian inclination gradually shifted to the United States from Britain. It has been said by author Helen Gordon McPherson that "Canadians have been so busy explaining to the Americans that we aren't British and to the British that we aren't Americans that we haven't had time to become Canadians".

Sir John A McDonald's regime was interrupted for a short while due to the reason that he had put his hands in some sort of political scandal involving the acceptance of bribes by 150 members of the Conservative government in the attempts of private interests in obtaining rail contracts and it led him to resign his position as the Prime Minister and he handed power to the Liberal government led by Rt. Hon. Alexander Mackenzie and then regained his power in a democratic election.

From the first Prime Minster Sir John A McDonald to the current Prime Minster Justin Trudeau Canada has been operating the government based on the political fabric without any major structural changes but with some cosmetic changes now and then. There has been no question so far in changing the British style parliamentary system to the presidential or any other system, except for the reformation of the house of Senate by advocating for elected Senators, rather than appointed ones. In spite of the British model unlike the Americans, still the Canadian government is not like the unitary government in Britain; rather it is a federal system of government. There are federal system of government around the world in Germany, France, United States of

America, India, Switzerland and Brazil. The degree of devolution of power between state government and the federal government varies, for example in India the federal government has a higher degree of power than that of Canada and in Canada the provincial (State) governments have substantial power and are also able to unilaterally with the majority of the vote from its citizens get way from Canada with some restrictions made by the *Clarity Act* by Jean Chrétien.

Freedoms and rights, especially freedom of expression, freedom of the press, and freedom of worship for Canadians has been protected extensively and none of the governments have tampered deeply into this, and the Canadian *Charter of Rights and Freedoms* of 1982 gave constitutional approval. Though the Harper government brought some restrictions under *Bill C51*, it was due to concern over radicalization. Though the U.S claims they are sons and daughters of liberty, many multi-ethnic groups in Canada, feel that they enjoy more freedom than their counter parts in the US. None of the registered political major parties are inclined towards a Marxist scientific socialist proletariat dictatorship system of government, and even the New Democratic Party with trade union backing is trying not to be inclined towards such a system of government. Canada is also very careful in not allowing any infiltration of external forces into the ideological conversation. Canada is very precise in maintaining social welfare benefits for low income earners, so that they would be pushed above the poverty line and not be attracted to socialist ideology.

In spite of this the registered Communist Party of Canada has Marxist philosophy as its core agenda and it is clearly mentioned in its constitution

"The Communist Party of Canada is the Marxist-Leninist party of the working class dedicated to the cause of socialism. It is a voluntary organization of like-minded people which strives to unite in its ranks the most politically advanced and active members of the working class and of other sections of the people exploited by monopoly who are prepared to work for the achievement of working class state power and the building of a socialist Canada. The Communist Party of Canada has no interests separate and apart from those of the working class from which it springs. Support and work for the Party program is the basis of membership in the Party....."

In the Canadian political structure the less powerful and most sensitive corner is about the head of State of Canada Her Majesty the Queen of Canada her Royal Highness Queen Elizabeth II. Let me read the heartbeat of today's Canadians through the 90th birthday greetings presented by the Canadian Prime Minister Justin Trudeau on April 21, 2016.

"Over the past 64 years, Her Majesty has stood with Canada through key moments of our country's history and, as our nation underwent change and transformation, has been a rock of stability and a steadfast keeper of tradition.

"Today we admire her devotion to duty, and are thankful for her deeply-held affection for our country and unwavering loyalty to all Canadians."

It is crystal clear that Canadians are not substantially ready for replacing the Monarchy as the head of state of Canada with an elected president, under a republic of Canada from a constitutional monarchy. We always make the commitment when taking the citizenship oath:

I swear (or affirm)
That I will be faithful
And bear true allegiance
To Her Majesty Queen Elizabeth the Second
Queen of Canada
Her Heirs and Successors
And that I will faithfully observe
The laws of Canada
And fulfil my duties
As a Canadian citizen.

Most Canadians have not yet considered whether or not it is necessary to invest their valuable time and resources on this issue when many other pressing issues are at hand. Some sections of Canadians are in a wait- and- see mode choosing to believe letting the Queen continue as long as she can and if she wishes to hand things over to another member of the royal family the statesmanship or remain until her last breath and then we will think over whether or not replace the monarchy as the head of state for Canada. There is a saying that "the queen will never make mistakes" It does not mean she is has divine powers; rather she does not have any responsibilities therefore there is no room for her to make right or wrong decisions.

I feel that a substantial number of new immigrants particularly from non-British countries have less concern about this issue and they do not attach a particularly deep meaning into it.

As far as the Quebecers are concerned, though they have not yet accepted the Canadian Constitution of 1982, that replaced the North American Act signed by her Majesty Queen Elizabeth II in Ottawa on April 17, 1952 but they have been governed in the name of the

Queen and her representative the Lieutenant Governor since February 6, 1952. The Quebec sovereignty movement does not recognise the Queen as Queen of Canada rather it represents the British monarchy or English crown. The aboriginal people who account for 1.4 million of 36 estimated populations in 2016 in Canada have mixed feelings and unsettled grievances.

Even in the United Kingdom there are those who are advocating for a republic and its primary goal is to replace the monarchy by an elected president. However, it is not yet clear how this will take place. Anyhow they have made a compromise in having the Queen as the head of state for Britain as long as she can and then the monarchy will have an abundant role in the British government.

The CEO, of this movement, Graham Smith, said at the time of the 90th birthday for Queen Elizabeth II "Headline polling figures mask what's really happening: a growing indifference to the royals, a greater sense of citizenship and disillusionment with the political system - and an active, organised republicanism that is increasingly clear about the way ahead."

Though, it has been in operation for the last few decades, still it was in existence in the mid-17th century in the United Kingdom. Anyhow it is a fast growing movement; still it has not penetrated deep enough in influencing the British citizens to replace the monarchy. Even it has to be brought forward, it has to pass through the process of a referendum and the majority of British citizens have to vote in majority. If it is successful automatically in Britain, it will alter the position of the head of Canada itself.

The second pending issue in the system of government is the structure of the house of Senate, the so called upper house, which is currently modeled after the House of Lords in Britain with slight variations. It is aimed primarily at having a check and balance system in the House of Commons that holds the actual power of the government and elected by the citizens periodically and at times they may make decisions that may be inappropriate for the nation but momentarily satisfy the voters and in the long term it may be harmful or when a nation in a critical situation like an economic crisis or at war certainly a second opinion is a must in the best interest of the nation. Any bill passed by the House of Commons has to pass through the Senate successfully and like Britain, they are not elected by the citizens and therefore they are not necessarily answerable to them directly, like elected politicians. Their period of time in the position is not limited and originally it was a life time position and then the Constitution Act brought the upper age limit to 75 years of age. The minimum age is 30 years old. Between 1867 and 1879 the average of Senators was below 60 years and then shot up to early sixties till 1896 and till 1967 went up to late sixties and at times reached 70 and then starting from 1968 till recently came back to below 65. The appointment of Senators is single headedly done by the Prime Minister and it is generally expected that they will be patriotic, mature, talented and people oriented citizens of Canada but the criteria is somewhat flexible. The regional distribution of senators was set by the Constitution Act 1867 but it also at the discretion of the Prime Minister and it is not purely on based a quota system.

The distribution of senators geographically is not purely based on the size of population and size of the area, rather it is correlated with the length of time being part of the confederation.

Distribution of Senators by province

Province	Date joined - Confederation	# of senators
Alberta	September 1, 2905	6
British Colombia	July 20, 1871	6
Saskatchewan	September 1, 1905	6
Manitoba	July 15, 1870	6
Ontario	July 1, 1867	24
Quebec	July 1, 1867	24
New Foodland	March 31, 1949	6
New Brunswick	July 1, 1867	10
Nova Scotia	July 1, 1867	10
Prince Edward Island	July 1, 1873	4
Yukon	June 13, 1898	1
Northwest Territories	July 15, 1870	1
Nunavut	April 1, 1999	1
Total		105

Over the years, there is doubt from many corners that the Senate has not met expectations and made substantial contributions for the tax payers in particular and the nation at large. The Senate first of all is not obliged to pay their gratitude to their Prime Minister who appointed them to that post.

Out of the three major political parties, the Conservatives and the Liberals are insisting on the reformation of the Senate but the New Democratic Party rejected the idea for any kind of reformation, rather they want it totally abandoned. Thomas Joseph Mulcair also advocated for the demolition of senate and former Conservative Premier of Alberta Brad Wall also supported it by saying "I think it's time to abolish the Senate. I think it's reflective of what Canadians are saying. I don't think reform is possible. I think abolition is also difficult, but it's " more doable than reform,"

According to the Constitution of Canada, it wouldn't be an easy task and it has to go through the provinces, House of Commons, the Senate and then the final approval from the head of state. That was the primary reason that Harper the former Prime Minister initially made some moves and later on could not do much and now Prime Minister Justin Trudeau has taken up the challenge. Let's wait and see how far he will be able to get. I would also like to mention that when he was chosen as a leader for the Liberal party he made a comment on the Senate on a regional basis. "We have 24 senators from Quebec and there are just six from Alberta and British Columbia. It's to our advantage," he told a French newspaper on May 2013 just after he became the liberal party leader on April 14, 2013. And it brought the Quebec interest first as he once said similarly In 2010, he told an interviewer he was tired of Albertans running the country and that Quebecers have made the best prime ministers" After he began to shoulder the responsibilities for the nation as a whole his attitudes began to be wider and broad minded. Of course Trudeau apologized for those comments when they surfaced in 2012 still it wasn't expected from such high calibre leader.

Canadian Prime Ministers

#	Name:	Term:	Time in office:	Elections won:	Left office:
1	John A. MacDonald	July 1, 1867 - November 7, 1873	6 years, 4 months, 6 d.	2	Resigned
2	Alexander Mackenzie (interim)[1]	November 7, 1873 - January 22, 1874	2 months, 15 d.	1	Elected
	Alexander Mackenzie	January 22, 1874 - October 17, 1878	4 years, 8 months, 26 d.	0	Lost election
3	John A. MacDonald (2nd time)	October 17, 1878 - June 6, 1891	12 years, 7 months, 19 d.	4	Died
	Nobody	June 6, 1891 - June 16, 1891	10 d.		
4	John Abbott (interim)	June 16, 1891 - December 5, 1892	1 year, 5 months, 20 d.	0	Resigned
5	John Thompson (interim)	December 5, 1892 - December 12, 1894	2 years, 7 d.	0	Died
	Nobody	December 12, 1894 - December 21, 1894	9 d.		
6	Mackenzie Bowell (interim)	December 21, 1894 - May 1, 1896	1 year, 4 months, 11 d.	0	Resigned

7	**Charles Tupper** *(interim)*	May 1, 1896 - July 11, 1896	2 months, 10 d.	0	Lost election
8	**Wilfred Laurier**	July 11, 1896 - October 10, 1911	15 years, 2 months, 30 d.	4	Lost election
9	**Robert Borden**	Oct 10, 1911 - July 10, 1920	8 years, 9 months	2	Resigned
10	**Arthur Meighen** *(interim)*	July 10, 1920 - December 29, 1921⁴	1 year, 5 months	0	Lost election
11	**Mackenzie King**	December 29, 1921 - June 28,1926	4 years, 5 months, 29 d.	2	Fired by GG²
12	**Arthur Meighen** (2nd time) *(interim)²*	June 28, 1926 - September 25, 1926	2 months, 27 d.	0	Lost election
13	**Mackenzie King** (2nd time)	September 25, 1926 - August 7, 1930	3 years, 10 months, 13 days	1	Lost election
14	**Richard Bennett**	August 7, 1930 - October 23, 1935	5 years, 2 months, 16 d.	1	Lost election
15	**Mackenzie King** (3rd time)	October 23, 1935 - November 15, 1948	13 years, 22 d.	3	Resigned

16	Louis St. Laurent *(interim)*	November 15, 1948 - June 27, 1949	7 months, 12 d.	1	Elected
17	Louis St. Laurent	June 27, 1949 - June 21, 1957	7 years, 11 months, 24 d.	2	Lost election
17	John Diefenbaker	June 21, 1957 - April 22, 1963	5 years, 10 months, 1 d.	3	Lost election
18	Lester Pearson	April 22, 1963 - April 20, 1968	4 years, 11 months, 28 d.	1	Resigned
19	Pierre Trudeau *(interim)*	April 20, 1968 - June 25, 1968	2 months, 5 d.	1	Elected
	Pierre Trudeau	June 25, 1968 - June 4, 1979	10 years, 11 months, 19 d.	2	Lost election
20	Joe Clark	June 4, 1979 - March 3, 1980	8 months, 30 days	1	Lost election
21	Pierre Trudeau (2nd time)	March 3, 1980 - June 30, 1984	4 years, 3 months, 27 d.	1	Resigned
22	John Turner *(interim)*	June 30, 1984 - September 17, 1984	2 months, 17 d.	0	Lost election
23	Brian Mulroney	September 17, 1984 - June 25, 1993	8 years, 9 months, 8 d.	2	Resigned
24	Kim Campbell *(interim)*	June 25, 1993 - November 4, 1993	4 months, 9 d.	0	Lost election

#	Name	Term	Minority lasted	#	Result
25	Jean Chretien	November 4, 1993 - December 12, 2003	10 years, 1 month, 8 d.	3	Resigned
26	Paul Martin (interim)	December 12, 2003 - June 28, 2004	6 months, 16 d.	1	Elected
	Paul Martin	June 28, 2004 - February 6, 2006	1 year, 7 months, 6 d.	0	Lost election
27	Stephen Harper	February 6, 2006 - November 4, 2015	9 years, 8 months, 29 d.	3	
28	Justin Trudeau	November 4, 2015 -		1	

#	Name:	Term:[3]	Minority lasted:	ended:	Result
2	Alexander Mackenzie (interim)[1]	November 7, 1873 - January 22, 1874	2 months, 15 d.	Election Call	Elected to Majority
11	Mackenzie King	October 29, 1925 - June 28, 1926	7 months, 29 d.	Fired by GG[2]	Meighen appointed PM
12	Arthur Meighen (interim)[2]	June 28, 1926 - September 25, 1926	2 months, 27 d.	No Confidence Vote	Lost election

	John Diefenbaker (1st minority)	June 21, 1957 - March 31, 1958	9 months, 10 d.	No Confidence Vote	Elected to Majority
17	John Diefenbaker (2nd minority)	June 18, 1962 - February 5, 1963	7 months, 15 d.	No Confidence Vote	Lost election
18	Lester Pearson (1st minority)	April 22, 1963 - November 8, 1965	2 years, 6 months, 16 d.	Election Call	Elected to 2nd Minority
	Lester Pearson (2nd minority)	November 8, 1965 - April 20, 1968	2 years, 5 months, 12 d.	Resigned	Trudeau becomes PM
19	Pierre Trudeau (interim)	April 20, 1968 - June 25, 1968	2 months, 5 d.	Election Call	Elected to Majority
	Pierre Trudeau (2nd minority)	October 30, 1972 - May 8, 1974	1 year, 6 months, 9 d.	No Confidence Vote	Elected to Majority
20	Joe Clark	June 4, 1979 - December 13, 1979	6 months, 9 d.	No Confidence Vote	Lost election
26	Paul Martin	June 28, 2004 - November 28, 2005	1 year, 5 months	No Confidence Vote	Lost election

27	Stephen Harper (1st minority)	February 6, 2006 – October 14, 2008	2 years, 8 months, 8 d.	Election Call	Elected to 2nd Minority
	Stephen Harper (2nd minority)	October 14, 2008 – March 25, 2011	2 years, 5 months, 11 d.	No Confidence Vote	

The Hon. William Lyon Mackenzie King was able to serve Canada for three full terms of majority governments and two terms of the minority government. His last minority government brought very significant constitutional issues and proved that the Governor General, the representative of the Queen of Canada is not necessary to be a nominal head or the ceremonial figure and this was proven by the Governor General Lord Byng of Vimy. Rt. Hon. Alexander Mackenzie's Liberal Member of Parliament seats won 101 in 1925 from 118 in 1921, whereas Arthur Meighen's Conservatives respectively won 116 in 1925 from 49 in 1921 The Progressive party position was also reduced to 28 from 58 and the overall total members of parliament were 245. Though Alexander Mackenzie lost his seat in the election and also his party's position was reduced from the second largest from the absolute majority in the previous election and gained power and in fact he was the one who advised the Governor General Lord Byng to dissolve the government and writ for general election in September and the election was held 29th October 1925. Still he did not resign and remained in office as a head of the minority government and the inclusiveness of the Progressive members of parliament did not go to the level of any coalition. At one point in time, when he discovered that it wouldn't work as well as he anticipated, but he wanted to continue in power but the Governor General told him "Well, in any event you must not at any time ask for a dissolution unless Mr. Meighen is first given a chance to show whether or not he is able to govern."

His contribution for the Canadians is comparatively remarkable at the crucial time when the global situation was so uncertain and unstable, the adverse effects of World War One (1914-1918) and the prolonged and severe Depression of the early 1930s, had been a major challenge for any ruler who would have been in a similar position and his powerful leadership made a tremendous contribution in overcoming those obstacles.

The direct or indirect involvement in the Beauharnais scandal that was on the corruption of given $ 70, 000.00 to the ruling Liberal party of Canada by the Beauhamois Light, Heat and Power Company in 1930s upset his reputation.

The scandal that was related with the Airbus jets purchase for the Government of Canada by the Government of Canada led by Brain Mulroney got some secret commissions. In 1995 the Royal Canadian Mounted Police accused Brian Mulroney and Frank Moors, the second Premier of Newfoundland of accepting kickbacks from Karl Heinz Schreiber, a dual citizen of Germany and Canada who was a businessman and arms dealer.

"I look upon it (wealth) as a solemn trust to enable me to serve my country without fear for the future...henceforth. I must dedicate my talent and my time and such qualities as I may have the fortune

That God has been enough to give me, to the interests of my country..." by Tory Leader R. B. Bennett

The reign of Mr. Stephen Harper, the former Prime Minister after having two minority and a majority government was over when Canadians voted for a majority government led by the Liberal Party headed by the so-called sexiest and cool headed, second youngest Prime Minister.

Justin Trudeau was chosen in the general election of November 4th, 2015 as the 23rd Prime Minister in the 43rd parliamentary election. It was an election that was eagerly watched by most of the developed nations, including the members of the North Atlantic Treaty Organization NATO, the G-20, and former SWETO and the United States of America in particular. Usually the parliamentary election in Canada is not keenly watched by the world except on three occasions and it was not due to the role of Canada, rather it was that Canada refused get involved in controversial issues or radical changes in both domestic and international politics. The New Democratic Party with its slight touch of left wing flavour became confident in its ability to capture federal power almost twenty years back. Being elected to form a majority government would have been observed carefully by both NATO and the members of the Warsaw Pact and the main reason is that the west would have been keen in its inclination to gradually bring Canada into their orbit deviating up to certain extents towards a state monopoly of the structure of the economy. Although the former soviet bloc and its allies have made slight changes in the system of state monopoly, they have not lost the roots. On the other hand they are sure that their influence in South America wouldn't be possible because Canada is not poor and less developed like them.

I presume that if the election had been held just after the terrorist attack in Paris, France in November 2015, it is likely that either one of the following would have happened; a sizable portion of the voters would have gone to the Conservatives from that of the Liberals and it might have resulted in recapturing of some of the seats where Conservatives lost with marginal votes and reduced the members of parliament by a few and kept either a slight majority government or minority government. There was only a slight chance of the alternative of a minority government for the Conservatives. If the election would have taken place a couple of months after the attack in Paris France, I think that the voters would have had ample time to reflect and allow Harper to continue his mandate for another term. I also consider the gravity of the first terrorist attack on Canadian soil on October 20th, 2014 and that of October 22, 2014 and I would venture to say that it was pure luck for Justin Trudeau and hard luck for Harper.

The replacement of the Harper government by the Liberals is the result of multiple factors.

The last election is the first in having 330 seats, an increase of 30 more seats to the total of 338 from 308 and over 1800 candidates mainly from 23 registered political parties at that time took part in the 19th October 2015 election. In spite of the party's inclinations for the candidates, eighty of them ran as independent candidates. They usually stand a better chance when no party has won the absolute majority. Some had been elected by the people through one of the major political parties but due to certain reasons they were expelled or voluntarily left. One example is that of Mr. Scott Andrews one of the former Liberal Party members of parliament elected in the 2011 election and served his constituency and then he was turned over due the allegations of sexual harassment by female New Democratic Party Members of Parliament.

Though this parliamentary election expresses the views and opinions of the majority of the voters, in a situation where a multiparty system exists, it is hard for having those of the majority expressed by the ruling party, due to the fact that every other party has a lesser number of members of parliament still it is not necessary to cast votes proportionately.

Though the women are slightly higher than men in population, only one third of them contested in this election, but it is an increase of 1.5% from the previous election of 2011. In all five main parties, as such the Liberal Party, Conservatives, Bloc Quebecois, and The Green Party, the New Democratic Party had around 33% female candidates and the NDP led the rest at 43% and then the Greens 39% The Liberals 31%, Bloc Quebecois 28%, and the Conservatives 20%. Although the three major political parties had full status with candidates, in each of the country's 338 seats, the Liberals were reduced to 337 candidates when Cherry Thomas quit after anti -Muslim and anti-Israel comments, she made long before she won the nomination, it became a serious issue for the reputation of her party.. Her comment had nothing to with the Canadian election directly, it was feared that it may antagonize the Jewish community. Usually the issues on Jews are very sensitive after the Second World War where over six million Jews were massacred by the Nazis. The Bloc Quebecois had candidates in all 78 seats in the province of Quebec. Since, it has been a party that has the great concerns of Francophone Canadians in particularly in Quebec though this does not mean that they do not care about other French Canadians in the rest of Canada. We also should acknowledge that they have equal rights and responsibilities to Canada like any other national parties. In fact the Bloc Quebec had the privilege for being the national opposition party between 1993 and 1997.

    a. Need for a change of government by general population. Justine Trudeau at an interview with Chief Mark Kennedy,

Ottawa Citizen parliamentary bureau, in London Ontario clearly mentioned that voters were seeking change, He further said that Harper's Conservatives might draw Canada into a ground war against ISIL in the middle east

b. Uncomfortable with hard line Immigration policies of the Harper's government.

c. Direct involvement in combat on the war against ISIS

d. Making laws favouring the rich at the cost of the middle class

e. Adverse effect of economic recession

f. Change in international trade relationships

g. Change on the principals on taxation.

h. Paul Martin's Liberal government was very successful in the economy. The federal budget returned balanced with a surplus. The corporate income tax was reduced in series.

i. Tough in nature on Foreign policy

j. The reviving Canadian image on the globe.

k. Expected a better American relationship

l. Approach against radicalization by Harper and criticized by Justin Trudeau in March 2015 in Toronto and also accused Harper's Tories of deliberately trying to " play on people's fear and foster prejudices, directly towards the Muslim faith" Later on to soften this accusation. He of fear and division, and pitting Canadians against one another. It is irresponsible and languorous further said that Harper playing the politics and not worthy of the office of a prime minister. There are consequences to the country from this kind political ploy"

m. Inappropriate spending claim by Senators

n. The so-called arrogant approach with colleagues

o. Over emphasis on Harper. Over focused on him. His attitudes in governing excess that of Ray Novak's and the Nigel Rights.

Jason Haney was put in forefront in gaining more votes from the east and south East Asians Canadians. It did not work well why. Though he was in very good term with them in certain sections of his contribution but overall his hard core immigration policies superseded and it turned against him. Candidates are accountable to the voters and the leader is accountable for members.

p. The back benchers voiced out when the party was in power that they were governed, not they have been a part of governing body.

It is not unusual for there to be such a major change in the voting patterns after one party has been in power for a long time. When one political party has been in power for a number of years, it is like a river that has been blocked; in due course, the water becomes stagnant and it is important to get the water moving again.

Justin Trudeau just after winning his seat at Papineau, made an appearance at a local subway station. Usually public transportation is patronized by younger workers in entry level career positions. The presence at the subway for a few minutes made a great psychological impact. It is a tactical move.

Prime Minster Trudeau determined to deploy more solders to Iraq as a Canada's role in the battle against Islamic CF18 fighters, even after the ISIS claimed responsibility for the Paris attack on November 13th 2015 - and it will surpass the contingent of 69 soldiers.

Brain Mulroney called Chrétien a "buffoon", Kim Campbell used the phrase " control freak." Chrétien's advice was to engage in a dialogue with variety of international leaders. Pierre Trudeau maintained an open approach. The Liberals campaigned from the left and govern from the right. The parallels between the Trudeau win in Canada in 2015 and the Obama campaign in the USA in 2008 are interesting. The Liberals got advice from the veterans of the Obama campaign. While the presidential system is more reflective of the voice of the people and has checks and balances between the legislative and the executive branches, this is not the case with our Parliament. In our case, both systems have been merged together and it is easier to make a decision and implement it very quickly. U.S President Obama had a difficult time and sent certain issues back and forth until they were finalized and implemented; one good example of this is the Northern Gateway Pipeline.

Chretien said Trudeau is a serious politician, like his father was but also got a lot of his political skill from his maternal side, Trudeau's grandfather Jimmy Sinclair, was a cabinet minister in Louis Laurent's Liberal government Jimmy Sinclair was quite a politician. He was a tall guy, good looking, comfortable with people"

"The regime under the leadership of Quebec is stronger than that of the westerners"

Justine Trudeau made poorly worded comment about the leadership partners in the Harper government in 2010. The Sun Media published comments on Thursday that Trudeau made in a November 2010 interview in French on the Télé-Québec program *Les Francs-Tireurs* (The Straight Shooters). In the interview, His comment of "Canada was better off in the hands of leaders from Quebec" was a momentary reaction of some Albertans politicians move at that time, but I do not think it was the best for a candidate who was pursuing the leader of a liberal party, one of the well reputed parties Now that he is the Prime Minister these comments cannot be justified

"Canada isn't doing well right now because it's Albertans who control our community and socio-democratic agenda. It doesn't work," Trudeau told interviewer Patrick Lagacé.

Liberal MP Justin Trudeau appears on the Télé-Québec program Les Francs-tireurs (The Straight Shooters) in November 2010. Trudeau's Liberal leadership campaign says comments about Quebecers and Albertans in the interview are being taken out of context. (Télé-Québec)

When asked whether he thought Canada was "better served when there are more Quebecers in charge than Albertans," Trudeau replied, "I'm a Liberal, so of course I think so, yes. Certainly when we look at the great Prime Ministers of the 20th century, those that really stood the test of time, they were MPs from Quebec. There was Trudeau, there was Mulroney, there was Chrétien, and there was Paul Martin. We have a role. This country, Canada, it belongs to us."

But his speech as the president of the party in 2015 is somewhat contradictory. "Canada's a great country and deserves better leadership. After ten long years, we know what get with Stephen harper; divisive politics that pits one region of the country against another. I believe that any prime Minister or -- anyone who wants to be Prime Minister-should be ready to fight to keep Canada together, not think of new ways to tear it apart. Liberals believe in a united Canada that looks forward with a shared purpose; a country that is strong not in spite of our individual difference, but because of Canada that looks forward with a shared purpose; a country that is strong not in spite of our individual differences, but because of them"

The impact of the hard core regime of Harper

The Harper Conservatives "tough on crime" strategy was one of the five priorities expressed at the Throne Speech of Stephan Harper, the Prime Minister on April 4, 2006 as " by proposing changes to the Criminal Code "to provide tougher sentences for violent and repeat offenders, particularly those involved in weapons-related crimes." and tightened the such laws and its implementations is more than even before and to Statistics Canada, the Crime Severity Index, the crime rate decreased by 3% between 2013 and it was the lowest rate recorded since 1969 even with the increase in population and continue in decreasing."

In some major areas this has earned mixed feeling and reactions. With the best intentions of maintaining peace and harmony for every citizen and others particularly the law abiding citizens being harmed or victimized over and over and those who get involved in unlawful activities have taken leniency in sentencing for the crime whatever the it may be have not controlled such activities or reduced them at the rate that has been expected. Therefore the hardening of sentences and punishments would result in curbing criminal activities and promote a better and safe environment for citizens and others who have been residing in Canada. Recently the crime rate in Canada has not been on an increase, rather, it is dropping. While the population in prison has been on the rise, the tougher laws on crime have been proposed and passed as law and implemented by the Harper government. The main areas where Harper government had concerns are:

- Imposing mandatory minimum sentences
  for drug-related offences and increase
  the maximum sentences for certain drug

trafficking offences;

- Institute a number of new mandatory minimum sentences for sexual offences;
- Implement new exceptions to eligibility for Conditional sentences to be served in the community;
- Increase restrictions on applying for pardons (now termed "record suspensions"); and
- Impose harsher sentences on young offenders.

The correctional service does have its own mandatory minimum sentences and they do not want those who enter the prison system to depart as they had entered. They are expected to correct themselves and become a better person for himself and for the nation. It was mentioned as a part of its vision and mission statement as "programs and services based on high standards to achieve positive change in offender behaviour and attitude".

The purpose of punishment and rewards has its own merits and modern theories encouraged by social sciences, and psychology emphasizes rewards over punishments. However, according to the criminal justice system the punishment for a criminal would discourage or prevent those who intend on getting involved in such activity. Practically it has both positive and negative impacts. I would cite an example in Toronto when John Tory the Mayor of Toronto was the leader for Progressive Conservative Party of Ontario in 2007 and I was the Candidate for Scarborough Center for the Progressive Conservative Party. We had a discussion on crime prevention with a group of young and middle aged Torontonians. In the discussion of a variety of topics related to the main topic at hand some of the participants who happened to have been sentenced and been in jail for one and more times were bold and frank enough in expressing their opinions. They mentioned that the first time they entered prison they regretted their actions and somehow they would try to reform themselves. But when they returned back to their respective communities, they were looked down upon and shown no sympathy and in some cases they were partially or totally isolated or treated badly. It reversed their previous change of heart and mind as such, it did not bother them much when they ended up committing another crime.

The community has to play a significant role through their community organizations and government agencies to assist those who have been in prison and it should not be left only to the correctional system. Those who have been in prison for a long time or repeatedly would find it hard to maintain positive changes. I do acknowledge that by having more prisons and prisoners is costly, and it is the taxpayers who bear this burden.

Mel Hurtig, in his new book entitled "The arrogant Autocrat; Stephen Harper's Takeover of Canada" describes arrogant actions both inside and outside Canadian affairs. At a news conference in October 2015 before the parliamentary general election, Mr. Harper mentioned at the time that the Senate had more Liberal senators that proposed some amendments to the Accountability Act and said "The behaviour of the Liberal Party is arrogant and anti-democratic," Jason Kenney, one of the key minsters of the Harper cabinet said about Trudeau during the election in 2015 - "I frankly don't see much difference between Pierre Trudeau's policies and Justin Trudeau's arrogant, anti-Alberta attitude that he's expressed more than once." And as mentioned, Trudeau commented in a 2010 French-language interview "Canada isn't doing well because it's Albertans who control both the community and socio-democratic agenda.' Of course Trudeau apologized for those comments when they surfaced in 2012 Justin Trudeau might have had a preconceive notion of the political background of Harper in relation with his Canadian Alliance Party and its roots in the Reform Party before the merger of the Progressive Conservative Party of Canada and Canadian Alliance Party of Canada. Though it was a merger of the two parties with a mutual understanding and shared values, still it appeared for many that the Alliance Party had the upper hand and its national vision and focus on its lingering agenda of the west should be promoted over the rest of Canada. Former Prime Minister Brian Mulroney called it "Reform in pantyhose". Anyhow, a silent truth was within the party itself by a few members that the original conservative flavour had been reduced to some degree. Justin Trudeau has a reason for the regional sentimentality for the west has some influences within the Conservative Party and it might have been impacted in the Harper regime.

The hard line nature of rule is the only way to bring effective and strong solutions for the accumulated and unsolved issues. A good example is that Mike Harris was able to bring back on track the Ontario economy and resolved certain abuses of the system and took it away from the brink from the regime of the Bob Ray, under the New Democratic Party. I do not think any other Canadian Prime Ministers would have faced internal challenges and also made historical changes for Canada than Prime Minister Pierre Trudeau. His approach was at times branded as arrogant in nature; still it was an asset for him in resolving the Quebec sovereignty movement, and the Quiet Revolution. His personality also helped him bring the Constitution and the Canadian Charter of Rights and Freedom of 1982 out but in addition his personality, his diplomatic skills also contributed to his great success.

Here are some criticisms on Harper's approach

a. Immigration broken hard nut bill C24
b. Terrorism C51 It is growing fast, changing tactics'
c. Counter terrorism reduction of oil price infiltration, Arab spring is a failure for those citizens and victory for the external forces.
d. Restricted relationship with U.S.A
e. Promoted family values in a very conservative manner
f. Proposed to Purchase of costly F34 at the time of recession.
g. Man of principle of respecting human rights and declined the invitation for attending the summer Olympics in China.

Conspiracy in the Process of Contemplation- Quebec sovereignty

Canadians, particularly Ontarians and Quebecers while feeling the pinch of the prolonged negative impact of the recession of 2008 and the uneasiness from extreme weather were somewhat relieved by the warm summer of 2013. Then all of a sudden, the time bomb called the Charter of Quebec Values went off and woke all of us up.

A proposed document entitled "The Charter of Quebec Values" from the Parti Quebecois; the minority provincial government for Quebec was leaked to the media and the core proposal in this charter is to ban public workers from wearing conspicuous religious symbols such as the turban, hijab- kippah or crucifixes in the work place. It appears that once it is brought forward as a bill and passed by a majority vote in the legislative assembly and then signed by the respective Lt.

Governor and becomes law, eventually the ban on religious symbols will be extended to other public sectors. Initially this restriction would apply to health, primary, pre-school, secondary school workers and provincial judiciary employees, including judges and law enforcement personnel. This idea did not come from out of nowhere however; it was one of the main items of the 2011 election manifesto of the Parti Quebecois. Mr. Bernard Danville the provincial minister of Quebec in charge for this mandate said on 10th September, 2013 that " it is a beautiful day for Quebecers" referring to the Charter of Quebec Values and that hopefully it would bring in another ray of hope for Quebecers in terms of protecting and promoting their age old traditional values.

The Provincial government claims that the ban in wearing these religious symbols in the workplace will create a conducive atmosphere in developing a unified Quebec society; by banning religious symbols, it is the theory that everyone will therefore work in the best interest of Quebecers from those who have roots from French ancestors and everyone else regardless of their ethnic origin and socio-economic or religious backgrounds. On the surface, it appears that this charter is promoting religious neutrality, secularism, and unity within diversity. Ms. Pauline Marois, the Premier of Quebec mentioned "Quebecers are open positive people and believe in defending each other's freedoms, not restrict them". Premier Marois also mentioned that it would bring Quebec together like Bill 101 aimed at protecting the French language. Equality between women and men is universal but is also an important value in Canada and Quebec. She further said that "it will become, I'm certain, a strong uniting element between Quebecers. We are moving forward in the name of all the women, all the men, who chose Quebec for our culture, for our freedom and for our diversity". According to her statements, this is not a new phenomenon; rather it began a half a century ago. If this had been the true vision, there would be no need for me to spend my time writing about this and you would not have to spend your valuable time reading it. I do not totally disagree with Ms. Marois and her sincerity, but I am concerned with the inner motives and the hidden agenda behind this proposed charter and its possible contradictions with the Canadian Charter of Rights and Freedoms. I also acknowledge that there is substantial support for the charter in other parts of Canada and it was revealed in recent polls that the level of support is high. The poll taken on 23/08/13 by New Forum Research indicated that 42% of Canadians support this proposed charter. In another poll, 32% of them supported it. Some of the supporting Canadians have the attitude of wait and see, and if it is passed into law and then triumphs over any legal challenges, then they will expect their provincial government to act accordingly.

The concern about religious expression is not limited to the proposed charter in Quebec. All around the world, there have been many suggestions as to how to deal with the discomfort around the issue of religious accommodation. For example, German Chancellor Angela Merkel alerted her citizens about the new waves of foreign influence and began to thwart such influence by preventing the creation of separate swimming pools for Muslim schoolgirls. The highest administrative court of Germany ruled recently that notwithstanding their constitutional rights to religious freedom, Muslim girls can be compelled to take part in mixed gender swimming classes at school. The court did not undermine the values of their faith and suggested that the Muslim girls swim in a full- body suit known as a "Burkini." In this case, the court might have taken the individual rights against the states obligation in educating children in a more conducive environment. Another powerful politician Mr. Thilo Sarrazin, co-author of a book about Germany condemned the ways of Arabs who live in the country The British media also gave a lot of coverage on the suggestion made by a Liberal Democrat Member of Parliament about a ban on women wearing veils in schools and public places. The spokesman for Mr. David Cameron declared that his leader is in favour in prohibiting veils in the schools.

There are over thirty million Muslims living in Western Europe and eight million in France. Most of them arrived from their former colonies as in the case of the Algerians, Tunisians, and Moroccans who are of Arab cultural background. Other Muslims living in France come from the Ivory Coast, Mauritania, Chad, and Niger of sub –Saharan Africa. These nations are part of the Francophone and others come from former British Colonies and are mostly members of the British Common wealth such as Zambia, Nigeria, Kenya, Uganda, Tanzania, and Sudan. There are also Muslim minorities in Germany, Austria, Switzerland, Holland, Sweden, Belgium, and Denmark. There are also old immigrants and converts in some pockets of the former Yugoslavia and Czechoslovakia and after disintegration with a bitter war and massacre new nations were born with Muslims taking the upper hand.

There are many Europeans who are not in favour of the penetration of foreign cultural influences on what they like to refer to as "their way of life". Though they might not say so publicly, sadly when given the opportunity, their views become more apparent.

Mr. Victor Armony, professor of sociology at the Universite du Quebec, Montreal said "the current debate is more dangerous than the one six years ago when the Quebec commission held hearings to study the accommodation of religious minorities. That led to the airing of anti-Jewish and anti-Muslim sentiment from some participants.

I had the privilege to speak with a prominent human rights lawyer while I was outlining this book in a vacation resort in Cuba and he too had some similar opinions. The leading Canadian politicians are very cautious and careful in expressing their opinions. The only politician who expressed his critical opinion faster than the others is Mr. Justin Trudeau, leader of the Liberal Party and a young and energetic politician. He said 'The world is laughing at Quebec over the blatant attempt to motivate fear of others. I do not think this is who we are and I do not think it honours us to have a government that does not know our generosity and openness of spirit as a people". Mr. Molar the Leader of New Democratic Party was concerned about not antagonizing the Quebecers who voted for the NDP in larger numbers than ever before in that province. However he should be aware that his silence speaks volumes.

The comment made by Mr. Harper, the former Prime Minister of Canada though it was very much expected from both the Quebecers and the rest of Canada was not overly exiting because he clearly said, while participating in a press conference in British Columbia that "I do not see the charter in its current form going anywhere, I think the common sense of Quebecers will force this towards a reasonable conclusion as the debate progresses". Therefore, this issue was not bothering him as others had expected. It reminded me about Mr. Jean Chrétien during the time of the campaign for the sovereignty referendum in Quebec in 1995. He was not panicked and stressed-out like Mr. Brian Mulroney who took it very seriously and worked around the clock. That being said, the results taught a lesson not only to Jean Chrétien but to all Canadians that certain issues have to be taken more seriously than others. I do not mean to compare the referendum with the current issue but there is much that can be learned from the past.

All the Federal political parties have expressed that this charter is unacceptable and somehow contradicts the Charter of Rights and Freedoms that it is discriminative and to a certain extent is offensive towards religious minorities. The majority of members in the Bloc Quebecois, the federal wing of the sovereignty movement support the Charter of Quebec values and there are those who oppose it like Ms. Maria Mourani who was born in the Ivory Cost in Africa, a former French colony and is of Lebanese ancestry and migrated to Canada and got herself well integrated into Canadian life. Since she was born and raised by French descendants, she might not have felt the gravity of the historical grievances of the Quebecers but might feel obligated to protect the interests of new immigrants and religious minorities.

Almost all of the mayors of the municipalities in the Island of Montreal are against this charter. Mr. Lionel Perez, Mayor of Cote-des- Neiges -dame-de –Grace condemned it and a Jew never hesitates in wearing a kippah to many important public events. He said " I am obviously a poster child for this issue" In Quebec the distribution of population by religion is 82.2 % Christians, Atheist and those who does belong to any religion 12.1%, Muslims 3.1%, Jews 1.1% Sikhs 1%, Hindus 0.4% and others 1%.

Apart from awaking ethnic nationalism, there is also another dimension in this charter that is supporting feminism and is against the subordination, oppression, inequality and suppression of the fundamental rights of women, regardless of their religious denominations. During the time of canvassing for the support for the Quebec referendum in 1980, many women's organizations fought for women's rights as well. Lise Payette, the first female mayor of Quebec brought up the oppression of women as a serious concern for all Quebecers. But gender equality is already an important part of the Charter of Rights of Quebec 1975.

Mr. Jacques Parizeau former Premier of Quebec from September 1994 to January 1996, has been a long time high profile supporter for the sovereignty movement and one who highly hoped for victory in the Referendum in 1995 and was thoroughly disappointed in the marginal defeat and blamed the defeat on money and ethnic votes, including European ethnic minorities who expressed a balanced view on the Charter of Quebec Values. His critical views appeared in the French newspaper Le Journal de Montreal. He explains that charter discriminates against its citizens because of their religious beliefs by banning religious symbols and clothing at work in the government departments. He further pointed out that the separation of church and state in Quebec has been long established. He also criticized the fact that the government has decided to leave the crucifix that hangs above the Speaker's chair in the national assembly. But the government says that it is a part of the province's history. They say that is but a symbol of history and has nothing to do with beliefs.

The national and Quebec Liberal party is against the referendum and the Quebec Liberal leader Philippe Couillard strongly denounced and said that it will become law "over my dead body" He further said " the big mistake that the government is making is to make people believe that, in order to defend what is specific about Quebec.

Over ten thousand people mainly from ethnic minorities held a demonstration on 14th September 2013 in Montreal, and signed a petition. It appeared to be a multicultural event with participants from the Muslim, Sikh, Jewish and Hindu communities and one of the banners carried by a group from a local mosque read "Multi-faith for peace". Despite this show of protest, still there is also silent support for the charter from the same ethnic groups, particularly from the women who value the promotion of feminism and are eager to have more freedom. The concept and the interpretation for feminism is based on fundamental human rights, religious interpretations, social values, economic factors and the system of government based on democracy that is built on the strength of every vote from its citizens, regardless of ethnicity, gender, religion and other social status.

When I was working in Nigeria,I was keen to know the structure and operation of their traditional values and at one point in time I happened to attend a meeting where the President Segu Saharay was making certain comments on education having been a school teacher himself had a sound background of both the traditional educational values of the Hausa and familiarisation with modern education. It was said that there were negative aspects in western education and what he knowingly said about modern western education itself is controversial. The core of the matter is not to encourage deviation from the norms of their society. The current rights for women in their family and public life have been considered appropriate and no other person has the right to make any attempt to even slightly alter it. Now the question is that if this was part of their ethnic culture and tradition or a vibrant section of their religious faith or if it was a customary value of the society where the religious beliefs have inherited. It is evident in the cultivation of the religious practises where it was planted, for example Sikhism in the predominant Hindu and Muslim communities, Islam in the Jewish context, Buddhism in relation to Hindus and paganism in the context of many religions. Apart from cultural and religious mingling, other factors such as the political and economic components also have an influence. The combination of colonial rule with economic domination forcefully converted many of their subjects of their colonies The suppressive rulers denied and repressed their age old religious freedoms and treated with partiality and gave undue rights and privileges for those who are committed in conversion. Economic domination as a single power that controls and dominates over others based on religious backgrounds also makes a huge impact. The other side of the story is the giving of priority to wealth over other factors. In this regard, Karl Marx is another extreme and in accordance with his theory of scientific socialism mentioned in his book, "Das-Capital" every move and aspect of human behaviour are basically influenced by economic factors and moving towards materialism is the final goal of life and nothing more than that. I have met Russians and Chinese in Africa and in Canada who were born and raised during Socialist rule and most of them have very little faith in religion. There is a fast growing trend in the profile of being spiritual but not religious. The spirituality program was enhanced in the curriculum fifteen years ago when the Catholic and Protestant instruction was removed from the curriculum and also abolished the religious school board in 1997. They do not visit the places of worship; observe religious ceremonies, fasting and the rituals. In some of the industrialized countries, like America, money and wealth speak louder than religion and other social factors. The growing rate of Atheists around the world also alarms religious organizations and they are not worried about any other issues related with religion. If we treat them as another sector, in Quebec they are second to Christians in number. We must also take into consideration the namesake religious people and for them religion is a label. The degree of accepting or allowing those values into the religious practise depends on the religious bodies, leaders and their strength.

It is crystal clear that this charter is a timely political manoeuvre in order to gain more support by awakening ethnic sentiments in order to secure popular support in the next election and form a majority government. They also know that the majority of new immigrants are not for Quebec sovereignty and they prefer to remain as Canadians first and then Quebecers. When compared to getting additional votes from the mainstream, losing the ethnic vote would not be a bad thing. For the Parti Quebecois, the loss of the ethnic vote would be nothing but short term pain for the long term gain. Furthermore, the charter also distracts from issues related to the economy, and unemployment among other things.

In closing, we must really question the motives behind the proposed Quebec Charter of Values. Does this Charter really seek to promote unity? Who has determined exactly what values the people of Quebec honour and uphold the most has everyone in Quebec been asked. Or is this charter in the end just another way for the sovereignty movement to gather more steam.

Hopefully, in time, the answers to these questions will become clear. In the meantime, it would serve all of us well to reflect on what the potential consequences of this charter could be, not only in Quebec but for the rest of us Canadians.

Canada with the United States of America

The New York Times, one of the most well reputed newspapers having a mass worldwide circulation has been terribly mocked online for an article published on 17th January 2016 declaring that Canada is a nation of backwardness. America's northern neighbour was described as "the country that gave the world ice hockey, the snow blower and

Labatt's beer "and which was widely viewed as "a frozen cultural wasteland populated with hopelessly unstylish citizens".

Describing our Right Honourable Prime Minister as a "6 foot 2 self-described feminist who has been a television actor, snowboarding instructor and amateur boxer" is offensive and appears to present an inferior and biased notion of our Prime Minister and it certainly hurts me as a Canadian.

I do not mind how some of the British media portrayed our Prime Minister with his photo depicting him engaged in practicing his boxing skills wearing his gym shorts, shoes and gloves and shirtless. I believe that the intent on showing his beautiful body was not meant to disparage or demean him; I think that the British media likely found it interesting that Justin Trudeau enjoyed boxing. When he was elected as the Prime Minister on October,19th 2015 some of the members of parliament commented that he was the sexiest Prime Minister. These comments and photos were blown out of proportion and have not made any serious impact.

Americans and Canadians, are still maintaining their relationship as cousins with the old immigrants who fled Britain under similar prevailing circumstance with the same objectives either together or by themselves during the same period of history. If the Americans had not revolted against the British Empire, the British loyalists would have remained a part of United States and Canada would have been the 51st state and the Acadians would have either merged with the States or would have won their own sovereign state after a bitter war.

Having root heritage values and sharing a common language, traditions and religion the British at the initial stage of the establishment of the states would have been close because of both being members of a homogeneous group rather than having multi ethnic groups with heterogeneous values. For some, the border between the two is not a barrier in sharing their values but just an invisible border. When I visited Britain, due to my pronunciation and actions in the way of speaking English I was spontaneously identified as being from North America and treated as an American. Americans in general are proud of themselves based on their own progress in their achievements and do not want to give undue recognition and credit for their ancestors back in Britain and they also feel they do not owe anything in such nature. They do not share deep rooted cultural values nor are they highly attached with the literature of those such as Shakespeare, Milton and other European English writers and other artists and they are strangers to many of their children.

The fast and deep entry of urbanization with the technological influences made many of them more engaged and involved in a busy life and this has produced and dominated their life style and slowly they deviated from their traditional values. The Americans also advocated for their economic superiority as of entire aspects of their life and they do want to value others as equal to theirs and bothered to go deep into accept their values. Third and fourth generation of Americans have its own identity.

The primary cause for the British descendants to flee included social victimization, lack of liberty, religious freedom, social inequality, oppression, dissatisfaction of the rule of the empire, and an element of economic wellbeing. When they left they were looked down as poor, underprivileged and unrecognized persons. They were not given a decent and emotional send-off for their departure as such they were leaving to a strange land with uncertainty; fear for their survival but with courage and determination. Some of them who were in similar situations did not have the resources and courage to flee, though they did not openly acknowledge this but recognized these actions as brave and bold and felt proud of it. Under normal circumstances, it is hard for anyone who has been living in a country where their forefathers had lived for generations with ups and downs but had some sort of sentiments and attachment for the land with its mountains, rivers, farmlands, lovely forest with birds, animals and sea shore. It has been universally seen and I have the privileged in confirm it by having contact with urban Canadians who have migrated from over two hundred nations around the world with many cultures, languages, religions and different backgrounds and the pushing forces. They have a soft corner for their ancestor's land and in some occasions, when someone makes negative comments of those countries makes these descendants quite uncomfortable.

But I did find some resourceful workers who have migrated as independent class of Immigrants for various reasons to North America and after their migration they re-established their life successfully both financially, and professionally. They do not have much regard and sentiments for their ancestor's land, rather they are proud of being North Americans. According to their view, they were the victim of the corrupted system of administration and they feel sorry for associating themselves with their traditional home land. These are naturalized citizens and at times they express more patriotic emotions than main stream citizens. Perhaps this is an exaggeration, but I have noticed it nonetheless.. Although they are a fraction of the population still we have to consider the other side of the story.

These controversial and opposite ideas could allow us to justify the Americans stance on the British at the time of their revolution and the British loyalists. The British loyalists suffered in the hands of the

American revolutionists who considered these people as deviating from their noble cause. A revolution against a well-established and powerful empire who had established their colonies around the world so the sun never set in their lands, with all required resources, weapons and man power would not be an easy task. They would not tolerate the slightest thoughts that were not supportive of their cause.

It might be a strategic plan not to plan more visits to African nations due to the fact that father of Obama was a Kenyan citizen and born and raised there. During his first election campaign it was questioned in some remote corners of the States how it was possible that a black man could become the President. Though it wasn't a deciding factor at that time and the major factors was getting out of the war in Iraq and Afghanistan and channel the money into boosting the local economy and resolving economic problems. The only way to achieve that target was to replace the Republican president by a Democratic one who had an alternative plans that suited their interest. The main cause of the victory at that time was more about getting rid of the Republicans rather than the merits of the Democrats.

Anyhow Obama and his spouse Michelle Obama played the cards well; after winning the second term they expressed from the bottom of their heart their sentiment for the African Americans and how they have been discriminated.

Obama has a mixed racial and genetic backgrounds, his father, Barack Hussein Obama, was Kenyan, of the Luo tribe. President Obama's mother, Stanley Ann (Dunham), who was American-born, had English, and small amounts of Scottish, Irish, German, Welsh, Swiss-German, and French ancestry whereas Michelle Lavaughn Robinson Obama was born to Fraser Robinson and Marian Shields Robinson and her paternal great-great grandfather, Jim Robinson, was a slave from South Carolina, as was her maternal great-great-grandmother, Melvinia Shields. One of her slave-owners sons fathered her first-born son when she was roughly 15 years old and his family had roots from the Protestant Irish. There is also another wave of her ancestors that has some links with Native Americans which was discovered in 2009 by genealogist Megan Smolenyak and the New York Times. They have in their heart the grievance that her forefathers bore, due to racial discrimination and slavery the pain that they underwent.

Mrs. Obama at Princeton University, said in her the speech. "While we no longer have segregated lunch counters, the reality is we still have racism in America."

At Tuskegee-university's 130th-commencement-ceremony she noted "No matter how far you rise in life, how hard you work to be a good person, a good parent, a good citizen... for some people, it will never be enough"

"You see, there are so many kids in this country who look at places like museums and concert halls and other cultural centers and they think to themselves, well, that's not a place for me, for someone who looks like me, for someone who comes from my neighbourhood. In fact, I guarantee you that right now, there are kids living less than a mile from here that would never in a million years dream that they would be welcome in this museum."

"And growing up on the South Side of Chicago, I was one of those kids myself. So I know that feeling of not belonging in a place like this. And today, as First Lady, I know how that feeling limits the horizons of far too many of our young people."

CHAPTER 4

Immigration And Emigration

1. The general trend

It is frequently claimed that Canada is a land of opportunities built by immigrants and immigrants are not only the backbone, they are the flesh and blood of the country.

Though Canada is geographically the second largest country in terms of size, and enriched with abundant natural resources and has a very stable government, still the great scarcity is inadequacy in the size of the population and its demographics.

Most parts of the north is sparsely populated because it is not conducive for comfortable settlement with less or normal efforts; still it is a land that has been built by new immigrants and they are one of the key instruments in economic growth. The fundamental immigration policies and strategies have undergone several stages of revisiting and revising its priorities on economic interests versus preserving and developing and expanding its own values and traditions in a very calculated manner. Its relaxation sounds, at times, like biased policies and when there is an economic pressure mounted on top, it becomes more of an open door policy.

Chris Alexander, the Minister of Citizenship and Immigration Canada, all of a sudden had to abandon his vigorous federal election campaign for Parliament that was scheduled to take place on October, 19th 2015 and that too demanded a forceful campaign due to the tough three way competition among the Liberals and the New Democratic Party. According to the various opinion polls it was a neck to neck fight, and left for, Ottawa on 3rd of September 2015.

A bomb shell was dropped by the international media with a photo of a corpse of the three- year- old Alan Kurdi on the sea shore in Turkey on September 2nd 2015. The mother Rehan Kurdi and Alan's brother, Galib Kurdi, 5, and eight other refugees also drowned in the sea while fleeing from their country of Syria on a boat due to the ruthless war between the ISIS Islamic militant group and their opponents, including locally recruited army and American allies. It was portrayed that his aunt, Ms. Tima a naturalized citizen of Canada, who settled down in Vancouver, long before this accident, submitted an application for the family of the child to claim refugee status and the response by the Minster and the Citizenship and Immigration department was not given in a timely fashion. Canada has to take the blame for the tragedy. Even the Canadian Broadcasting Corporation (CBC) mentioned this with other major Canadian Medias. Mr. Alexander was bombarded heavily with questions, but he proved that he had not ignored or dumped the letter without giving due respect to her concerns and sent it to the appropriate section of his ministry and they could not instantly complete the processing due to the fact that the application was incomplete. Later it was learned that Ms. Tima applied for refugee status not for the victim's family but rather for her older brother Mohammed.

The Opposition parties took advantage of the issue and attacked the government and had an almost a roundtable conference among the leaders of the main political parties and an emergency meeting about, how to resolve the internationally provoked refugee issue at our level and what could have been done in our part. On the surface it appears to the common man that the government has not taken any immediate action or is not concerned over the current issue and rather more committed in participating in the war against ISIS with the United States of America and its allied nations that involved.

Already, both the Liberals and National Democratic Party are not in favour of Canadian involvement in the war that was initiated by the United States, rather they aim to provide more humanitarian aid for those who are affected. The NDP always advocates for non-interference in such wars directly or indirectly; even its late leader, Jack Layton opposed the Canadian men-in- uniform training Afghan soldiers during the war between 2001 and 2014. At that time, the NDP had not reached the level of a national party that would be able to form a government. But the results of the federal election 2011 elevated it to the level of one of the major parties that would be able to form at least a minority government, if not a majority one sooner or later. It is very clear that the proposed sympathy and called for round table conference during the middle of the election period was to please and gain more votes from new Immigrants and encourage those multi- ethnic Immigrants, both the visual and non-visual minorities, who arrived after the gates were opened wider for them by Pierre Trudeau in the 1970's and also not to be tempted by the penetration of the conservatives particularly by Jason Kenney whose actions in this regard was once commented as " curry in a hurry". Though he has been trying to get closer to the ethnic voters, particularly the East and south east Asians who are the fastest growing group and outnumber the Europeans and other particular regions that supply more immigrants, his tightening of Immigration policies during his period as minister of Immigration did not please many and earned mistrust more than before and as usual Asians are not very vocal in expressing their dissatisfaction and slowly,, quietly swallowed these bitter pills. I am not racially biased but when I looked at the preventive methods of the anticipated fear of mass immigration of Asians during and immediately after the construction of the Canadian Pacific Railway and other major railway lines by levying the head tax for the Chinese and the restricted navigation paths of the ships that brought the Asians are hard memories to erase.

These would be immigrants to Canada were expected to complete their journey without a break in between India and western Canada and the hidden motive was to block, if not totally stop, these people from entering Canada entirely.

`I do not mean to say that our immigration system is perfect and examples of these are refugee cases that were rejected because there is no established fear for life or expected persecution for the individual who applied for refugee status in Canada and are sent back to their respective countries. But when they were returned, they were tortured and in some cases murdered. In some countries they were legally welcomed back but behind the scene the respective governments through its forces and some kind of agents did the same thing. In some cases, countries like England reconsider their cases and grant asylum. However, cases such as these are but a small percentage.

I would also like to look at the other side of the coin. Fraudulent refugee cases are also rampant, for example, during the current refugee crisis in Syria, some Pakistanis who have been working either on a temporary foreign workers contract or other means, had abandoned their respective passports and obtained fake Syrian passports with their photos through illegal means and tried to escape to Europe. It is true that ineligible refugees take advantage of the generosity of the refugee accepting countries. This could be a weakness in the system. it may insignificant for officials to differentiate falls refugees from the genuine ones and they might have considered that it is not worth investing more resources, energy and time for it. Though they knew well that this deception has been on for a while, it may reach a point that ends up weakening the system with their social norms, economy, and national security. Recently some of the politicians and leaders who advocate that to maintain the identity of the nation should not be altered in New Zealand mentioned that " we accept the children and women, not male refugees and it meant the refugees from the Middle east in particular but not men and let them go back and engage in fighting." It all became a serious issue in accepting refugees because a couple of terrorists disguised themselves as innocent victims of the war or conflict and seek for refugee status and they had been granted such status, particularly Canada is one among them that became a victim and it was pin pointed by the American security and intelligence sources. Holland and Denmark are also afraid of accepting them and an outcry was made. The infiltration of such terrorists at times affects the genuine refugees and it is very costly for the respective governments to invest more resources and time. Furthermore whenever those governments apply vigilant modern techniques with ultra-modern equipment, those terrorists also take an extra step and somehow defeat the mechanism.

The agents for human trafficking have been using many techniques and most of those agents are primarily aimed at maximizing their profits and they also know well that all the doors are not going to be opened as they want and sooner than later those governments will take counter measures to curb the situation. They are least worried of the calibre, motive, and ethnic background and as long as they make money out them, it is fine for them. Some of the advanced agents are operating internationally like international operation of the finance, insurance companies. They conduct classes and training for the illegal immigrants with sample credit cards, social insurance cards, papers, traffic rule, bank cards, greeting customs, and so on. They even show them videos related places, cities, and institutions of the country where they are going to be landing.

They are also smart that some of those refugee claimants had been living in safe locations and leaning their life well, but to have a better life and make use of the wonderful opportunities at the targeted refugee accepting nations, they pretend to be the victims. They had no knowledge of those victimizing men-in- uniform or the rebels where they were stationed what kind of methods of their operations and dealing with the public, the suspected enemies. But the persons at the refugee hearing at the level of the government know very well and are well informed and trained periodically. In some occasions they questioned the so called refugee claimants even on the color of the exit passes handed to the people in the controlled areas by the rebels and some of the socialist countries when they were screened allowed to exist and also the conditions made for the exits.

The human traffic agents are also aware of the sensitivities of time and place at the border points of the destinations where those immigrants land. They know where, when and how to smuggle their clients. For example even the Israeli government smuggled Otto Adolf Eichmann, the right hand man of Hitler during the operation of the massacre of the Jews in Germany out of Argentina, dressed as an ordinary man. When the country was in preparation for its 150th Independence Day celebrations, the attention on other routine matters were at a very low level and he was captured and instantly brought out of the country to Israel. Human smugglers are aware that on Christmas night and New Year's Eve the border agents are normally in a relaxed mood and wouldn't be vigilant and it would be the best time in crossing the border and they make good use of this time.

The reasons for this type of immigration are many. For example, there are the pushing forces of armed conflict, natural calamities such as drought in East Africa, the tsunami in south east Asia in 2004, the volcanic eruption in the Philippines, the earth quake in Haiti and governmental terrorism, social non acceptance of people in the Lesbian/Gay/Bisexual/Transgender (LGBT) communities, lack of women's rights, and denial of religious freedom. Another reason for mass migration is the desire for a better life in developed nations because of the higher exchange rate for the money that they earn in their own country for the same work done is elsewhere, like the semi-skilled workers in construction industries and domestic work in the Middle eastern countries just after the Organization of Petroleum Exporting Countries (OPEC) used petroleum as a weapon against western nations who extended according to most of them undue support that caused huge damage to their survival, dignity, preserving their traditional values, economy and political stability and reduced the production level and artificially increased the price based on the demand and supply formula. Due to mass developments in infrastructure, there was not only a shortage of middle level skilled workers locally but also there was the unwillingness of some to engage in such hard work. This provided an ample opportunity for such workers in Pakistan, India, Sri Lanka, the Philippines, and Bangladesh to work and though their earnings were less than the natives for the same work with similar or higher qualification, skills and experience, still it was higher that their colleagues back in their respective homelands.

There is a high rate of underemployment and unemployment and over production of high school and college graduates, and university graduates and some of them wouldn't mind switching their jobs from their field of expertise and some do not mind doing menial jobs for their survival. Even in western countries new immigrants who have been unable to find jobs in their field of expertise engage themselves in doing manual jobs. For example, in Canada, those who received their immigration status on the point system in most cases were able to have their credentials accepted or they underwent upgrading to meet the respective requirements and found jobs. But a sizeable number of them were not able to do this due to their family commitments, age and other factors and are working in minimum wage jobs; for example, there are physicians, accountants, teachers, and engineers working as taxi drivers, pizza delivery employees, security guards and other fields that do not require their high calibre qualifications and experience.

The penetration of capitalism is also a pushing and pulling force when it comes to immigration and mass migration. Capitalism has even reached into socialist countries such the eastern European nations, the former Soviet bloc, and the People's Republic of China, a country that has a five thousand year old civilization and its own political system, culture and economic structure. Mao Tze Tung through the Cultural Revolution established China as a socialist nation where most of the properties were owned by the state and discouraged abundant accumulation of wealth has now partially accepted private enterprise and is also one of the leading countries in terms of the number of millionaires and billionaires. If Chairman Mao was around to see what has happened to China in recent years, he would likely be very shocked but possibly quite pleased.

The mobility of the global investment of Capital has brought a dramatic change in the internal and external mobility of human resources. The investment in manufacturing industries, mining, consumer good production and distribution, various sectors in service industries such as Financial services, tourism transportation, communication, domestic work, professionals, and entertainers. I would cite some examples as such China, today's number one economy in the world has been heavily making investments in African and South American and Middle Eastern countries very quietly with long term plans of establishing political and economic strength and shines as number one not only in economy rather that of global power and its investment certainly it wouldn't disappoint them. In fact I brought it to the attention for the western world and Canada and America in my second book on Canada entitled "Canada A Nation In Motion"

The modern means of communications and computer industry both the hardware and software has brought the investment operation function so close and it also encourages the mobility of Capital and migrants from north to south and east to west and vice versa.

The multi-dimensionality of global migration is complex and its dynamics are very unique it is confined within a unified frame work and its distinctive look and migratory process varies from time to time and country to country and the level of migrants range from manual labour to the skilled worker and also from refugees to illegal immigrants.

But the immigration changes forwarded by the Harper government in this regard starting from the first of January 2015, the system of recruiting skilled workers under the system of "express entry" that does not allow the first come first processed and grants permanent residency status. Rather the companies and economic sectors as a first have to have taken all reasonable and possible steps in recruiting such employees locally. They have to apply through job banks. On the other hand the potential foreign workers either within Canada or outside workers who got themselves registered under this system will be pulled out and invited to apply for the permanent resident status under the skilled worker category in the Independent class and then if they meet all other requirements they will be granted the status and after migrating into Canada they do not have to look for in any available sectors and jobs in their field of expertise and also in order of the chosen the province on their priority basis. It is a brand new system as far as Canadian Immigration policy is concerned and it is too early to judge its effectiveness and it sound more beneficial for new Immigration who will have job satisfaction to continuing in the field where he or she has the expertise and skills and also for the country in utilizing their expertise skills for in the best interest of the economy and optimizing his /her potential and what is the point of allowing them to migrant and grab the jobs of those who are local and unemployed. It is a winning situation for both sides.

There is a new trendy wave of immigrants migrating not for the benefit of their personal or family life but, for a designated common cause, at any cost, even against the interests of the nation that gave them privileges and rights and accommodations. The terrorists from South

America, the Middle East, Europe, and Asia are operating quietly in the USA, Canada and in most of the western European countries and countries that are emerging world super powers, like India and China. These terrorists are determined to be a part of groups or organizations that plan and execute their agenda at any cost and do not hesitate in making use of every available resource and they do not mind sacrificing their comforts even at the cost of their valuable lives in the capacity of suicide bombers without hesitation and without even expecting a reward in this world or in heaven.

I have personally had some opportunities in terms of associating with some of these groups, in Ethiopia at the time when the Ethiopians were fighting for an independent nation during and after Emperor Haile Selassie's regime, under the rule of Mengistu Haile Mariam's ruthless rule. Though I was not a supporter for either of them, I was working in a mighty secondary school and spoke Amharic fluently and had integrated with the locals very well. Because of these things, I was able to understand the situation and sensed certain political motives. I noticed that some of my teachers and ordinary citizens were engaged in some anti-governmental activities aimed at over throwing the emperor and conducted secret meeting in the jungle during most of their weekends and holidays, yet managed their duties perfectly well. I, being a foreign contract worker, carried out my assignments as guided and left the activities of the teachers during their off time alone as it was none of my concern. I also noticed that security agents were everywhere and they were vigilantly monitoring at all levels and took action ruthlessly like most of the tyrannical monarchies.

The Eritrean Independence Network was also very effective and those who were working for their movements outside of the Eritrean territory but within Ethiopia were almost doing the same things as the anti-Emperor movements but these ones were well organized and better equipped. But when came to sacrificing their lives, it was not to the same degree.

During the regime of Mengistu Haile Mariam though he was ruthless in eliminating all opponents he also potential rivals who were right hand personnel in high ranking position in the forces. Their tactics were such that once someone had to be eliminated when she or he was a potential threat to their power, they prepared a fabricated list of false accusations and then assassinated by accusing them of treason, misuse of public properties, money, abusing human rights, working in collaboration with anti-national and government forces, the Central Intelligence Agency and so on. Mengistu did it twice by assassinating two of the leaders General Tafari Banti the head of state for the period between November 28, 1974 and February 1977 and a senior co-revolutionary leader, Colonel Atnafu Abate. Even after the dedicated sacrifices that were made by the Eritreans and Ethiopians, Mengistu made use of the people and the country at large for his own fame and finally when the crisis and opposition mounted he deserted the nation and escaped from the situation to Tanzania for asylum, like Idi Amin from Uganda, and Marcos from the Philippines to the USA.

Power struggles at many times supersedes the national interests and some Canadian politicians are not exempted though, I do not want go deeply into this subject, not because of any adverse effect but it is already known by many of us, due to the freedom of the press. Anyhow, let me cite some examples in a very brief manner. Jean Chrétien and Paul Martin and Brian Mulroney and Joe Clark at times had their manipulative attitudes push them to advance political considerations for self-gain rather than the national interest.

Let me focus on the general shift in the immigration trends and immigration policies around the world in comparison with Canada. We are adapting toward the fast and fundamentally changing trend brought to us by globalization and it has left no stone untouched, starting from bedroom affairs to space traveling to applying for visiting Mars. Information technology has brought the global village into the global family level. Love affairs are initiated by internet connections and developed between two persons from one corner of the world to the other without even knowing the political and historical background of each other's countries and ends up in marriage in some cases and in the rest without having any legal and social commitments, remaining in the status of boyfriend and girlfriend.

In the past, immigration was more or less a domestic affair, this is no more and it has the national stage. Regional organizations of groups of countries like the European Union (EU) consists of 27 nations (after the departure of Britain on June 23, 2016) which was grouped with originally six nations and today it has reached the stage of the number one economic force. it used to have a slave trade between Africa and mainly with Europe and the so-called new world. And reached to the level and became the global immigrants and that has the core of attraction today. Immigration is mainly focused on two main areas such as economic benefits and the advantage of having additional human resources and then uplifting or replacing the decline in the natural increase of the population and filling the gap that has been created. The baby boomers are now the largest and most active group.

There are restrictions in international trade by a quota system, import duties, designation of countries, trade embargos, from some countries due to political, human rights and various other reasons, restrictions of non-member nations from the free trade agreements, but when it comes to Immigration though it appears that there are restrictions and limitations, it is freer than trade these days. Involving and evolving global Immigration activities in the globalized world is no longer just an immigration matter that is confined within the Immigration department alone.

2. Globalization on immigrants and Immigration

International migration in 2010

Categories	% or # of Immigrants	Total population
Estimated number of International Migrants	225 Millions	7.2 Billions
Percentage of world's population who are migrants	3.1%	
Top five destination countries by numbers		
United States of America	42.8 Million	323, 725,000
Russia	12.7 Million	146, 600, 000
Germany	10.8 Million	81, 770, 900
Saudi Arabia	7.3 Million	32, 248, 200
Canada	7.2 Million	36, 048, 521
Top five countries with the highest share of international migrants (including temporary foreign workers) per total population		
Qatar	86%	2, 587, 564
United Arabic Emirates	76%	9, 856, 000
Kuwait	68-8%	4, 183, 658
Jordan	45.9%	9, 531, 712
Singapore	40.7%	5, 535, 020
Bottom five countries with the lowest share of international migrants per total population		
Indonesia	0.1%	258, 705, 000
India	0.4%	1, 285, 913,123

Romania	0.6%	19, 861, 400
Nigeria	0.7%	186, 988, 000
Japan	1.7%	123, 960, 000
Permanent foreign-born population as percentage of the total population (year 2009)		
Australia	31%	24, 092, 095
New Zealand	27%	4, 692, 246
Israel	25%	8, 515, 100
Canada	24%	36, 048, 521
United States of America	13%	323, 725,000
Top source countries for immigrants		
Mexico	10 Million	122, 273, 473
India	9 Million	1, 285, 913, 123
Bangladesh	6-5 Million	160, 827, 548
Internally displaced persons in the world in 2010	27.5 Million	
Number of world refugee, 2010	15.5 Million.	

The migrants in 2010 appear as only a fraction of 3.1% of the total world's population of 7.4 Billion but we also have to take into consideration that the world's population just after the end of the Second World War rapidly increased. After a very destructive war, people were fed-up in engaging in war,except for fighting for independence from their respective colonial masters that too was encouraged by relaxing the rigid colonial rule in order to win the support from the subjects so that they would stand a better chance in winning the war and not to inflate their colonies by the opponents and even like Britain extended a promise that they would have some sort of independence and it all motivated them for moving towards an independence movement. But most of the promises given by the colonial masters blew away with the winds and they have to initiate wars for their independence and finally won around the 1960s.

The reborn nations began to rebuild and they initiated the development of infrastructure, including Better health facilities, compulsory education coupled with patriotic Sentiments reduced the death rate significantly and increased the life expectancy. It has made a very positive impact of the population in general. The under age of 15 has demographics has occupies the lion's share of the total population and it continues even today and their focus on education and at least partial elimination of child labour brought down the Mobility of people and reduced the percentage of migrants.

In the available history of migration this number is very high, with slightest variation due to the unavailability and accountability of documented procedure in place in many other of today's developing countries. Out of the 225 million more than a half of them landed in countries where language, culture, Traditions are very unfamiliar and also sizable number of them migrated into sophisticated developed Parts of the developed nation from rural areas where they had less social amnesty but accustomed with Nuclear family system.

Saudi Arabia a holy country for all sectors of Muslim and economically mainly depending on crude oil, a single commodity being one of the five nations that received more Immigrants and compared with its overall and that too sparsely distributed with the oil wealth was able to accommodate more immigrants, In 2015 oil either has been used as a secret weapon of reducing the power of certain evolving radical Arab nations or in a natural phenomenon, the price has been reduced more half and it wouldn't attract more immigrants anymore decades and also the substitution for oil has been another contribution factor for the less importance for exhaustible sources of energy and the USA has committed in meeting its self-sufficiency goals for in oil use in a few years' time and began to export crude oil than importing from Canada and Saudi Arabia.

The rest of the five are developed nations

When such changes are rapidly penetrating into our life, the Immigration and Immigrant policies also had to fundamentally change sooner than later. The European nations are having continuous and long historical fabric whereas Canada, America and Australia are mainly built by Immigrants and are known as lands of Immigrants. Are all those Immigrants abundant their ancestral roots, including the natives who were the first human settlement made in Canada over 30,000 years ago Do they have dual loyalties, are they expected and exclusively obliged to commit exclusively for their new nation Canada and unconditionally embrace their new mother land. How far all Canadians who have arrived from all six continents belonging just around two hundred nations and speaking over 160 languages get integrated with the norm of the Canadian mainstream. Do they have to disconnect from the homeland of their ethnicity, if not how far they have to share? Encourage or discourage the magnitude of shared loyalty between the two. How elastic on integration and transformation in adapting to the committed new land from that of their land of birth or habitually living land in the past.

I, do understand that at early stage of migration they come with high expectations of better life with flexible efforts, easily able to accumulate money, free land and the freedom to live the way as they wish, self-liberation from their rigid cultural barriers and so on. Immigrants, who have come from war zones and disaster areas, who want to breathe

the air of freedom, sleep without any fear of attack and the ability to keep their precious belongings with them. There are some who escaped from mass attacks by both the rebels and the army or navy and walked through unknown forests, bush, jungles, the land of dangerous animals enjoying wild freedom and wouldn't discriminate man from those other animals when it comes to hunt and eat or for the purpose of self-protection. Life is a challenge for the survival of the fittest and walking with no aimed or targeted destination. There are almost living like a primitive man, not having any long term plan, living day by day. Whatever they brought with them gets exhausted and at times starving with no food to fill the stomach, no water to satisfy the thirst, at times some of those refugees ate the corpse of fellow refugees. Some of them are wounded and there is no medicine for treatment or cure and they died in their journey and no respectful burials and at times left for animals to have meat without any struggle in killing them. The pain in the body can be cured up to certain extent, but that is in the mind and soul in fact almost all of them are psychiatric patients, and no way of keeling but up to a smaller degree of curing is possible. I have met some of the surviving victims of World War Two and after having close conversations, I discovered that even after seventy years, they still carry the pain after living comfortably in a safe land for decades.

Another group of victims who were imprisoned or detained and tortured inhumanly and they faced a situation that the question of life and death could meet them at any second and not living rather surviving minute to minute at the mercy of their captors. All around the world, it is being done from the east to west and north to south both the so called democratic countries and dictatorship ruler's nations with the exception of a few nations like Canada and Scandinavian countries. But the countries like Britain, France, Italy, Germany, Holland, were worse during their colonial rule with their colonies. That is why three Canadians' who have permanent resident status in Canada and have all eligibility to become naturalized citizens by going through the process and I believe they have a solid reasons and portrayed in a sensitive way and either they have any other citizenship or intended in holding a citizenship of their ancestor's land. All three of them said that they cannot do what they do not believe in it and it does not go alone with either religious or conscientious belief. Taking oath as " to be faithful and bear true allegiance to Queen Elizabeth the second Queen of Canada, her heirs and successors" Ms. Simone Topey, 47, a Jamaican born, Rastafarian said outside of the Ontario court of appeal yard on April 8, 2014 that " I want to be real to Canada, I want to be loyal to the country. I am trying to become a citizen not a subject". Mr. Dor Bar- Natan, 48 is Jewish and a mathematics professor at University of Toronto., do say like Simone Topey said taking oath to any person is prohibited by their religious faith. He even said that "To become a Canadian citizen, I am made to utter phrases which are silly and ridiculous and offensive. Finally and later on he found an alternative approach as Dror Bar-Natan became a Canadian citizen by reciting the prescribed oath. Immediately afterwards having the Citizenship oath handing the judge a letter stating, "I hereby completely disavow whatever I thought the first 25 words of the Citizenship Oath conveyed when I took the oath." The third person was Michael McAteer age 80, a permanent resident of Canada and having met all the criteria to qualify to apply for Canadian citizenship and being Irish said that taking the oath would violate his conscience.

When George W. Bush was invited by a group to deliver a speech in Vancouver British Colombia there was a protest against him for the very reason that he was a war criminal. Recently when the Israeli Prime

Minister was about to pay an official visit to the United Kingdom over one hundred **thousand British citizens signed a petition against his visit for the reason that If this would happened to the leaders of the countries that they claim that they are the protractors and advocators for democracy and we are the sons and daughters of the liberty.

Anyhow in comparative teams it the degree of variation in the principle of fundamental human rights, freedom of expression, rule of law, is so wide between these countries and many others. Canada is a vibrant county has no or very minimal degree of fear, insecure feeling, human dignity, rule by law, low level of discrimination on race, social, open minded, manipulation of rules, ethnicity, color, ethno-religious conflicts, nitrate, antagonizing attitudes, religion and gender.

3. Unspoken truth on immigration

I do accept and give due consideration for anti-sentimental attitudes and advocating provocations against new Immigrants from visible minorities and their slow speed of integration and forming an isolated society in a certain areas as Chinatown, Polish town, Indian bazaar, and reconfigured the demographic pattern, though a small portion of the currently displaced 210 million people left their traditional home and living elsewhere. Though their activities in various capacities in a low profile and low priority in nature, still it is somewhat reshaping the existing centuries old system particularly in the urban areas. The anti-Immigrants the primary concern is that it should not even slightly alter the Canadian values and it should not be compromised if the transitional loyalty is inescapable, unbridgeable and uncompromised and provocative. They do necessarily feel that they are to be obligatory in demonstrating exclusively, unconditionally making their commitments for this nation. The globalization through social medias also made it easier in maintaining their emotional attachment with their former homeland and how far it slow down or prevent from having due emotional attachment with this nation.

The conventional notion of Immigration and immigrate is out dated and does not address in the current globalization that empowered moment of people access the borders of world's nations. ' It has been pin pointed by many but former Immigration minister Sergio Marchi said ' we need a clear and practical vision of the kind of nation we want to build' He would have done more in this regard but his sudden growth and supportive of rival group within the party against Jean Chretien should have been prompted in sending him to Italy with another assignment that was not very familiar to him but clearly he was taken from the direct politics and it would be a tactical political move with the party by Mr. Jean Joseph Jacques Chrétien at that time.

At the recent times Mr. Jason Kenney, former Minister for Immigration brought certain radical changes in a very sugar coated way and it was praised and bitterly criticized systematically. We tightened so hard that up to a certain extent the people who entered into this country through the loop hauls such as the bogus refugees, so called family members on marriages of conveniences, under the family class sponsorship,. On the other side he made it easy and somewhat faster for the economic class Immigrants for their migration process and removing failed and other removal cases of the immigrants caused a burden for the tax payers money in keeping them and consuming the resources in the same department contribute a portion in the back log in the refugee processing. Mr. Chris Alexander continued in the same path vigorously within his short period of time as the minister for citizenship and immigration Canada. His radical change was on

Canadian citizenship and he made it clear that "Canadian citizenship is not a right rather a privilege'.

They want drastic change in the policies and system and its operational pattern on Immigration and as to what extend it could be can be defined easily. Could it be an over haul the system, change it from orthodox notion to that reflect and accommodate needs for the 21st century, maintaining the conventional system and maintaining it at contemporary level And also the following issues have to be defined mathematically, objectively and clearly, through it is not in the hands of the Immigration sector and it depends of the government policies on such as economic, foreign, demographic,. The complexity of immigration policy should not easily do. Anyhow the number of annual intake, the categories and its quartos, their skills and language capabilities, processing time, eliminating back logs, national security, cost effectiveness, temporary workers, foreign students, geographical distribution, emigration level. What immigration model suites at the best interest of the economy and local market expansion. How do we promote Canadian nationalism under multiculturalism? How do we maintain the balance of unity in diversity? How to dismantle home grown terrorism?

These days the majority of them migrate from Asian countries, particularly the skilled workers and investors from China and India and these two nations are fast growing and shaping into a super power status and China has over taken United states of America in economy and reached number one in the world. Furthermore it also began to control the international affairs and graph from a portion of the USA and not much from Russia due to two main reasons as such that they both being built up by practicing same ideology the Marxism and that helped them in overthrowing feudalism and brought to the modern world by passing capitalism, though they relaxed from a ridge socialist system of economic structure. As far as India is concerned it has so far not so reached the overall growth in economy, military, foreign investment, diplomatic, influences in oversee like China. India would have gone far ahead than what it is now, if there is a dictatorship system of government where they could make use of both the man power and the resources in achieving their end, but in a democratic system of government, with freedom, disputes between the labour unions and government and private sectors. Anyhow, it will be another influential world's power and will have to have a say in the Canadian affairs as well.

The Philippines is another supplier of man power to Canada and most of the Western nations as domestic workers, a job most westerners or Chinese or Indians have paid very little interest. What we all have to look into is that migration and demography is not a separated link like a water tide compartment from the rest of the socio-economic sectors, politics and the cultural values. Therefore, in an integrated approach, we have to expand our areas of concern in a wider range integrated with other spectrums so that a gain in one sector should not cause a damage to the rest. Some of these countries have hidden agendas and what appears on the surface is glamorous, innocent, and accretive but underneath the buried hidden agenda is critical and bring more harm than expected. Though Canada is very careful at its end but we shouldn't undervalue or underestimate the strength of the merging powers. It could be not only on immigration but also in the sector on investment, social Medias, and trade.

These days rigidness on the ideological approach or its rivalry attitude have been very much relaxed and softened and the capitalist countries wouldn't mind in nationalizing some private sectors and at the other end the socialist nations have deviated from wholesale socialist system and slowly get into capitalist private enterprise in China, Albania, Hungary, Bulgaria, countries from the former Soviet Union, Yugoslavia, Czechoslovakia, Poland. Though Cuba has re-established its diplomatic relationship after more than a half a century, still remain as a socialist system of government.

It is no more a straightforward business of migration and migration exercise rather it is more complicated and the mode, means and its objectives have taken a multidimensional approach starting from forced migration to self-motivated migration. These days crossing the manmade boarders between the nations has no more significant impact on a modern man life and he wouldn't take it very sentimental and serious matter in deserting his forefathers traditional home land, partially in the global village we share many things instantly around the world. I would cite a simple and properly an insignificant matter for people in serious nature that of skin tight pants which was somehow introduced by a set of fashion designers, either in the city of Paris or New York and do you believe that it has penetrated all nook and corners of the globe, regardless of their race, religion, ethnicity, language and the interesting part is that in some of the traditionally prioritized societies such in India it entered into their traditional pants as a latest fashion. Only the customs and Immigration and border security agencies are pretty serious in processing the papers for immigrants. I have been traveling for the last four decades in five continents and noticed that the method of processing at the port of entry has changed into a modernized well equipped, faster level but the attitudes and the sentiments remain unchanged. But I have seen the type of passengers apart from the business class has changed dramatically. Those days the affordability and need for travel by plane was so prestigious and only a highly dignified person would be able to imagine doing it. I do remember when I was recruited by the Ministry of Education in Africa, I had to travel from

Sri Lanka by plane and I had to wear a three piece suit and it was very common and almost all of the passengers are in similar dress. In contrast, today people are dressed up in jeans, slippers and all sort of workers and travellers join as they travel by bus in a small town.

There are various components for simplified and easy going levels of movement among the people around the world as a global village, not a global cosmopolitan city. One of the common trend around the world is the process in the elimination of class and status deference and consider follow human being is a human being like myself, apart from educational and economic achievements. Those psychological changes brought into the modern societies and the prestige, aristocratic venerability feelings have been considered out dated and the modern generation has looked down on it.

The second main factor is the democratic rule in progress around the word that too after the decolonization around the world since 1960's and today an ordinary man if not practically treated equally with the wealthy and man with higher portion in many of the developing nations and the corruption in rigging the election, still all citizens have been somewhat recognized and extended status and recognition.

Let's ask a question. Do immigrants need receiving countries more that those receiving countries need them? Or do they need new immigrants more than they need them?

4. Biased on Ethnicity

Insight of the objective criteria for accepted new immigrants even at the stage of having influenced by the globalization still certain elements make its influence in having a subjective decision of flavoured immigrants being given favourable chances in migration. It has been lingering by various factors such as religious inclination, ethnic integrity, linguistic sentiment, cultural base, color sentiment, educational advancement, modernisation in life, and historical background. Mr. Ben Carson one of the potential Republican candidates for the US presidential election for 2016 made a statement in which he clearly mentions that a Muslim should not be the President of United Stated of America. "I would not advocate that we put a Muslim in charge of this nation. I absolutely would not agree with that," Though it has not been related to the new immigrant phenomena still it reflects the religious biased sentiment for a candidate who has been preparing himself to be a candidate for the presidents under the Republican Party. On the other hand Israel is not prepared to accept the Syrian refugees but in a clever way portrays to the world that the terrorists may be infiltrating under the disguise of innocent refugees but there is an element of racially biased thought lingering around and it is the naked truth but legally we may not be able to challenge it by the constitution or the international law. In the former socialist countries it has taken a different dimension as such there are racial, religious, linguistic and other defences brought down to the lowest level and impounded by the socialistic ideology. For example in the former Yugoslavia the Catholic, Orthodox Christians, and the Muslims have their religious sentiment in their heart still they were treated as a co member in the socialist society and the ideological outlook over powered their religious and ethnic backgrounds. After the socialist government of dismantled and a new political system based on the free enterprise and economic factor made these nations empowered by their religious sentiments. In this case still they sentiment is replaced by the religious and ethnic sentiment and still they risk a discriminative unspoken truth.. After the dissolution of the former Czechoslovakia they have been created as separate countries and this took effect on 1st January 1993 and became eight federated entities, and the separation had a strong ethnic base. They became six republics as Slovenia, Croatia, Bosnia, and Herzegovina, the republic of Macedonia, Montenegro and Serbia. In a similar manner the former Yugoslavia was also dismantled.

Though many of the receiving countries of the immigrants by constitution and rules and regulations do not mention any form of segregation, favouritism, and elimination or exclusions of new immigrants based on these categories. But the smart way of implementing so called unbiased implementations of the policies on accepting new immigrants is an open secret they do shed some light on these fundamentals.

There is a cold war going on in these countries between capitalizing the human resources at the highest level while biased on those factors. Then demarcation goes up and down due to the necessity of having such man power and the degree of inclination on those factors. At times the politicians have a tug of war with the economist, nationalist, and patriotic citizens. the certain cases the politicians many were manipulate in winning the heart of mass level of waters by arousing their ir sentimental values

5. An evolving Immigration policy

It has been considered as the government of Canada and academics that from the natives till recent refugees from the Syria all of us, including the natives have migrated from all corners of the globe. But to some of the prominent native leaders, they are not to be included among the rest of the Canadians as immigrants and they are the original sons and daughters of the soil and also the recognized and documented history should begin with the arrival of the Europeans in the late 15th century and it deprives them of their history in this land and the history of this nation should go back centuries and treated equally, rather not given the blessing for their history. This is in a way touches the sensitivity of the immigration and migration history of Canada. It appears that their concern is that Canadian history should treat the first part as undocumented and we are unable to document prehistory and the so called ancient history is unacceptable and given all reason is backed by limp excuses.

Anyhow, let me begin with the evolution of the migration and emigration at the northern part of British North America, the current territory of Canada. It was been originally focused towards France and England, the two of the main superpowers or rather the colonial rulers and originally a trading center in an unknown land in the new continent America. At the time of their thin waves of communication with the North American continent they primarily did not have any serious commitments or interest in permanently settle down and be a hinterland for their respective colonial powers, rather doing business and making profit and build their nations at the expense of materials gathered from here.

As far as the Immigration and emigration polices are concerned that it is a part of their colonies and they have kept the authority for themselves and their subjects. It was the time in the 15th century the class system was more powerful and within the French and the English and obviously the privileged class had taken the upper hand and the leftover of the under privileges were given, let alone the Irish and Scottish who have been a part of the British Empire. Let me classify the major classifications of the Canadian Immigration periods.

1. Pre- historic period; the original settlers of this land, the natives.

    a. From hunting to agriculture, to settlements from wandering

2. The period of the European settlements 1497 till the British conquered the New French and French entire colony in North America. In 1760. Rivalry between the British and the France

3. The North American British colony 1760-1867 A single ruling colonial power

    a. The Industrial revolution 1760-1820 in England and its influences in emigration

    b. Period of the American Revolution 1776-1789, the exodus of the British Loyalists.

    c. The French Revolution 1789-1799 and its impact

    d. The American invasion of Canada (the North British North American Colony) 1803-1815

6. The Independent Canada 1867 till 1918 the end of World War One

The Canadian Immigration Act 1869 though it dealt with certain restrictions on immigration, the main focus was ensuring the safety and protection of the immigrants during their journey by ship. The father of our nation and the first Prime Minister Sir John A Macdonald was highly interested in having huge settlements in the west so that the prairie grassland could be converted into a bread basket for Canada and also be a market for the industrial goods produced in upper and lower Canada and also a source of raw materials for the industrial sectors of those regions. Unfortunately, it did not work as he anticipated, because a substantial number of new immigrants from England did not engage in farming prior to their emigration and this trend continued till the end of the century.

7. The Royal Commission on Chinese Immigration 1885

As a preventive measure of anticipated influx of Chinese immigrants this commission was appointed to prove the necessity of regulating Chinese Immigrants to Canada. In fact they came to do the hard labour job in construction of the railways on the western section of the Canadian Pacific Railway and most of the Europeans would not previous to do so and it was not only demanded job in an open air but also it was one time job and would not be made permanent. I believe the notion that the European settlers in particular and the trade Unionists, usually did not like having the idea of more Immigrants and it will somehow put their demand low and the politicians who mostly danced to the tune of the voters in British Columbia was that they were not in favour of the influx of the Chinese Immigrants and they also gave some reasons for it was the Chinese Immigrants were immoral, prone to disease and primarily incapable assimilation. The commission recommended imposing a $ 10 duty on each Chinese person seeking admission for entering into Canada.

The Chinese Immigration Act 1885 was the beginning of somewhat discouraging the incoming Chinese immigrants to Canada by an exclusive levying tax based on ethnicity and it was the first and last in its kind and the primary reasons given for justifying the Act is very general and hard in objectively accepting by critics. The reasons expressed by some of the Canadians, particularly in the province of British Colombia was that the Chinese Immigrants were lagging behind in the assimilation process with the main stream Canadians and their habits, way of living and poor living conditions were peculiar in nature.

The first wave of Chinese arrived in Canada in 1858 from the grass roots level and majority of them did not having literacy even in their own languages and migrated mainly from the southern part of China, particularly from the province of Guangdong. They too faced hardship and poor living condition in their own country such as suffering from famine, persecuted by rebellions and somehow wanted to get out of it and also given a magnified picture of easily finding gold in the gold mines in British Colombia.

The second wave arrived in 1880s at least with a realistic hope of finding employment at least as labourers in the rail way construction. They were treated not equality with other European workers and paid only three quarter of what a European origin workers being paid and also assigned to do demanding, dangerous manual work such as carrying rocks, working with explosives and so on.

Almost at the end of the construction of the Canadian Pacific Railway, they faced an economic recession and the unemployment rate went up and the local people thought that the Chinese Immigrants were ready to take away their jobs with long working hours in a lower working conditions and at a cheap labour and it fuelled the anti- Chinese turmoil and pushed the politicians to make more restrictions on the arrival of the Chinese Immigrants. It became an issue of economic matters rather than other social factors at this moment. The Chinese Immigration Act, 1885 levied a head tax on every Immigrant of $ 50 and then this was amended three times with restrictions within two decades as such 1887, 1892, 1900 and 1903. In 1900 the tax was increased to $100 from $50 and $ 500 in 1903.

1900. It was the year the increase of the discriminative and discouraging of Chinese Immigrants by increasing the head tax to $100 from $ 50.00 and increased again in 1903 to $500

The discriminative Immigration policy continued, even after many restrictions were relaxed and some of them were not removed until 1967, even though the Chinese Exclusion Act was repealed in 1947. One of the primary reasons was that China, under the leadership of Mao Tze Tong based on scientific socialist ideology and the process of implementation was more depressive of capitalism, Imperialism and the system of western democracy. Its influence also is another reason that certain restrictions on China continued till 1967. The Immigration act brought all nations under one umbrella on its Immigration policy and all existed restriction on Chinese Immigrants vanished by itself in a very silence manner. The final nail was hammered by former Prime Minster Stephan Harper made an apology at the parliament on 22nd of September 2006. It was officially presented as:

"On behalf of all Canadians and the government of Canada, we offer a full apology to Chinese Canadians for the head Tax and express our deepest sorrow for the subsequent exclusion of Chinese immigrants"

He further allocated for financial benefits for the living spouses of the deceased living Head tax payers. In spite of this apology and the monitory compensation, some expressed their grievances and said it would not compensate the suffering and the humiliations that those Chinese underwent. On the other hand the Canadian government collected around 23 million dollars from about 82,000 head tax payers and its equivalent to one billion dollars.

8. Gentlemen's agreement 1908

The Citizenship and Immigration has acknowledged the positive contributions trended by the new Immigrants by saying that

"At no time has immigration played a greater role in Canadian history than during the twentieth century. In fact, without the immigrants who have settled in all areas of the country since the turn of the century, Canada would not be the culturally rich, prosperous, and progressive nation that it is today. The flood of people that poured into Canada between 1900 and 1914 and the dramatic changes in immigration patterns that occurred in more recent decades created a present–day population that bears little resemblance to the population in 1900."

1900- Preferable immigrants were farms who could adopt themselves in the farms in an virgin land who would be able to prepare the land for farm and initiating cultivation and successfully in having Immigrants for south of border the United States of America, Britain and Northern Europeans

1900-1921 Mostly from Eastern Europe, particularly from Russia pre the October Revolution and during the error of Czarist regimes who were the victim of the persecution.

Immigration Act of 1906, the essence of the act was to discourage and prevent and control or prevent certain group of people who were addressed as the undesirable Immigrants and also the power was given to the government to deport those who already arrived with two years of their landing. Though such practise was there but it has got the legal blessing from this act.

In 1906-06 4,700 Indians and 2,300 Japanese arrived. It created turmoil and anti-Asian demonstrations were held in the western coast of British Colombia. This resulted in the following:

It was crystal clear that until the second half of the twentieth century, Canadian Immigration polices had under gone many changes and some them were justified as appropriately fair and acceptable, but compared with the current conditions of freedom, fundamental human rights, impartiality, fairness, equality, anti-racism, ethnic non bias and so on, it was the other way around. The discriminative, restricted Immigration policy kept many non-Europeans, out of the scene and conveniently expressed they are incapable assimilation with the British and French norms of the descendants and also not totally prepared and committed in getting integrated. There was no room for the acceptance and promotion of cultural diversity. In fact at the time of high demand for the labour forces, they were extremely careful in weeding out the undesirable people and preventing their entry entering into the British North American colony.

During the colonial era particularly during the 15th century till the end of the first half of the twentieth century, the major and predominate European colonial rulers, such as the French, Portuguese, Dutch, German, Spanish and The British were competing each other in colonizing the American, Asian, Australian and African nations in having sources of exploiting their natural and other resources for the betterment of their own nations. At their initial stage they just wanted to establish trade centers and maximize their profits and probably not getting interfered in their local politics or even establish any settlements. They have also taken the advantage of the inter-tribal rivalry and the power hunger of the so-called monarchies, emperors, Chiefs, tribal leaders with ineffective equipment and weapons as their capital and sold guns and whiskey and in return they got abundant land and slaves. It was an unexpected and adventurous opportunity in their deeply rooted system. It also turned their primary purpose of trading with India in purchasing spices and having fur and gold in North America. They also capitalized the humanitarian and other services of the Christian missions as being loyal to them and tolerate their authoritative invasion and having at times curial treatments, because they are also being Christens. The loyalty is a high powerful weapon that wills not only helping in having their support but also keep them in not initiating anti-colonial masters activates and they were made to believe it is also a sin.

The essence of the Immigration Act of 1906 was to discourage, prevent and control certain groups of people who were deemed undesirable immigrants from settling in Canada. Furthermore, power was given to the government to deport those who had already arrived within two years of their landing.

9. The Royal Commission on Italian Immigration 1904-1905

At times the Canadian Government took adventurous initiatives to protect immigrants from undue exploitation by middlemen or travel agencies. The travel agencies in Italy, Montreal and New York in the early 20th century known as Padroni were taking all the initiative in recruiting, making arrangements for passage, finding jobs, and preparing immigration documents. Their services certainly benefitted both the sending and receiving countries. If not for them, Canada would not had the inexpensive and hardworking European labourers from Italy and many Italians would not had the opportunity to have a better life especially those from the southern part of the country where, at the time literacy rates were low and there were few job opportunities. Many of these labourers ended up working for the Canadian Pacific Railway.

But the Padroni capitalized on the ignorance of these people and their immediate need for a better life; immigrants were charged extravagantly and more workers were recruited to maximize their profits. They also made exaggerated and false promises about the living conditions and opportunities only to find that when they arrived in their new country, there were no jobs and they found themselves on the street. In parallel to the Royal Commission of Italians in Canada, the Italian government also expressed its concerns and sent Commissioner Egisto Rossi to visit Canada and visit wherever Italian Immigrants were living and reported on the situation of overall life, including their employment, working conditions and so forth.

The Canadian government took the situation very seriously and appointed a Royal commission on Italian Immigration to investigate the exploitation of Italian labourers by the employment brokers. In fact Canada had a very close link with the Italians in the later part of fifteen century. The Italian Canadians are amongst the earliest Europeans to explore and enter into this new continent. The Italian explorer John Cabot navigated and discovered the coast of Newfoundland for the British Empire. Another Italian John Verrazano, in 1524 explored a part of Atlantic Canada for the French, the British rival in colonization and international trade, and there were Italian Missionaries who settled into Canada as well.

The British Empire had a wonderful relationship with the Italians even at the beginning of 19th century in 1812. When the Americans tried to invade the British North American territory in both Upper and Lower Canada, Britain hired Italian mercenaries to fight against the Americans.

At the end of the war, as a gesture of appreciation, they were given land and other assistance in settling here. Italians from the developed northern part of Italy migrated mainly to cities like Toronto and Montreal and were not primarily involved in farming or railway construction and engaged in craftsmanship, aesthetic arts, teaching and the hotel industry. Italians continued to migrate to Canada for the entire 19th century and this continued until the beginning of the First World War. In fact in 1913 almost 119, 770 Italians were residing in Canada.

But in the late 19th and early 20th centuries, Italian immigration decreased. Canada had a very high regard for the Italians who helped them and as far as their calibre of discharging their duties was concerned, there was not any issues. But their influence in organizing trade unions became a thorn in the flesh in the relationship with their employers.

Unlike France and some other European countries, North America has been concerned about the issue of mobilizing and organizing the labour force under one umbrella. In order to address the issues and concerns of the labourers, the capitalist economy was modified by blending it with the political system and creating the welfare state as a system of government so that the workers who were in the grass roots level would not be influenced by labour union activists. The second concern from the public was that the Italians were involved in organized crime in the style of the Mafiosi and if this were to be allowed it would be a social disaster and a challenge to public safety. This fear has carried on into our modern times because in recent years, there have been inquiries into the connection between the construction industry and the most powerful organized crime clans. However, it must be said with great emphasis that those involved in organized crime are a very small minority and the majority of Italians are proud and patriotic citizens of this country who speak up against this sort of activity.

Italians in Canada also faced hardship due to having sentimental relationship with their families, friends closer and up to certain extent, their nation and during the Second World War Italy was in the enemy camp that supported the German Nazis. Benito Amilcare Andrea Mussolini, ruled Italy between October 31, 1922 and July 25 1943. Although he was elected as a democratic leader and carried out his duties accordingly, in 1925 he left all of constitutional obligations behind and became a dictator. He was also a strong supporter of the Socialist International movement and Canada and some other western nations, including England and France avoided having too close of a diplomatic relationship with him. Though a few Canadian Italians were sympathisers and active with the Fascists, many were minding their own business but still had a buried sentimental attachment to their country of origin and around two hundred of them settled down in the eastern townships of Quebec and in Southern Ontario. At the end of WWII, any negative feelings about the Italian community dispersed and over a half a million Italians arrived as new immigrants.

At the end of the First World War the western world was in a deep recession and Canada was not the exception and in many sectors layoffs superseded recruitment in many sectors of production. Despite the situation, over 29000 Italians somehow managed to enter into Canada as labourers and sponsored family members and immigrants from Italy had overtaken those of Britain.

The number of Italian Canadians is 1.5 million, only about %% are in the rural areas and the rest of 95% of them were residing in cities such as Toronto, Montreal, Vancouver, Hamilton, St. Catharine's- Niagara, Ottawa, Windsor, Calgary, Edmonton, London, Winnipeg, Thunder Bay, Sudbury and Oshawa. Their geographical distribution is somewhat similar to many other ethnic enclaves like Chinatown, Little Portugal and

J-Town. These enclaves are called Little Italy and have the Italian flavour in restaurants, bars, wine shops, clubs, grocery shops and churches and even if we parachuted an alien from outer space and dropped it in that vicinity, he would be able to spontaneously recognize that he was in Little Italy.

Over three quarters of the new Italian immigrants who arrived and settled in Canada after the Second World War were not come from upper class families; rather they came from the working class and engaged in working in construction, factories, and other low paid jobs. But with determination and the sacrifice of some of their comforts in education and investing their hard earning money in business and other industries they made the second and the third generations prosperous. In 1980s, over 86% of them own their homes and some of them are worth over millions of dollars and it is above the general population.

1900- Preferable immigrants were farmers who could adapt themselves in the farms in a virgin land who would be able to prepare the land for farming and initiating cultivation and successfully in having Immigrants for south of border the United States of America, Britain and Northern Europeans

1900-1921 Mostly from Eastern Europe, particularly from Russia pre the October Revolution and during the reign of the Czarist kings who were the victims of the persecution.

10. The Important turning points in 20th century

1. The Gentlemen's Agreement, 1908
2. The First World War, 1914- 1918
3. The Russian revolution October 1917
4. Immigration amendment act 1919

5. Empire settlement act 1922

6. Chinese Immigration act 1923

7. Railway agreement 1925

8. Canada 1930 till the end of the second world war in 1945

    a. World War 11- 1939-1945

9. Revolving Canada and its Immigration policy 1945-1978

    a. Citizenship Act 1947

    b. The Korean War 1950-1953

    c. Immigration Act 1952

    d. The Vietnam War 1954-1975

    e. Immigration Regulation 1962

    f. Immigration Regulation 1967

10. Modern policy in implementation April 28, 1978-2016

    a. Canadian constitution Act 1982

    b. Multiculturalism Act 1971, 1988

11. Syrian Refugees 2015-2016

It was crystal clear that until the second half of the twentieth century Canadian Immigration polices had undergone many changes and some them were justified as appropriately fair and acceptable, but compared with the current condition of freedom, fundamental human rights, impartiality, fairness, equality, anti-racism, and so on, it was the opposite. The discriminative and restricted Immigration policies kept many non-Europeans out of the scene and it was conveniently expressed that they were incapable of assimilation with the British and French norms of the descendants and also not totally prepared and committed in getting integrated. There was no room for the acceptance and promotion of cultural diversity. In fact at the time of high demand for the labour force, they were extremely careful in weeding out the undesirable, not favourable, not prioritised people in entering into the British North American colony.

During the colonial era particularly during the 15th century till the end of the first half of the twentieth century, the major and predominate European colonial rulers, such as the French, Portuguese, Dutch, German, Spanish and The British were competing with each other in colonizing the American, Asian, Australian and African nations in having sources of exploiting their natural and other resources for the betterment of their own nations. At their initial stage they just wanted to establish trade centers and maximize their profits and probably not getting interfered in their local politics or even establish any settlements. They have also taken the advantage of the inter-tribal rivalry and the power hunger of the so-called monarchies, emperors, Chiefs, tribal leaders with ineffective equipment and weapons as their capital and sold guns and whiskey and in return they got abundant land and slaves. It was an unexpected and adventurous opportunity deeply rooted into their system. It also made their primary purpose of trading with India in purchasing spices and having fur and gold in North America. They also capitalized the humanitarian and other services of the Christian missions as being loyal to them and tolerated their authoritative invasion and having at times cruel treatments, because they are also being Christians. The loyalty is a highly powerful weapon that will not only help in having their support but also keep them in not initiating anti-colonial master activities and they were made to believe it was also a sin.

The colonial network made an extensive link in developing their trade, the exploration of minerals and mining, the cultivation of commercial and cash crops by clearing the virgin lands and converting the farms where crops were being cultivated for local needs into cash crops. One example of this is the conversion of land for rice paddy production into coffee, tea, sugarcane and tobacco plantations. Investments were also made in developing infrastructure, such as building roads, bridges, churches, and office buildings by clearing the forest land into settlement areas, along with processing raw materials like fur into leather, and iron ore into steel. These raw materials would be processed and made into consumer products which would then be sold back to the people who lived in the colonies so that the Colonial powers could collect the tax revenue. For example, tea that was grown in India would be shipped to Britain were it would be packaged and sold back to the people of India in British tea boxes at an inflated price. The British North American territories had undergone a similar process and this had a big impact on emigration and migration and it superseded trade in commodities on the surface but it had an impact on strengthening the hold of the colonizers. This also helped in the political manoeuvres of the United States of America which had become an independent nation due to the American Revolution and this was slap in the face to the British. But this just made the British tighten its grip on their remaining colonies even more and the government implemented policies to prevent any future revolutions. Britain was multitasking in terms of keeping its northern part of the British North American territory loyal for its long term benefit and also quelling any desire for independence. They had the confidence that things would not get out of hand because the British loyalists who left all of their belongings and privileges, including the farmers who left better arable land and knew that the land in which they were going was not of the same quality were loyal to the British Crown. Loyalty superseded everything else, but in spite of it this there was room for suspicion and a mild fear of the infiltration of the idea for advocating for independence.

Although Britain had colonies all around the world in five continents, still Australia, New Zealand and Canada have been viewed as special and as such they have remained as an extension of their settlements even after they depart from their rule and even if they are not a member of its Common wealth organizations an umbrella unit. Even though The United States of America left any sort of formal bindings with Britain after they won their independence on 4th July 1776 and the British Common Wealth was formed in December 1949 and currently has 53 sovereign nations but only 16 of them still hold the Queen of England as their head of State and recently seven out of eight states are in favour of becoming a republic and replacing the Queen with an elected head of state. Australia is going to be the first to get out of the formal legal binding as having the Queen of England as the head of state, after the formation of the British Common wealth Nations- Organization. New Zealand is also considering the same.

Though many factors are behind making and executing Immigration and emigration policies and acts in Canada, all throughout the economic interest is a forceful determining factor and at times the socio- ethnic interest superseded, still the economic interests stand firmly and starting from the second half of the twentieth century its importance had become significant and had substantially gained its priority.

The fundamental change in the structure of the economic activities and the major shift to the service industry, mining, transport from farming and livestock and also the modernization of farming with the industrialization in agriculture demanded more capable and suitable man power man power and when it couldn't be met with their traditional and preferable source countries such as England, Ireland, and Scotland, whether they liked it or not immigrants from other European nations were accommodated and as a last resort, immigrants from Asia. The diversification of the modes of production also reflected in terms of the type of immigrants and their socio-ethnic backgrounds. It also converted remote villages into small towns and the small towns into larger ones and then to the level of cities with complexity of various socio-ethnic background and industrialization brought urbanization and almost a half of the new immigrants remained in those urban areas. In spite of the high density wave of immigrants settling in the urban areas, still the attraction to agriculture was also in the lime light, due to the encouragement given by the government in providing free land, free or subsidized passage, loans and other facilities and also providing a broader and wider market for their yield by having railway transportation that linked so-called upper and lower Canada where those products had a huge market.

The attraction of the urban life at that time was strong and the idea of having material comforts with better social amenities such as pipe born water, electricity, roads, hospitals, schools, and steady income without the need to depend on nature for high temperatures and rain for the crops in the rural areas made the cities seem like paradise. Even today the attraction and thirst for the city life by rural people and the agrarians and new immigrants continues to be very strong.

In spite of these attractions however, there is another side of the coin. City life has its own nature and notions. Historically, Canadian cities like many in other industrialized countries were not well equipped with social amenities. Sanitation was poor, air pollution was caused by coal and other cheap sources of energy, there were inadequate health and hygiene facilities, there was also a high infant mortality rate. Working conditions were poor and at times quite dangerous with little to no protection, there was no job security, the workdays were long with very little time off, and the scarcity of workplace benefits or compensation made life in the cities challenging. Unskilled labourers particularly those who were on-Europeans faced the additional hardship of racist discrimination which was not seriously investigated and very often these labourers worked in occupation that were deemed dirty, difficult or dangerous.

Canada had a peak number of immigrants between the period of 1896 and 1914 and it accounted for over three million members of the population. In fact in the year of 1913, a year before the beginning of the First World War, Canada granted permanent resident status for 400,870 new immigrants and this accounted for 5.3% of the Canadian population.

New Immigrants attained the permanent resident status.

YEAR	1900	1901	1902	1903	1904	1905	1906	1907	1908	1909
Number	41,681	55,747	89,102	138,660	131,252	141,465	211,653	272,409	143,326	173,694
% of Population	0.8	1.0	1.6	2.5	2.3	2.4	3.5	4.2	2.2	2.6

1910-1919										
YEAR	1910	1911	1912	1913	1914	1915	1916	1917	1918	1919
Number	286,839	331,288	375,756	400,870	150,484	33,665	55,914	72,910	41,845	107,698
% of Population	4.1	4.6	5.1	5.3	1.9	0.4	0.7	0.9	0.5	1.3

The statistics of the new Immigrants in corresponding to the population of Canada there was a steady increase in new immigrants and the percentage corresponding to the national population as well. In 1990 the landed new immigrant was 41, 681 and 0.8% of the population the gradual increase reached to 138,660, and accounted for 2.5% and in 1907 it was 272,409 to 4.2% and there was slow down in 1908 and 1909 respectively.

148, 326 and 173,694 and regained and reached the peak of 400,870 in 1913 and accounts for 5.3% of the population of 7, 632,000 and in 2011 the new Immigrants were 248,747 and accounts for 0.7% and total population was 33, 476,688. Then the beginning of the First World

War in 1914 and its interruption had a very big negative impact on the economy and immigration declined at the end of the war in 1919. The higher ratio of the new immigrants had a very positive impact on the demographics and other sections of the Canadian fabric.

12. Immigration Act 1906

The Immigration policies and the governing body of the government and the reaction from the public and the lessons that they learned from past experiences prompted the development of checks and balances periodically. It was crystal clear that there were certain elements lingering in this evolution process that protected, preserved, encouraged and promoted the British foundation of the Canadian fabric in the social, political, economic, cultural, and linguistic values. The open door approach in the later part of the nineteenth century somehow allowed the so-called unlikeable, unfavourable immigrants some status narrowed down exclusively to the British and then when the demand for immigrants came due to the potential for settling other parts of the country and the establishment of various industries, again the doors would open slightly, but when the need was fulfilled, the doors would close again in the form of restrictive immigration policies.

Unlike today where the rule of law determines what the various levels of government in democratic societies are allowed to do this was not the case in the early 1900's.Each level of government could, for the most part do whatever it saw fit and there was active interference in the executive body at the judiciary level. This was not treated as undue interference and this influence was visible at the department of immigration. The government had abundant power in making arbitrary judgements on immigration matters. The government had the power to prohibit entry of any class of immigrants that they deemed undesirable.

13. Gentlemen's Agreement-1908

As far as the evolution of the Immigration policies of both America and Canada are concerned the west and the east of the land had its own nature and priorities as such the entry of Europeans via the Atlantic Ocean to the east was welcomed and encouraged with certain discriminations for some s while in the west particularly British Colombia in Canada and California in America where the influx of Asians as cheap labourers was somewhat discouraged and restricted.

Simultaneously both America and Canada had to restrict the incoming Japanese, due to the fact that the reaction of the public was not in favour and there was the fear of them over taking the immigration pattern. The antagonism lit the flame and the media also added fuel into the fire. Arbitrarily some local government bodies reacted seriously and interfered in the policies of the federal government. One example of this is the San Francisco school board which arranged for all Asian descendant or origin children to be placed in a segregated school and it brought in very sensitive and discriminative measures that wounded Japanese and other Asians. The President was concerned about the challenges faced from growing Russian power in the Far East and wanted to have a strong foot in Japan to prevent it. He was making all possible efforts in neutralizing the opposition. The formal withdrawal was brought forward to the San Francisco school board on March 13, 1907.The former president of the US. Theodore Roosevelt negotiated for a gentlemen's agreement with the Japanese government in 1907-1908 it amended the immigration agreement of 1894. Japan denied passports to labourers seeking entry to the United States. But the Japanese travel agents and other agents abroad made use of the loopholes to enter America through other means. They sent the labourers who intended to migrate to America via Canada and Mexico where such restrictions did not apply.

Canadian Immigration, under the Ministry of labour made a similar attempt like the United States of America by having a bilateral gentlemen's agreement negotiated between the Labour Minister for Canada Rodolphe and the foreign minister Tadasu Hayashi for Japan and Japan voluntarily limited the number of immigrants to a quota of 400 annually.

14. Continuous Journey Act 1908

Another blow for Asian immigration to Canada was aimed at the East Indians. We should bear in mind that India was not an independent nation like Canada is or the United States of America for at that time it was a British colony and India had no independent rights or freedom in deciding its own affairs. Though overtly it appears like other reactive measures but practically it was targeted in denying, rights and privileges to Indian labourers who wanted to migrate to Canada. Though this legislation appears very polite in its intention, that of imposing travel restrictions; those who wrote and passed the legislation knew what they were doing. The *Continuous Journey Act* stipulated that would be immigrants would have to start their journey from the country of their citizenship where the tickets were purchased, to the targeted sea port in Canada without having a break in-between. It was very clear that there were no steamship services between India and Canada and due to the standards of navigation at the time, such a journey would have been impossible.

It was said that the public had serious concerns and some expressed the influx of Indians is as an 'Indian invasion' and 'Hindu Invasion'.

Most of the Indians in British Colombia were Punjabi Sikhs and their religious dress and the men with their bearded faces might have appeared quite strange or even threatening to Canadians of European heritage. The community built a Gurudwara in 1908 in Vancouver, with the Khalsa Diwan Society which was their religious non-profit organization that administrated, advised and helped their community which was very similar to how the Roman Catholic Church worked with their respective communities but the Khalsa Diwan Society did not exert as much control over the personal lives of its members. This organization mobilized the community in British Columbia, Canada and found alternative ways for their fellow Indians to have passage into Canada. One of the ways of reaching Canada by bypassing the continuous journey restriction to Canada was to reach the United States of America and cross the border illegally to take refuge in the Gurudwara. The *Continuous Passage Act* remained in effect until 1947.

Mr. Stephen Harper, former Prime Minster made a formal apology for the 1914 Komogata Maru Incident. A Japanese steamship called the Komogata Maru began its navigation from Hong Kong, a British colony of a 99 years of lease by the British government to Yokohama, Japan and reached its final destination Vancouver, British Colombia in 1914 carrying 376 passengers from Punjab, India another British colony and these immigrants also claimed that by being British subjects they had the right to enter into Canada. But in 1914, Canada was not a British colony, rather an independent nation. The passengers had to wait for two months to disembark and had to remain on the ship. Among them 24 were admitted and the remaining 352 were not allowed and the ship was forced to return to India and all of them were British subjects. Finally when the boat sailed back to Calcutta and was met by police, 20 people were killed as they disembarked while the rest were jailed. This is one of the acts of exclusion of immigrants of Asian origin

Mr. Harper was speaking to a crowd of about 8000 people and almost all of them are Indian origin Canadians, predominantly Sikhs in Surrey British Colombia. The community leaders were not pleased with the way the apology was made in a public place, rather than in Parliament and commented on how similar apologies were made in Parliament for the Chinese Head Tax in 2006 and for the hardships faced by native students at the residential schools. The president Jaswinder Singh of the Descendants of Komogata Maru Society said that the apology was unacceptable and that it needed a full apology. Anyhow the intention of Mr. Harper was to remove a very deep stain in Canadian history.

Mr. Harper made another apology to the families who lost family members in the Air India bombing in 1985. He described the disaster as "institutional failings" on June 23, 2010 and Indian Canadians did not pay much attention to this.

Justin Trudeau, the Prime Minister followed the footsteps of former Prime Minister Stephen Harper in apologizing for the Komogata Maru incident of 1914. It was proposed to have such an apology given in Parliament on May 18th 2016 and preceded accordingly and it has been welcomed and appreciated by the Sikh community.

Initially the Prime Minister expressed his concern, by saying "As a nation, we should never forget the prejudice suffered by the Sikh community at the hands of the Canadian government of the day. We should not and we will not,"

Although the majority of the passengers were Sikhs there were 24 Muslims and 12 Hindus on the Komogata Maru and all were British subjects. This was one of many incidents in the history of the early 20th century, in restricting and excluding of Asian immigrants. However, this drama lasted a short while because the ship arrived in Vancouver, B.C on May 23, 1914 and left the port on June 23, 1914 and reached Calcutta, India on September 26, 1914 with 352 people and 24 of them were allowed to enter into Canada.

In fact similar apologies were made on other restrictive immigration issues by Canadian politicians and religious leaders outside of Canada. For example, in 1988 Prime Minister Brian Mulroney made an apology to the Japanese Canadians for Canada's internment camps during the Second World War when Japan was considered an enemy. He also offered admission of wrongdoing to the Italian Canadians who were not treated appropriately, under the War Measures Act in 1990.

On 29 April 2009, Pope Benedict XVI apologized to Native Canadians for the abuses –physical and sexual made on native students at the residential schools operated and administrated by the Catholic Church and other missionaries.

15. Immigration Act 1910

One of the fundamental elements of this act was that it gave power for the concerned minister, an elected officer in prohibiting immigration based on racial origin. Not only did this Act prevent the admission of immigrants of certain races, it also gave power to the minister to strip them of their immigration rights and privileges and deport them as well. The concentration of such powers limited the say of the judiciary and gave more power to the executive bodies.

The so-called undesirables "owing to their peculiar customs, habits, modes of life and methods of holding property and because readily assimilated"

Though it appears that this Act arbitrarily interfered with the fundamental rights of individuals, its implementation shows that the focus on certain races and nationalities that was directly or indirectly connected to the concerns around safety and interests of the nation. On March 14, 1929 for example, there was an Order in Council to prohibit immigrants of the Hungarian, German, Austrian, Bulgarian or Turkish races except by special permission.

The Asian race also suffered due to this Act. In 1919, Asians were prohibited from entering into Canada with the exception of farm labourers, domestic workers and the wives and children of Canadians of Asian origin males to be sponsored from 1923. In 1930 the privilege given for such labourers and domestic workers was removed and this continued until 1956. Later on in 1956, there was an agreement made between Canada and three South Asian countries India, Pakistan and Sri Lanka, which was then known as Ceylon was made. It did not completely eradicate immigration from these countries, rather, it established a quota respectively 150 immigrants came from India, 100 and 50 from Sri Lanka though the number was increased by 300 from India in 1958 and this continued until 1962.

16. Naturalization Act 1914

Another restriction but neither for entry nor for deportation rather attain naturalized citizenship and retain it. The residential criteria of 3 years was increased to 5 years and the criteria of good character and the added qualification of having adequate knowledge of either English or

French the two main official languages of the Canadian government and it was not a criteria at the beginning for most of the British North American colony had the British and the French and few others who had little or no linguistic qualification on one of these languages. But at the beginning of the 20[th]century. According to the census 2011 there are over 200 languages have been spoken at homes in Canada.

Facts and figures 2014 – Immigration overview: Permanent residents

Canada – Permanent residents by province or territory and language ability

Total by language ability

Language ability	2005	2006	2007	2008	2009	2010	2011	2012	2013	2014
English	133,037	133,112	127,173	140,004	142,904	160,344	144,545	144,532	135,277	152,510
French	12,066	12,562	12,823	12,692	13,696	16,839	16,420	16,664	15,186	13,732
Both French and English	23,010	22,656	24,099	24,624	27,932	28,949	25,972	25,795	22,132	22,628
Neither	94,125	83,294	72,606	69,872	67,638	74,553	61,796	70,895	86,425	71,507
Language ability not stated	0	0	0	0	0	0	0	0	0	1
Province or territory not stated	4	16	52	52	0	2	14	17	3	26
Total by language ability	262,242	251,640	236,753	247,244	252,170	280,687	248,747	257,903	259,023	260,404

Geographic distribution

The following table details the population of each province and territory, with summary national totals, by language spoken most often in the home as reported in the Canada 2011 Census ("Home language").

Province/territory	Total population	English	%	French	%	Other languages	%	Official language(s)
Ontario	12,722,065	10,044,810	78.95%	284,120	2.23%	1,827,870	14.36%	English (de facto)
Quebec	7,815,955	767,415	9.81%	6,249,080	79.95%	554,405	7.09%	French[8]
British Columbia	4,356,205	3,506,600	80.49%	16,685	0.38%	670,095	15.38%	English (de facto)
Alberta	3,610,185	3,095,255	85.73%	24,690	0.68%	379,550	10.51%	English
Manitoba	1,193,095	1,007,325	84.42%	17,950	1.5%	125,285	10.5%	English
Saskatchewan	1,018,310	938,170	92.13%	4,295	0.42%	59,240	5.81%	English
Nova Scotia	910,620	868,765	95.40%	15,940	1.75%	18,510	2.03%	English (de facto)
New Brunswick	739,895	512,115	69.21%	209,885	28.36%	9,310	1.25%	English, French
Newfoundland and Labrador	509,950	502,475	98.53%	1145	0.22%	5,000	0.98%	English (de facto)
Prince Edward Island	138,435	132,200	95.49%	2,465	1.78%	2,925	2.11%	English (de facto)
Northwest Territories	41,040	36,485	88.9%	555	1.35%	3,620	8.8%	Chipewyan, Cree, English, French, Gwich'in, Inuinnaqtun, Inuktitut, Inuvialuktun, North Slavey, South Slavey, Tłı̨chǫ[12]
Yukon	33,655	31,025	92.18%	820	2.43%	1240	3.68%	English, French
Nunavut	31,765	14,440	45.45%	245	0.77%	16,820	52.95%	Inuit language (Inuktitut, Inuinnaqtun), English, French[13]
Canada	33,121,175	21,457,080	64.78%	6,827,860	20.61%	3,673,865	11.09%	English, French

Source: Statistics Canada, 2011 *Census Population by language spoken most often and regularly at home, age groups (total), for Canada, provinces and territories.* (Figures reflect single responses).[14]

17. Immigration Act 1919

After the First World War many colonies were left with the task of rebuilding not just physical structures, but the entire system of infrastructure, the educational system and the economy. At this point, Canada was not ready to receive more new immigrants when the local people were left out of the workplace due to the interruption caused by the war, and the nation was in a deep recession.

Furthermore, the negative sentiments around Italy, Germany and Japan also impacted negatively on preventing immigration from those countries and these feelings polluted the social and political atmosphere and politicians were very careful in making sensitive decisions on immigration and emigration. This was reflected in the policy of prohibiting immigrants of any nationality, race, class, or occupation because of their "peculiar customs, habits, and modes of life and methods of holding property".

At the time, such policies were directed towards "enemy" countries that had participated in the First World War such as the Austrians, Bulgarians, Hungarians, and the Turks but also included people with disabilities, those who had been injured in the war, people with infectious diseases, criminals and those who were 15 years old and who could not read English or French

Throughout the evolution of Canadian immigration, the balancing of material interests versus the preservation without substantial dilution of the socio- cultural life of the British in particular and Europe in general was delicate. Most of the Immigration Acts prior to 1967 reflected these interests sometimes quite discreetly, and at times bluntly when it was seen fit. When the priority was given to the economy the prioritised groups were favoured; but when the economy settled, the immigration policies were adjusted accordingly.

Canada and many other western nations were heavy affected by the October 1917 Bolshevik Revolution in the newly formed Soviet Union. At the same time in Winnipeg in the construction industry and metal work factories, over 30,000 workers walked off the job in a labour dispute and many of these workers had migrated from Europe. The blame was passed on those foreign workers. In Germany and France, labour unions were strong and well established but this was not the case in Canada or the United States. This walk out by the workers in Winnipeg led to immigrants from those respective European countries being "blacklisted" due not only to concerns around unionization, but the also the fear of Socialism.

18. The Empire Settlement Act, 1922

The British government at this time was concerned with rebuilding its economy and also resolving the issue of mass unemployment that the decision was made to make use of its colonies such as India, Australia, South Africa and some other colonies in Africa and Asia including Canada itself a former colony. 34,750 British were sent to Australia, 12, 890 to New Zealand and another 3000 were sent to other colonies and about 165, 000 British immigrants in many categories arrived into Canada and its number was greater than what other British colonies received.

19. Railway Agreement, 1925

Canada felt the pinch of the economic recession during and just after the First World War and then began to rebuild its economy and expanded in the sectors of reconstruction, building new infrastructure, and expanding agricultural. However, there was inadequate man power and this was partially caused by the emigration of Canadians to the United States of America who were seeking better accommodations in particular farmers who found the farm land and mild climate were more conducive to successful agrarian practices.

There was a demand for a more liberal immigration policy so that new immigrants from other parts of Europe would be able to be recruited to meet the shortage of manpower in a faster, cheaper and easier way. Prime Minister Mackenzie King considered their request as reasonable and also beneficial and gave permission in establishing certain privileges for the Canadian Pacific Railway and Canadian National Railway corporations in recruiting foreign workers into Canada. It opened the gates wider for central and eastern Europeans, particularly from Latvia, Lithuania, Estonia, Poland, Russia, Yugoslavia, Austria, Romania and also Germany. There were also some restricting measures for the best interests of their sectors of production but it appeared that it was based on racial background. For example, they did not allow Jews in this category, not because of their race, rather it was the perceived impatience in working or holding the responsibly of being farmers. In other sectors such as industrial, the calibre of people needed was somewhat flexible and different in nature from farmers in western Canada. It was another milestone in extending the immigrant territory further from the British and French.

This was a short lived program due to the Great Depression which gripped the entire world and dismantled and destroyed entire economies. The tightening of the inflow of new immigrants was inevitable and this also protected some of the local economic interests.

As the 2008 recession fire was lit by the United States of America the Great Depression also started there when the stock market crashed on October 29, 1929 and spread out to the world in a short time. By 1932, the worldwide GDP fell by around 15%. The Canadian economy was in very bad shape the unemployment rate was so high that 30% of Canadians were out of work and 20% of them became dependant on government assistance. The national income fell 58% of the 1929 level. The economic major industrial nations suffered also suffered badly.

The Change in Economic indicators 1929-1932

Item	United States	Great Britain	France	Germany
Industrial Production	-46%	-23%	-24%	-41%
Wholesale prices	-32%	-33%	-34%	-29%
Foreign trade	-70%	-60%	-54%	-61%
Unemployment	+607%	+129%	+214	+232

The economic recession had a very high impact on migration and emigration as well and Canada was not ready to entertain new immigrants while many local people were struggling for their survival and the resource countries were also aware of the worldwide situation and therefore did not dare to take any initiatives. Canada limited its acceptance of new immigrants from the desirable categories from the United States, Britain, Australia, New Zealand, and South Africa and Ireland, preferring those who were able to stand on their own feet and under no circumstance be a burden to the tax payers. There was decline in newcomers who gained permanent resident status in Canada starting from 1931 and in comparison with 1930 it was 104, 806 in 1931 it came down to 27, 530 and in 1936 it was 11,643 and came down further in 1941 as 9,329 and began to remain in 1946 a year after the Second World War as71, 719 and shot up over one hundred thousand persons starting from 1948

It is important to mention that the relationship with the French Canadians and the Canadian government was quite cordial. French Canadians who had gone back to France or migrated to the United States were welcomed back into Canada during this time. But France was in need of more manpower in the army and its related areas to protect against German expansionism and thus discouraged emigration; but to those who desired to emigrate, they were encouraged to go to one of the French colonies. The Canadian government made some efforts to bring back French Canadians to have them settle in Quebec.

Permanent resident in Canada -immigrants

YEAR	1930	1931	1932	1933	1934	1935	1936	1937	1938	1939
Number	104,806	27,530	20,591	14,382	12,476	11,277	11,643	15,101	17,244	16,994
% of Population	1.0	0.3	0.2	0.1	0.1	0.1	0.1	0.1	0.2	0.2

1940-1949

YEAR	1940	1941	1942	1943	1944	1945	1946	1947	1948	1949
Number	11,324	9,329	7,576	8,504	12,801	22,722	71,719	64,127	125,414	95,217
% of Population	0.1	0.1	0.1	0.1	0.1	0.2	0.6	0.5	1.0	0.7

The citizenship Act, 1947

20. Citizenship

"I swear (or affirm)
That I will be faithful
And bear true allegiance
To Her Majesty Queen Elizabeth the Second
Queen of Canada
Her Heirs and successors

As at I will faithfully observe

The laws of Canada
And fulfill my duties

As a Canadian citizen"

Our beloved head of State is the Her Majesty Queen Elizabeth the Second, Queen of Canada, the longest serving monarch in the British Regime is our head of state even though there is a vocal minority of those who want this country to be a republic. Although there were three people who hesitated to recite the oath by mentioning her Majesty, it was due to their grievances not against the Queen herself; rather the acts committed by the British monarchy on various occasions. So far these three refused to become naturalized citizens of Canada and made their case at the Supreme Court of Canada and the court declined to hear the constitutional challenge and as custom, the court did not give the reason for its decision. They made some move to challenge an Ontario Court of appeal ruling. The ruling written by Justice Karen Weiler for the three –judge panel, said that the citizenship ceremony does not violate the appellants' freedom of expression because " they have the opportunity to publicly disavow what they consider to be the message conveyed by the oath" after they take it.

In response to it Mr. Dror Bar-Natan, a mathematics professor, in Toronto, a permanent resident in Canada and a citizen of the United States of America said that "I think it is silly" he further said the notion of taking a vow and then publicly disavowing it 'I misunderstood the law in Canada, I thought vows had meaning".

He also said that "I wish to affirm my allegiance, my true allegiance to Canada and the people of Canada, but also to disavow the royalty part and only the royalty part of the citizenship oath"

The second landed immigrant is Michael McAteer, journalist, an Irish born resident of Canada since 1964 and the third person is Simone Topey a Rastafarian claims that swearing the oath to the Queen would violate her freedom of religion.

Anyhow, the Canadian Citizenship Act was enacted on June 27, 1946 and it came into effect on January 1st 1947 and prior to this those born in Canada and naturalized citizens held the status of British subjects and if it was required, they held the British passports. Since Canadians were considered British subjects like the British and other British subjects of the British Commonwealth, they also have the extended rights as British subjects; they were not required to have any naturalized rights authorization to be in Canada. In spite of this however, there were other criteria that Canada established so that one could become a member of the family such as good character, basic linguistic skills in either English or French and the residential status.

The First and the Second World Wars insisted that Canadians be able to act on their own rather than be under the symbolic rule of Britain and Paul Martin Senior, who was a cabinet minister, introduced the bill in parliament on October 22, 1945 and gave a very sensational and meaningful introduction.

Our "new Canadians" bring to this country much that is rich and good, and in Canada they find a new way of life and new hope for the future. They should all be made to feel that they, like the rest of us, are Canadians, citizens of a great country, guardians of proud traditions and trustees of all that is best in life for generations of Canadians yet to be. For the national unity of Canada and for the future and greatness of this country it is felt to be of utmost importance that all of us, new Canadians or old, have a consciousness of a common purpose and common interests as Canadians; that all of us are able to say with pride and say with meaning: "I am a Canadian citizen."

t. 1414 Foreign born Canadian population

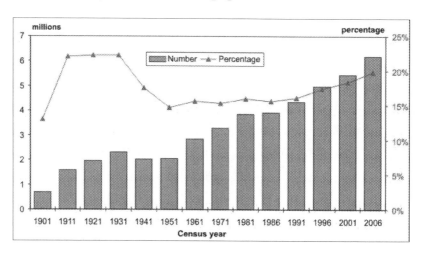

Sources: Statistics Canada, censuses of population, 1901 to 2006. (**In 2011 it is 20.6%**)

21. The Citizenship Act 1977

The Citizenship Act that came into effect on 15th February 1977 brought a broader outlook to the Canadian Citizenship Act of 1947. Both the citizens of Canada by birth, regardless of their country of origin and the status of their parents and naturalized citizens were granted equal status and were entitled to all the rights and freedoms and subject to all of the duties of a citizen. The previous Act which gave some priority for the British subjects over aliens was removed and the right to attain dual or multi citizenship while having Canadian citizenship was not a right or privilege until the implementation of this Act.

The Minister for Citizenship and Immigration Canada John McCallum brought forward an act of Citizenship on February 2016 that revoked some the fundamental changes made by the previous government as Bill C24 which became an act and then began to be implemented in June 2015. The short lived Act reversed many of the changes to the previous Act and removed certain barriers and allowed for greater flexibility and made it easier to attain citizenship, rather than losing it for potential citizens. He made the intention of the changes clearly in that they would encourage potential would be Canadians to attain Canadian citizenship and also those who attained it shouldn't feel that their citizenship was not secure and at any time might be revoked with additional powers allowed for the Cabinet Minister, an elected executive person by the Act brought forward by the Harper government in June 2015.

"A Canadian is a Canadian is a Canadian. It's not up to the government to revoke citizenship. We want to facilitate the process of people becoming Canadian citizens while retaining program integrity."

"As it was lingering in 2015 in some corners that "Canadian citizenship is not for sale" at that time when the Citizenship Bill C24 was in discussion in parliament. It was the reflation of the hardliners in support of the restrictive bill. It has been discovered a thousand of naturalized citizens might have abused the system my misrepresenting, interpreting of given false data or information on the application and attained the citizenship and it has be reviewed and if it is necessary to be revoked if this a very serious case in nature and the federal court continues to remove the citizenship of those involved in organized crime, war crime and crime against humanity will continue in the future as well.

One of the prominent immigration Lawyer Lorne Waldman said those who face citizenship revocation on the grounds of misrepresentation are still not entitled to a hearing – a practice that is under a legal challenge in the federal court.

Mr. Chris Alexander formerly of Citizenship and Immigration Canada clearly mentioned that "citizenship is not a right, it's a privilege" at the time when the Citizenship law that was passed and became law on Friday June 20, 2014. It somewhat alienated Canadian values in terms of accommodating new comers from the initial stage of the processing of the documents for the newcomers, regardless of which of the categories he or she belonged to. Even welcoming the refugee claimants either at the border or within the country or from elsewhere, Canada has never had the notion like most of the receiving countries in Europe who clearly state that when the circumstances that pushed refugee claimants for seeking asylum is approved regardless of their established lives in their respective countries where they claimed refugee status, they will be sent back to their home land. Canada has a vision that the eligible refugees will be permanently settled down here and reaches the level of attaining the status of a naturalized citizen. When we claim for those who had already attained naturalized citizenship and intend to do so will be altered in that citizenship is only a privilege not a right dilutes the rich Canadian values.

Those who want to become Canadian citizens fall into separate groups each with their own interests and values. Some view the Citizenship oath as just a ceremonial action and do not otherwise pay it much attention. Whereas there are others for whom Canadian citizenship is a convenience; these people receive their citizenship and return to their country of origin, returning to Canada only when the time is right for them. Furthermore some engage in activities that are against Canada's national interests and this is why the tory government had to tighten the Immigration laws. Anyone who wants to be a citizen of Canada should have a serious commitment to this country and to being a Canadian and not abuse the rights and privileges for an inappropriate agenda. Furthermore they should realize that the rights that they enjoy also have certain responsibilities and obligations. Canadian citizenship is not a gift and as quoted in the media it is "Not for sale".

Privileges can be revoked in certain circumstance but it is not easily revoked. In most of the world's major revolutions, it was a key point to turn the privileges of the people into rights as was done during the French revolution in 1789 and in the declaration of the U.S Constitution which says that:

"We hold truths to be self-evident, that all men and created equal, that they are endowed by their Creator with certain unalienable Rights, that among these are Life, Liberty and the pursuit of Happiness"

In spite of this being at the top position, Canadians do not have the restriction that USA has as such. Anyone who wants to become President for example has to be a natural born U.S citizen. Someone may be an American citizen of they are born abroad if both parents were citizens of the United States, but in Canada there is no such restriction for naturalized citizens to become the Prime Minster of Canada and our former Prime Minister was born in Scotland. When President Richard Nixon had to vacate his presidency due to the Watergate scandal in 1973, Dr. Henry Kissinger was on the top of the American political ladder, but he could not replace Nixon because though he was an American citizen, he was not a natural born citizen of America.

There are residency requirements for people who want to be Canadian citizens and not for ones who are born in Canada. This has been in practice since May 22, 1868 and periodically it has been expanded and contracted and starting from June 7, 1919 to 14 February 1977 it was five years.

In the U.S.A the requirement is a continuous stay in the U.S.A for at least five years after receiving permanent residence status and in the case of the spouse of an American citizen it is at least three years. In the United Kingdom, someone who wants to apply for British citizenship he /she must live in the United Kingdom at least 6 years prior to applying and then within that period the applicant should have resided outside of Britain for more than 450 days and then in the last twelve months within the 6 year period the applicant must not have been outside of United Kingdom more than 90 days. In the case of the spouse, the residential criteria are lenient like the USA. In Germany, one has to live in Germany at least eight years before applying for naturalized citizenship and in France it is five years. The continuous physical presence will also disregard short visits out of the country for six months or less in many cases. In Australia, one has to have a residential stay with a valid visa for four years immediately before applying which must include the last twelve months as a permanent resident. The cumulative stay will prove that the applicant has made his commitment to establish or make efforts to establish his life in this country. That is why the citizenship law that was popularly known as Bill C 24 brought in another criteria in that a resident needs to have lived four of six years in Canada, including at least half a year physically in Canada for four of those six years and in the previous case the residential criteria required three of the four immediate period of applying for the citizenship was enough, regardless of the compulsory stay of six months in a year of any particular years. It was only a means to prove that the applicant has shown his /her commitment and is capable of being a loyal citizen. Among those countries the USA and Canada, New Zealand are brand new British descendant nations and except for the USA the rest have certain things in common and also still have the British Queen as their head of State.

From	To	Residential criteria
22 May 1868	04 May 1910	2 years
5 May 1910	6 June 1919	3 years
7 June 1919	14 February 1977	5 years
15 February 1977	10 June 2015	3 years
11 June 2015	Now	4 years

Citizenship by birth is another section of Canadian citizenship has been in discussion for a while and may in the future be a hot topic for discussion and some changes would be made, but it has taken the attention for the common man to the elites Today there are only thirty countries around the world granting birth right citizenship in which two of the developed nations are the United States of America and Canada. They are as follows

Birthright Citizenship

	Birthright citizenship	Nations recently repeated	
1	Antigua and Barbuda		
2	Argentina		
3	Barbados	Australia	2007

4	Belize	New Zealand	2005
5	Bolivia	Ireland	2005
6	Brazil	France	1993
7	Canada	India	1987
8	Chile	Malta	1989
9	Columbia	United Kingdom	1983
10	Dominica	Portugal	1981
11	Ecuador		
12	El Salvador		
13	Fiji		
14	Grenada		
15	Guatemala		
16	Guyana		
17	Honduras		
18	Jamaica		
19	Mexico		
20	Nicaragua		
21	Panama		
22	Paraguay		
23	Peru		
24	St. Kitts and Nevis		
25	St. Lucia		
26	St. Vincent and the Grenadines		
27	Trinidad and Tobago		
28	United States of America		
29	Uruguay		
30	Venezuela		

A non- Canadian couple boarded an Air Canada fight in Calgary on Saturday May 9th 2015 to reach their final destination Tokyo, Japan and while the flight passed over Canadian land and ocean territory which is around 22.2 km from the coastline and entered into international airspace a baby was born at the altitude of 35,000 feet from the Pacific ocean on the flight and finally landed at the Narita International Airport in Japan. The baby was granted Canadian citizenship and although the child was not born in Canadian territory per se it was given Canadian citizenship because the airline is a Canadian registered enterprise.

Usually a woman who is over 36 weeks pregnant under normal conditions wouldn't be allowed to board an airplane but this was an exceptional case because the baby was born premature.

Babies born in Canadian airspace are granted Canadian citizenship, regardless of parentage. In 2014 a flight from Qatar airways took off from Miami, Florida and during the flight a pregnant passenger went into labour and the flight had to be diverted to Gander Newfoundland and the baby was born in Canadian airspace and the baby was given Canadian citizenship. According to the 1944 Civil Aviation Convention if a baby is born outside of the territorial jurisdiction of any country, the baby is registered as a child born in the country in which the aircraft is registered and gains the citizenship of that respective country. However, the citizenship laws of the country also apply. For example, with births that occur on French or German airlines, the baby is issued a birth certificate from their respective country but is not granted citizenship status spontaneously.

Regardless of the parents immigration status in Canada, be they in a deportation, removal or departure order, on a temporary resident visa or refugee claimant except for diplomatic immunity all babies born in Canadian waters, airspace or land would be granted citizenship by birth. However, the parents would not gain any special immigration status in Canada due to the citizenship of the child by birth in Canada.

In spite of this however there are some cases where pregnant mothers enter into Canada on some form of visa including tourism under the pretention of visiting for other purpose though their primary purpose is to give birth in Canada and gain citizenship for the child and in the long run it would benefit them. Furthermore, when the child reaches over the age of 18 if he meets the other criteria for the ability to sponsor his parents as a citizen of Canada, they would be able to migrate to Canada eventually. These babies are referred to as anchor babies. In the United States of America one out of twelve newborn babies are born as anchor babies or born by illegal immigrants and the estimated number of illegal immigrants in the United States is around 13 million. In Canada it is not significant in number and it is below 500 a year and accounts for 0.14% of the 360,000 total births per year in Canada. It has not yet became an organized business in Canada but in the United States of America it is a flourishing enterprise in some communities such as the Chinese and Turkish. For example in California such agencies charge around $14, 750 dollars to take care of the pregnant mother and have the baby born in the States while providing food, lodging, entertainment and attending to other needs.

Canada does not restrict its citizens from having dual or multiple citizenships. Certain naturalized Canadians choose to continue if allowed by their country of birth, to have the citizenship of their country of birth without denouncing it. This has its own privileges such as the ability to participate in politics as candidates, or voters, holding their properties, not having hassles in obtaining visas and extending them and paying for the fee, having the rights for education, health and social services and also doing business with the rights and privilege of fellow citizens, not as foreigners. There are naturalized Canadians or bale to have their citizenship of their country of origin abundant their citizenship of their country of origin because of certain other obligation such as to have been obliged to participate in compulsory military training and also paying taxes for their foreign earnings like the United States of America.

There are some prominent politicians who have dual citizenship. The National Democratic Party leader Thomas Mulcair, though born and brought up by Canadian parents in Canada, is married to a French citizen and obtained French citizenship as the spouse of a French citizen. In case he was to become the Prime Minister of Canada his loyalty and commitments may be questioned especially if there was some sort of conflict between Canada and France. There are also recent cases of former and present members of parliament in the past and present holding dual citizenship. They have dual citizenship with Syria, United Kingdom, Greece, France, Pakistan, Argentina, Portugal Macedonia, Brazil, Japan, China, Tanzania, and Paraguay and so on.

22. Immigration Act, 1952

I would quote from McCarran in the senate on March 2, 1953 on the veto by U.S President Truman on the Immigration and Nationality Act of 1952 that is somewhat similar to the trend on immigration that Canada was dealing with.

"I believe that this nation is the last hope of Western civilization and if this oasis of the world shall be overrun, perverted, contaminated or destroyed, then the last flickering light of humanity will be extinguished. I take no issue with those who would praise the contributions which have been made to our society by people of many races, of varied creeds and colors.... However, we have in the United States today hard-core, indigestible blocs which have not become integrated into the American way of life, but which, on the contrary are its deadly enemies. Today, as never before, untold millions are storming our gates for admission and those gates are cracking under the strain. The solution of the problems of Europe and Asia will not come through a transplanting of those problems en masse to the United States.... I do not intend to become prophetic, but if the enemies of this legislation succeed in riddling it to pieces, or in amending it beyond recognition, they will have contributed more to promote this nation's downfall than any other group since we achieved our independence as a nation."

23. Immigration Act, 1952

Immigration Act, 1952 did not make any fundamental changes on the open door immigration policy nor was it extremely restrictive on migration from certain designated nations. It reinforced a wider range of powers such as the discretionary power over decisions of admission and deportation with the ability to grantor cancel immigration permits and also overturns the decisions of immigration officers and immigration appeals boards to the Citizenship and Immigration Minister. Furthermore, it also extended more power to the executive body from the judiciary as such they were able to retain control over immigration, the act continued to bar judges and courts from reviewing, reserving or otherwise interfering in immigration proceedings, unless they related to a Canadian citizen or a person with Canadian domicile. In spite of mobilizing more power for the elected executive body, still the creation of the Immigration appeal boards has given room for seeking justice from the government. The side-effect of this accumulation of power rather involving in an extended manner in day to day activities has taken the time and resources for planning, making appropriate polices, and researching and other assignments.

Additional restrictions from the previous ones treated homosexuals the same way as drug addicts and drug traffickers from entering into the country as a kind of social clean up, not allowing them to pollute the well-established society

24. Immigration Regulations 1962

It is another turning point in the evolution of our immigration policy, in which Canada has realized that Canada as to get in line with the global changes in modernization in technology and push backward in the element of the racial sentiments and look for skilled workers, regardless of their ethnic or regional backgrounds. The Minister of Citizenship and Immigration Ellen Fairclough almost followed with Prime Minister John Diefenbaker's bill of rights in 1960 which rejected discrimination on the basis of race, colour, national origin, and religion or sex. In spite of it still there was degree of discrimination exhibited by those immigrants from the preferred nations in Europe. When it comes to family class sponsorship by the Canadians abroad, there was also ethnic discrimination based on the geographical distribution from the selected countries in Europe, America, selected countries in the middle East permitted to sponsor children over the age of 21, married children, siblings and their siblings families and unmarried orphaned nieces and nephews under the age of 21. It was also aimed at eliminating or restricting the inflow of unskilled Asians.

It is very appropriate at this junction to comment on what was said on the restrictions on migration during the period of the economic depression in the 1930's by Harold Fields of The American Journal of International Law, 1932

"The doors which once were opened wide are now but slightly ajar. The countries that boasted of their liberal attitudes toward new settlers-particularly the countries of the Western Hemisphere are much more strict in their boundaries for permanent settlement"

The Immigration Act 1952 gave more room for discriminative practices which included Asian immigrants without immediate relatives in Canada, gay persons and persons with mental disabilities.

25. White Paper on Immigration, 1966

The White Paper was a review of the Immigration policy and recommendations for creating a more effective immigration policy that could meet the economic demand as a priority. The growth of diversified economy with manufacturing, professional management positions and technical occupations increased the demand for more skilled man power for its operations and future growth and also for a local and steady market for the industrial products. The focus slightly shifted from the ethnic and unskilled manual labour force to skilled workers with more emphasis given to what was suitable for the economic demands and also to minimize the number of unskilled workers so that there would be no additional burden for the locally unemployed unskilled workers. The minister for the newly formed department of Manpower and Immigration Jean Marchand had the intention of curbing the influx of immigrants under the family class sponsorship, and it is necessarily required the skills, rather than family ties.

26. Immigration regulations: Order-in-Council PC 1967-1616-1967.

The major share of immigration has turned towards having immigrant who would be able to make very effective and efficient contribution for the economic growth that would be able to match the fast industrialized growing economy and it became more objective and calculative in the process. It brought down the point system in which whoever meets the criteria would be able to migrate and make positive contributions while improving their earnings and uplifting their life.

The advantage of the surplus skilled workers and recently qualified persons in developing countries, in addition to the developed world became the source countries for supplying those skilled workers. It is a winning situation for both the sending and receiving countries and there are three categories of suppliers as the influx of the skilled workers from the East European countries after the collapse of the governments and disintegration of the Soviet Union, Yugoslavia and Czechoslovakia in the early 1900's. The second wave came from India and China where the education system and rapid economic growth produced a mass scale of skilled workers and the state of the economy was unable to accommodate at this juncture and their emigration in fact helped in two ways as such; earning a foreign exchange and the lowering of the local competition in the labour market and reduction in the unemployment sector. The third group is from the traditional supplier from Europe and the USA and it has been reduced due to the fact that their own development is able to accommodate them in the labour market and also having a lower birth rate does not supply more young adult skilled workers even for their local market.

Modern technical education is shared around the globe and the curriculum is very much uniform and it does not matter much from where and in which language the knowledge and skills have been imparted to the students and the minimum requirement for linguistic capabilities for the technical field compared with humanitarian subjects and social sciences is not deeply required. It matters a little whether or not it was taught in Japanese, English or Mandarin, provided having substantial linguistic skills either in English or French.

I do not believe that the current source countries will continue to supply such large numbers of skilled workers in the forthcoming decades as it is now, due to the tremendous economic growth in these respective countries and slowdown in the birth rate. Maybe in the future there might be a shift to Africa and South America since the growth of the natural increase in population is higher and a portion of those skilled workers may emigrate in more numbers. The flexibility in the global labour mobility would not have any hardship for both the source and receiving countries.

Recently the former government addressed the issue on how to make use of the skilled workers for their benefit while getting higher degrees of benefit from them for the nation. Quite a good number of these new immigrants in the skilled worker categories felt that the honey and milk does not flow into their bucket, instead plain water flows into it and that too is interrupted. They have to do odd jobs and after having a good position in their field of expertise, fine status and having job satisfaction, then coming into Canada with high hopes and to get a license to practise in their field of expertise, to undergo certain courses and training that too with the family responsibility in a strange environment is a strain and to switch for a new job is somewhat painful.

Anyhow, the Harper Government introduced an alternative system of processing as the express entry process and on January 1, 2015, the

Government of Canada implemented the Express Entry Immigration system under the Economic Class including the Federal Skilled Worker Program. It is aimed at neither tightening nor loosening the entry of the immigrants under the skill worker category, rather proper and high binomial usage of the skilled workers in the interests of the soon to be immigrants and the national economy. Under the point system whoever is professionally qualified, experienced and meeting other criteria's for migration were processed on the basis of first come first served. Under the express entry system whoever could meet the shortage of manpower wherever such calibre persons would not be found locally, new immigrants would be sought to meet the need immediately. Under this system, federal skilled workers across 347 occupations are included. In such operation there is a possibility for someone who applied later may gain the chance in migrating with having permanent resident status, than those who applied for another sector of employment with higher qualifications and experience.

This is focussed more in the interests of economic advantage and Canada like any other countries that recruits skilled workers desires to have the best of the best so it would maximize the advantages both immediately and in the long term.

There is a mismatch between migration of the skilled worker immigrants and the utilization of their potentiality at the labour market not only in Canada but also in many other countries that have them as number one priority in having such immigrants. Let me compare Germany with Canada and gauge the similarities. These days, Germany not only among the European Union but in all of Europe is the most popular destination for skilled workers. The rewards that they have been given as ways for the jobs that they have been discharging, mostly not at the field of their expertise is very low and they earn a low level of job satisfaction. It is rampant among the non-European Union immigrants to be somewhat forced to engage in a low profile jobs because the German companies do not pay due attention in recognizing their qualifications. According to a Report by the Berlin Institute for Population and Development, immigrants to Germany are now more highly qualified than the average Germans. The percentage of the academics that migrated to Germany between 2010 and 2010 was 355% compared to 20% in the native population.

When it comes to the temporary foreign workers the so called "Guest workers" between 1955 and 1973 they came mostly from Turkey, Spain, and Greece and had lesser academic qualifications.

According to Citizenship and Immigration Canada the following six factors are considered:

Under the new rules, qualified applicants are evaluated against six factors to determine their eligibility for immigration to Canada. Applicants must obtain a total of 67 points out of a possible 100 in order to qualify. The selection factors are:

Education; Language; Employment experience; Age; Arranged employment; Adaptability;

The new program seeks to select candidates with the highest probability of economic settlement success and contribution to Canada. It maintains previous criteria with modification to the relative importance and point structure for each selection factor.

Selection Factors:

To be selected under the FSW program, applicants who possess sufficient work experience and language proficiency must accumulate a minimum of 67 points on the skilled worker selection grid, which allocates points for education, language, employment experience, age, arranged Canadian employment and adaptability.

Education – Maximum of 25 points

The maximum number of points awarded for education is 25, with maximum points awarded to applicants with doctoral degrees. Foreign credentials will be evaluated by a designated third party to determine their Canadian equivalent and points will be awarded based on that equivalence. At this time, organizations designated for credential evaluation are:

Comparative Education Service: University of Toronto School of Continuing Studies;

International Credential Assessment Service of Canada;

World Education Services;

Medical Council of Canada.

Language - Minimum threshold of 16 points, Maximum of 28 points

Only applicants capable of demonstrating an intermediate to high level proficiency in one of Canada's official languages, English or French, will be considered. Applicants who meet the minimum threshold must score at least 16 points under this selection factor.

Higher language proficiency can lead to an allocation of up to 24 points.

The benefits of bilingualism are considered marginal to an individual's successful economic establishment in Canada and the new point system limits points for a second official language to a maximum of 4.

Employment Experience – Minimum of 9 points, Maximum of 15 points

The new program requires a minimum of 1-year to qualify and the maximum consideration is 6-years.

Age – Maximum of 12 points

Up to 12 points will be allotted to candidates between the ages of 18 and 35 years. Each year above the age of 35 will reduce the allocation by 1, with no points being awarded as of age 47.

Arranged Employment – 0 or 10 points

Points are allotted to individuals with a validated offer of employment in Canada. In an effort to streamline labour market related processes and reduce processing times for employers and their potential employees, the Arranged Employment Opinion process will be replaced with the Labour Market Opinion (LMO) employment validation process which is generally used in processing applications for Canadian work permits.

In order to validate an employment offer and obtain points for this selection factor, a candidate's proposed employer must demonstrate to

Human Resources and Skills Development Canada that the hiring of a foreign worker will have neutral or positive economic effects on the local labour market.

Candidates with a validated employment offer will gain 10 points under this factor, and an additional 5 points in the Adaptability selection factor for a total of 15 points.

Adaptability – Maximum of 10 points

Applicants who have at least 1 year of full time Canadian work experience in a managerial, professional, technical or skilled trade occupation will be awarded maximum points. As mentioned above, a validated offer of employment will provide 5 adaptability points. Other considerations awarding points under this selection factor include: A close adult relative living in Canada; Applicant or spouse has studied in Canada; Spouse has previous Canadian work experience; Spouse has knowledge of one of Canada's official languages.

Skilled Worker Selection Grid

Factor	Score	Final
EDUCATION		Max. 25
(Canadian equivalence established by a designated third party)		
Doctorate		25
Masters or professional degree		23
Two or more post-secondary degrees, of which one is three years or longer		22
A three year or longer post-secondary degree		21

A two-year post-secondary diploma, trade certificate or apprenticeship			19
A one-year post-secondary diploma, trade certificate or apprenticeship			15
Secondary School Educational Credential			5
LANGUAGE (Abilities: Speak, Read, Write, Listen)			Max. 28
1st Lang	Very high proficiency (per ability) (CLB 9)		6
	High proficiency (per ability) (CLB 8)		5
	Intermediate proficiency (per ability) (CLB 7)* *Minimum threshold required to apply		4
	Basic or no proficiency		0
	Possible maximum (all four abilities)		24
2ndLang	Basic proficiency or higher (per ability)		1
	No proficiency		0
	Possible maximum (all four abilities)		4
EXPERIENCE (NOC Skill Level O,A,B)			Max. 15
One year* *Minimum threshold required to apply			9
Two to three years			11
Four to five years			13
Six years or more			15
AGE			Max. 12
18 to 35 years			12
36 years			11
Less one point per year until 47 years			

ARRANGED EMPLOYMENT IN CANADA		Max. 10
HRSDC-confirmed permanent offer of employment		10
Applicants from within Canada holding a temporary work permit that is:		
Validated by HRSDC, including sectorial confirmations		10
Exempt from HRSDC validation under international agreements (e.g., NAFTA)		10
ADAPTABILITY		Max. 10
Applicant has a minimum of 1 year skilled Work experience in Canada		10
Applicant has previously studied in Canada		5
Spouse has previously studied in Canada		5
Spouse has previously worked in Canada		5
Family relation over the age of 18 in Canada		5
Arranged employment		5
Spouse is proficient in an official language		5
Total		100

CIC policy confirms that the Federal Skilled Worker Program, while well-tailored to select highly educated individuals, does not favour applications from the skilled trades. In an effort to ensure the Canadian labour market attracts sufficient trades workers, qualified trades' candidates may now apply for permanent residence under the Federal Skilled Trades Program.

27. Multiculturalism Policy, 1971

The Multiculturalism Policy is more than an Immigration Act. Like the previous Immigration Acts which had multi- dimensional purposes and deviates from the outlook of Canada in terms of its conservative and narrowed vision on its ownership in monopolizing the social structure of this nation to a more liberal vision which was accommodating of various cultures, without having any room for alteration of the strongly built framework of the Canadian fabric. It was a statement presented by the late Prime Minister Pierre Trudeau in the House of Commons on 8th October 1971 as the government policy.

It was intended to respect the cultural freedom of every individual and provide recognition of the cultural contributions of diverse ethnic groups to Canadian society and also assist individuals in overcoming discriminatory barriers, encouraging intercultural exchange and assisting immigrants in learning French or English. It has been made clear that no one traditional cultural values of the immigrants has to be tolerated, rather it must be accepted was a very positive move for the multi-cultural communities to make more psychological commitments to Canada. In fact still comparatively such commitments from many multi-ethnic groups is below expectations and this is another issue that has to be addressed. The second part is their cultural contributions to the Canadian society. It means that Canadian society refers to itself as the mainstream which has its unique and well rooted traditions and norms. The Canadian society has been well established and developed and the simple truth is that sooner or later the other ethnic groups whether they like it or not will be to a higher degree absorbed without any force. Therefore in the long run, automatically the preservation, innovation and promotion of their multi- ethnic cultural will be superficial on the surface and this has been witnessed. Either way, cultural practises of many cultural groups are being recognized and accepted in its given place.

Though this does not have the expected impact on the second and third generations, still it is a moral boost and encourages mainstream Canadians to have an accommodative attitude that makes the multi-ethnic groups feel more at home. Comparatively with other nations who accept multiethnic immigrants at the grassroots level mainstream Canadians have such positive attitudes to a very high degree. In Europe, multiculturalism is on the verge of becoming a sickly person and almost a failure. Starting from 2016 when those European nations faced an influx of refugees from the Middle East and Africa and their inelasticity of their way of life somewhat irritated some sections of the local people at the grassroots level sparked anti-immigrant feelings and pushed their respective governments to make some limitations. It does not mean that they were not sympathetic towards those refugees or were unwilling to help them. It is a two way street in that both the mainstream and the multi-ethnic groups have to understand each other and get into the integration processes. Though the major share is on the multiethnic groups, still this has to go both ways. The Canadian government on multiculturalism policy made the commitments to assist cultural groups in their development. On the other hand the multiethnic groups also accept the norms of the society and explore the opportunity in getting integrated with the mainstream while preserving their culture and traditions.

Marginal note: Multiculturalism policy

It is hereby declared to be the policy of the Government of Canada to o **(a)** recognize and promote the understanding that multiculturalism reflects the cultural and racial diversity of Canadian society and acknowledges the freedom of all members of Canadian society to preserve, enhance and share their cultural heritage;

o **(b)** recognize and promote the understanding that multiculturalism is a fundamental characteristic of the Canadian heritage and identity and that it provides an invaluable resource in the shaping of Canada's future;

o **(c)** promote the full and equitable participation of individuals and communities of all origins in the continuing evolution and shaping of all aspects of Canadian society and assist them in the elimination of any barrier to that participation;

o **(d)** recognize the existence of communities whose members share a common origin and their historic contribution to Canadian society, and enhance their development;

o **(e)** ensure that all individuals receive equal treatment and equal protection under the law, while respecting and valuing their diversity;

o **(f)** encourage and assist the social, cultural, economic and political institutions of Canada to be both respectful and inclusive of Canada's multicultural character;

o **(g)** promote the understanding and creativity that arise from the interaction between individuals and communities of different origins;

o **(h)** foster the recognition and appreciation of the diverse cultures of Canadian society and promote the reflection and the evolving expressions of those cultures;

- o **(i)** preserve and enhance the use of languages other than English and French, while strengthening the status and use of the official languages of Canada; and
- o **(j)** Advance multiculturalism throughout Canada in harmony with the national commitment to the official languages of Canada.

Federal institutions

(2) It is further declared to be the policy of the Government of Canada that all federal institutions shall

- o **(a)** ensure that Canadians of all origins have an equal opportunity to obtain employment and advancement in those institutions;
- o **(b)** promote policies, programs and practices that enhance the ability of individuals and communities of all origins to contribute to the continuing evolution of Canada;
- o **(c)** promote policies, programs and practices that enhance the understanding of and respect for the diversity of the members of Canadian society;
- o **(d)** collect statistical data in order to enable the development of policies, programs and practices that are sensitive and responsive to the multicultural reality of Canada;
- o **(e)** make use, as appropriate, of the language skills and cultural understanding of individuals of all origins; and
- o **(f)** Generally, carry on their activities in a manner that is sensitive and responsive to the multicultural reality of Canada.``

Since the slowdown in the natural increase in population and also not having the possibility of new immigrants in mono cultural ethnic groups, the necessity of maintaining multiculturalism in a well-balanced manner and the growing number of voters of multi-ethnic groups certainly the politicians will focus on promoting multiculturalism as well.

It has made a tremendous change in having a more open and generous mainstream that is welcoming to new immigrants. It has made a clear vision for future immigration policies. In fact after this Act there were changes now and then, particularly during the Harper government when Jason Kenny was the minister for Citizenship and Immigration Canada from October 30, 2008 to July 15, 2013 there were a lot changes in a restrictive manner but more numbers of immigrants were allowed to enter into Canada. The Liberal party was able to capitalize and gain more immigrant votes on the October 19, 2015 election and formed a majority government.

Immigration source countries
One hundred years of immigration to Canada (1901-2001)

Date	Event	Top countries of origin of immigrants to Canada
1900 to 1910	Settlement of the West	From 1900 to 1910 1. British Isles 2. United States 3. Russia 4. Austria 5. Galicia
1911 to 1920	World War I (1914 to 1918)	From 1911 to 1920 1. British Isles 2. United States 3. Russia

1921 to 1930	Pier 21 in Halifax opens in 1928	From 1921 to 1930 1. British Isles 2. United States 3. Poland 4. Russia 5. Czechoslovakia 6. Finland
1931 to 1940	The Great Depression begins in 1929	From 1931 to 1940 1. United States 2. British Isles 3. Poland 4. Czechoslovakia
1941 to 1950	World War II (1942 to 1945) and the arrival of displaced persons/refugees (1947 to 1950)	From 1941 to 1950 1. British Isles 2. Poland 3. United States 4. Netherlands 5. Italy 6. U.S.S.R.
1951 to 1960	Hungarian refugees begin to arrive (1956)	From 1951 to 1960 1. British Isles (25%) 2. Italy (16%) 3. Germany (12%) 4. Netherlands (8%) 5. United States (5%) 6. Poland (4%) 7. Hungary (3%)
1961 to 1970	Americans of draft age; 11,000 Czechoslovakian refugees arrive from 1968 to 1969.	From 1961 to 1970 1. British Isles (21%) 2. Italy (13%) 3. United States (10%) 4. Portugal (5%) 5. Greece (4%) 6. Federal Republic of Germany (4%) 7. Other West Indies (3%) 8. Yugoslavia (3%)

1971 to 1980	Refugees accepted from Uganda and Chile (1972 to 1973); Indochinese Boat People (1975 to 1981)	From 1971 to 1980 1. British Isles (13%) 2. United States (10%) 3. India (6%) 4. Portugal (5%) 5. Philippines (4%) 6. Jamaica (4%) 7. People's Republic of China (4%) 8. Hong Kong (4%)
1981 to 1990		From 1981 to 1990 1. Hong Kong (7%) 2. India (7%) 3. British Isles (6%) 4. Poland (6%) 5. People's Republic of China (6%) 6. Philippines (5%) 7. United States (5%) 8. Viet Nam (4%)
1991 to 2000	1997 marks the fiftieth anniversary of the Citizenship and Immigration Act; 7,000 refugees from Kosovo arrive in 1999.	From 1991 to 2000 1. People's Republic of China 2. India 3. Philippines 4. Special Administrative Region of Hong Kong 5. Sri Lanka 6. Pakistan 7. Taiwan 8. United States

28. The Immigration Act 1976

This act set a clear vision for the entire nation by putting provincial and regional issues into consideration and the size, type of the demographics by consulting the provinces by the citizenship and immigration department before finalizing the immigration policy. In fact it limited the power of the Immigration Minister in making decision unilaterally, though Immigration is a federal responsibility still the input from the provinces is highly required and their concerns addressed.

The second vision was the immigration and emigration section of the government categorized immigrants into three major sections based on the needs for the nation and their backgrounds and other humanitarian and compassionate grounds and they were clearly grouped as refugees, family class sponsorship and investors and skilled workers. The Act took effect on April 10, 1978; it was amended 30 times, including some major changes in 1985 and 1992 and replaced in 2002 with the Immigration and Refugee Protection Act. More focus was on the skilled workers and investors and the point system for the skilled worker was clearly designed. The family class sponsorship was subdivided as immediate family as sponsoring the spouses and children and the next one is assisted relatives as such, parents, grandparents and dependant family members. The third category focuses on humanitarian obligations as defined by the 1951 United Nations Convention. They too were in three categories: the government sponsored refugees and private sponsorship; in fact the Syrian refugees who were brought in 2015 and 2016 were from both categories. The third category was refugee claimants who came and claimed refugee status inland and at the border by air, boat and crossing the border by land.

29. The Canadian Multiculturalism Act of 1988

The Canadian Constitution Act 1982 the highest law of the land was a historical and most significant move in Canadian history. Prior to this Act, Canada was The North American territory and the brand new nation of Canada came to be on July 1st, 1867. The following constitution was signed by Queen of Canada Elizabeth II from a land that had no written constitution on March 29, 1982. It also included the Canadian

Charter of Rights and all these changes might have applied pressure to develop a more effective and efficient implementation of the Canadian multiculturalism policy. It revised the earlier multiculturalism policy and placed more emphasis on protecting the cultural heritage of all Canadians, reduced discrimination and encouraged the implementation of multicultural programs.

An extract of the relevant portion from Canadian Constitution Act

Preamble

WHEREAS the Constitution of Canada provides that every individual is equal before and under the law and has the right to the equal protection and benefit of the law without discrimination and that everyone has the freedom of conscience, religion, thought, belief, opinion, expression, peaceful assembly and association and guarantees those rights and freedoms equally to male and female persons;

AND WHEREAS the Constitution of Canada recognizes the importance of preserving and enhancing the multicultural heritage of Canadians;

AND WHEREAS the Constitution of Canada recognizes rights of the aboriginal peoples of Canada;

AND WHEREAS the Constitution of Canada and the Official language Act provide that English and French are the official languages of Canada and neither abrogates nor derogates from any rights or privileges acquired or enjoyed with respect to any other language;

AND WHEREAS the Citizenship Act provides that all Canadians, whether by birth or by choice, enjoy equal status, are entitled to the same rights, powers and privileges and are subject to the same obligations, duties and liabilities;

AND WHEREAS the Canadian Human Rights Act provides that every individual should have an equal opportunity with other individuals to make the life that the individual is able and wishes to have, consistent with the duties and obligations of that individual as a member of society, and, in order to secure that opportunity, establishes the Canadian Human Rights Commission to redress any proscribed discrimination, including discrimination on the basis of race, national or ethnic origin or colour;

AND WHEREAS Canada is a party to the International Convention on Elimination of All Forms of Racial Discrimination, which Convention recognizes that all human beings are equal before the law and are entitled to equal protection of the law against any discrimination and against any incitement to discrimination, and to the International Covenant and Political and Civil Rights, which Covenant provides that persons belonging to ethnic, religious or linguistic minorities shall not be denied the right to enjoy their own culture, to profess and practise their own religion or to use their own language;

AND WHEREAS the Government of Canada recognizes the diversity of Canadians as regards race, national or ethnic origin, colour and religion as a fundamental characteristic of Canadian society and is committed to a policy of multiculturalism designed to preserve and enhance the multicultural heritage of Canadians while working to achieve the equality of all Canadians in the economic, social, cultural and political life of Canada.....

30- Immigration and Refugee Protection Act, (IRPA) 2001.

Canadian Immigration and emigration policies were evolving mainly into two factions as such the preservation and promotion of the Canadian norm and culture, traditions and linguistic values of English and French until 2001. When radicalization deeply entered into the United States of America, the most powerful and highly watched local and international security was attacked and the financial and political capitals,of the western world were also on their attack agenda, they began to alert themselves and became vigilant in its immigration. The September 11, 2001 altered many Western nations and also made the Canadian government alter national security and tighten some sections of Immigration, border security and so on. A new Immigration Act was passed on November 1st 2001 and came into effect on June 28, 2002.

The Immigration Act, 1978, was based on the structure of the second half of the 20th century was overhauled twice and amended more than 30 times and the Immigration and Refugee Protection Act, 2001 was designed to address current global trends on immigration and emigration and the protection of Canadians from within and outside of Canada. It is also highly concerned with the protection of Canadians by weeding the inappropriate inflow of immigrants in the form of international students, refugees, foreign investors, skilled migrants, illegal immigrants, temporary resident visa holders, family class immigrants and no stone was left untouched. The wide range of power and responsibly was given to them, so that they would be able to carry out their assignment effectively. The IRPA is empowered with rights and responsibilities to shoulder the great toll in weeding out any source from within Canada or abroad who are a danger to the Canadian public. The IRPA was designed to carry out its assignments in four sections as such: the Immigration and Refugee Board, enforcement of the Immigration and Refugee Protection Act, refugee protection and immigration to Canada.

The main part of it is as follows

- **Increases and strengthens powers of detention.** The government wants to increase the number of persons detained and the length of detention.[1] IRPA expands the provisions concerning detention without warrant and extends the power to arrest and detain persons who cannot establish their identity (s. 55). Refugee claimants without proof of identity could be detained if they refused to cooperate with measures to establish their identity;

- **Expands the inadmissibility categories** on the basis of security (s. 34), human or international rights violations (s. 35), serious criminality (s. 36), organized criminality (s. 37), health reasons (s. 38), financial reasons (s. 39), misrepresentation (s. 40), non-compliance with the Act (s. 41) and inadmissible family members (s. 42). Neither the Act nor the regulations define terrorism, although it is a grounds for inadmissibility under IRPA;

- **Restricts the right of immigration appeal.** IRPA removes all right of appeal and power to review removal orders against any person, even a permanent resident, who is inadmissible on the grounds of security, violating human or international rights, serious criminality and organized criminality (s. 64);

- **Toughens penalties for persons who break immigration laws.** Tougher maximum penalties for organizing illegal entry into Canada, and very severe penalties for the new offence of human trafficking, etc. (s. 117–121);

- **Strengthens removal orders.** IRPA requires persons who have been issued enforceable removal orders to leave Canada immediately (s. 48) and prohibits them from returning (s. 52). The government will also increase the funds for deportation measures.[2]

- **Strengthens interdiction provisions.** IRPA increases the penalties for traffickers (s. 117–121) but does not distinguish between persons who are motivated by humanitarian concerns and those motivated by other factors. Someone who helps a family member flee persecution can be refused a refugee claim hearing or lose permanent residence without possibility of appeal.

The delay in processing the refugee's applications and deportation, removal and other such order costs more for the tax payers and endangers the safety and protection of the public. It is already believed that in one such incident a delay in executing such orders due to certain technical reasons was an uncovered plot.

They were given power to detain, arrest, and deport anyone based on mere suspicion or secret evidence on their activities and plans to launch terrorist activities.

d. 25 Changes to citizenship Act (June 19, 2014)

These changes were intended to enhance loyalty from would be citizens and these changes were meant to bring more meaning into the potential citizen's new life beyond the oath taking ceremony. There were some changes made and some Canadians, particularly among some new immigrants felt that the changes went too far in tightening the citizenship criteria.

Which was higher than other industrialized countries such as the United States (2.9), the Russian Federation (1.8) and France (1.2)?

Arrivals at inland and ocean ports in Canada, 1903 to 1907					
	1903	1904	1905	1906	1907[1]
	number				
Country of origin					
Great Britain and Ireland	41,792	50,374	65,359	86,796	120,779
European continent and Iceland	37,099	34,785	37,255	44,349	56,652
United States	49,473	45,171	43,652	57,919	74,607
Total	**128,364**	**130,330**	**146,266**	**189,064**	**252,038**
1. Nine months.					

Source: Statistics Canada, *The Canada Year Book, 1907.*

31. Are the Current New Immigrants Assets or a Burden

"I have two degrees and strong work experience, but I spent a year underemployed in Toronto and over a year unemployed in Vancouver. I have since moved to Calgary, where opportunity is everywhere." Brendan Baines, 28- The Globe and Mail, 29th May 2012

Although the above statement is partly a reflection of the current economic recession in Canada and the adverse effects from the deep recession in the United States of America and in Europe, there are other contributing factors to consider when it comes to underemployment or unemployment. The out numbering of baby boomers in the job market by new immigrants to Canada is another important factor.

In spite of what some politicians, academics, and immigration critics may say, it is acknowledged that this nation has been built by the sweat of immigrants and that Canada is a land of immigrants. However, in contrast, there is some research that has done by certain academics which considers new immigrants both in the recent past and now, as burdens or liabilities to the nation and the work force.

Their conclusions are mainly based on economic input and its returns by new immigrants to Canada. Professor Herbert Grubel of Simon Fraser University mentioned in his research piece entitled

"The Fiscal Burden of Recent Canadian Immigrants" that in the year 2002 alone, the costs and benefits received by the 2.5 million new immigrants who arrived between 1990 and 2002 exceeded the taxes they paid by 18.3 billion. Another critical author on immigration, Daniel Stoffman was not in favour in accepting the current level of immigration and concluded that if it continues as it is, it will have a very negative impact on those who were born in 1980- 1995 in terms of their future job prospects.

A similar study was made by Mr. George Borjas of Harvard University himself an immigrant to the USA and a world renowned immigration economist clearly states that immigrants do not benefit the economy. He also recommended in his book entitled 'Heavens Door" that the United States should reduce its intake of new immigrants by half. In Britain, a report produced by the House of Lords in 2008 to the government recommended the reduction in the intake of new immigrants to below 190,000 from what had been planned. The report also mentioned the side effects of allowing such a large number of new immigrants in terms of social amenities and housing.

In most cases, the private enterprises would prefer to have more immigrants so that they will have an ample supply of workers. Based on the theory of demand and supply, the higher the supply in comparison to the normal demand it would be easier and cheaper to have new immigrants in the labour force for there will be less demand for better working conditions and higher wages. Whereas on the opposite side the labour force as a whole would prefer that there be fewer immigrants in order to preserve local jobs and the benefits that go along with them.

These days the Independent Class Immigrants are on the top of the list of preferred class immigrants while pushing the ethnic and regional preferences down to an extent. Still, there is concern over the number of skilled workers and investors among the overall number of independent class immigrants. For example in 2001, the principle applicants from the Family class was 38.8%, in the refugee class it was 11.3% and 49.8% in the Independent class. Among all these three categories, almost half of the total immigrants in the Independent class are the principle applicants and has outnumbered the rest. In spite of it, if we look into a micro analysis, 62.1 % of the total of immigrants was granted permanent resident status in 2001. This is a great percentage in the overall immigrant categories. Still 50.2% of them are dependants such as spouses and children and it is not necessary for them to be skilled workers. This could be a financial burden or the expenses could be seen as par for the course when sponsoring dependants.

There is also another argument that new immigrants are ready to work for less pay and more hours and that the employers are aware of this and try their best to exploit the situation in their favour and that this has an adverse effect on the local labour force. In fact, this is really a question of the distribution of wealth from the income generated from business and it has not contributed much on the negative side on the national economy as a whole. Once Statistics Canada's study concluded that if the labour supply increased by 10% then wages would decline by 3%-5% and this would affect young Canadians in particular.

Should we really worry about the number of immigrants that Canada should have in relation with checking and balancing the flow with the natural birth, death and emigration rates? Or are we to assess the potentiality of the natural resources and other economic factors and its contribution to the overall economy.

Recent immigrants, earlier immigrants and the Canadian-born collectively express high levels of positive identification as citizens of Canada and there is a significant variation in sharing between their sense of belonging to their ancestral heritage and that of being a Canadian who belong to the categories of recent immigrants, earlier immigrants and the Canadian-born. Although there is a certain degree of positive identification as citizens of Canada, there is an element of being attached to the homogeneous ethnic group in their local communities. There is a war among all ethnic groups in those three categories in drawing a demarcation line between the Canadian values and that of their own that they brought from their home country. This issue has many faces and some values are compatible to Canadian, some are similar and can be easily bent and manipulated, whereas others can be held rigidly. Usually the third generation of new immigrants absorbs the main values of Canadians in their day to day life to the greatest extent. But none of the ethnic groups including the First Nations, the Quebecers, the English, Irish, and Scots, though they have been residing in this country over the last five hundred years are proud and determined to maintain their cultural values. Their primary concern is that the cores of Canadian values are those of their root heritages. There was a silent message passed on when there was an influx of new immigrants from Southern and Eastern Europe and Asia. In the history of immigration to Canada it was challenged when measures were brought forwarded in limiting the influx of certain ethnic groups entering into Canada. However, when looking at differences between the three groups, there is an increased tendency in absorbing Canadian values. It also depends on how they distinguish the importance of it. Some of the ethnic groups who have mainly arrived in this country are primarily attracted by the high standard living, high economy, political stability, and the high level of peace and harmony in society. They would also make a positive conclusion that the Canadian culture and way of life are also superior to theirs and in the psychological war, the Canadian values win.

It also depends on how far each ethnic group identifies the economic superiority and impact of it on their culture. Some of them are still strongly convinced that though they are in a disadvantaged economic condition, still their culture is always superior. I have for example, met a couple of Greek Canadians who have similar beliefs even at a time of economic instability. Earlier immigrants and recent immigrant respondents who strongly identify with their community are significantly more likely to identify as citizens of Canada. This suggests that micro-community identification may play a significant role in influencing macro-community identification. For recent immigrants, ethnicity is a significant variable which appears to have an impact upon response patterns.

I believe that there is no much contradiction between identifying as a citizen of the world and identifying as a citizen of Canada. And those who have accepted the concept of a global citizen are significantly more likely to positively identify as a citizen of Canada.

The tremendous increase in the ethno-cultural and linguistic diversity of immigrants to Canada over the past forty years also provide insight into feelings of belonging, perceptions of settlement as psychological security, self-esteem and feelings of being at home in the world. A very strong or somewhat strong sense of community implies that identities are generally understood to be constructed, multiple, dynamic and relational as opposed to being essential or predetermined. Some fear that globalization will continue to blur national boundaries, further directing identities away from a strict focus on national affiliation.

We are quite concerned about the rapidly growing number of baby boomers and the challenges that the Canadian economy is going to encounter but we also have to deeply consider the next generation. The children of the baby boomers who were born between the periods of the 1980's onwards are another rising economic force. Although their growth rate is generally declining, they are a vital part of the human resources in the future of this nation.

We also have to take into consideration the we cannot be picky all the time and the supplier nations with qualitative man power will not remain static in their current surplus of educated and skilful man power and their fast economic growth as such the Chinese at 8-9% and Indians at a 7-8% growth rate will be able to absorb their local manpower and the increase in local employment opportunities and the improving standard of living would discourage them in looking for a venue where they could utilize their potential. When the local demand increases and supply of local man power slows down by the decrease in the birth rate, certainly there will be a slowdown in supply and the receiving nations have to go back and encourage and improve the incentives. But should there be a more aggressive approach in terms of restricting the immigration policy? Or should we look over the whole future of this nation taking into consideration future plans, size of the demographic patterns, age distribution, limitation of the local migration, current and future economic plans of the historically preferred nations, cultural globalization and the shift from the ridge cultural practice among other factors?

This is not a matter that is mainly confined to the immigration policy makers and the inclinations of the government towards one particular direction. Canada has historically depended on immigrants and it is not fair to act drastically on the matter of the migration of certain group of people and then making an apology. It does not mean that I do not give due respect to Prime Minister Harper for making an apology for the Chinese Head Tax and the Komogata Maru incident where a ship full of Indian immigrants was not allowed to dock in Vancouver in the early 20th century. As far as Canada is concerned, immigration is a vital part of the country and is in a constant state of change. Some of these changes both now and in the future might not necessarily be comfortable or pleasant but will hopefully respond to the growing needs and changes in this nation and we as Canadians will be able to handle them.

8. Broken Padlock

The nature of the European new immigrants at the initial stage was more intended in towards the exploration of new land, expanding the international trade, mining valuable minerals but not a large varieties of minerals that were not in popular use as after the introduction of the industrial revolution which demanded for more iron ore, copper, uranium, crude oil, zinc and others such as old out 4660 minerals that has been approved by the International Mineral Association.

The escape was limited but enthusiasm and the high pressure for accumulating wealth abroad prompted their adventurous journey Most of their voyage was not well financed by the government like that of Christopher Columbus (1492-1504) by Spain. The British explorer John Cabot arrived with certain facilities after the arrival of Christopher Columbus.

The ownership of the land of Canada is disputed to a certain extent between the natives and the European settlers and this issue has not been fully resolved and I don't believe that there is any chance of this dispute being put to rest in the near future. When we refer to the term "Europeans" it does not include every part of the entire European continent. Thou the diversity increased the initial stage of the settlements was mainly restricted to the English in the United Kingdom and the French in France. Although the Portuguese, Spanish and some other Europeans had some form of contact with Canada in the 15th century the organized settlements were established by the French and the English. The British were the ones who took the initiative to have settlements built by clearing the forest, constructing roads, bridges and other infrastructure. The expansion of the settlements slowly encouraged more people to utilize the blessed land and make a new life with more comfort. Once they were organized, the settlers came to realize that Canada was a land of golden opportunities though during that period of time they had no idea that from these small communities a nation would be created. In these early days most of the people settled in small pockets in certain regions. The concept and the boundaries of Canada were so narrowly drawn and they wanted to have the ownership and the access to the land. Within their ethnicity, they were aware that the explosion of the population and the unsustainable economic conditions along with the fact that people from other European nations were looking for fertile land for resettlement fostered a desire to migrate quickly. Though such an urge existed within other ethnic groups around the world they did not have the means of transportation along with the capabilities and the resources for exploration. It is fair to say that they had the desire but not the means. At that time 2 countries were becoming powerful in terms of expanding their colonial rule and other countries like Portugal, Holland, Germany and Spain had not reached this point.

Protective measures to ensure priority for certain ethnic groups as opposed to others was a constant battle so the door for migration to Canada was narrowly opened for these two groups of people and it was closed to the rest including the Irish, the Scots and the Welsh from the so called United Kingdom. So the immigration policy during that period of time was based on very narrow ethnic lines. The gates were however open to criminals, prisoners and lay men from the same ethnicity but they hesitated to accept missionaries, scholars and able men who could make a very positive contribution for building this nation from other ethnicities. We should also not forget that it was a time when these Europeans confronted and faced some threats from the natives and felt that their settlements were not fully secure therefore it was easier for them to spend their energy protecting themselves rather than others from different ethnic though I do not think that this would have been the only reason for this kind of immigration policy.

These settlers were quite ambitious and very hardworking and they made tireless contributions. Not only did they make their lives better but they made it more comfortable and they also realized that they themselves would not be able to utilize the abundance and natural resources of the land on their own and began inviting people outside their own ethnicity who had certain skills and who were experts in certain areas such as arable farming and raising livestock. Furthermore they felt that their precious positions were secure and that they would not be challenged by new immigrants. Furthermore they began to realize that in order to get a higher yield they needed extra man power and that the resulting benefits from the expansion of the economy would equal more benefits for themselves. It was at this stage that their eyes were opened to the idea of expanding their settlements beyond people of their ethnicities.

Though they were ready come out of their narrow shell and look forward to inviting the new immigrants, still they did want non-Europeans to come and deviate from their similar cultural background. Although they had a lot of differences such as language, culture, the fine arts, habits and living patterns they considered that the root of their cultural civilization was the same. They all had a similar fundamental way of living and their linguistic inter-relationships and human values were similar so they preferred to pick up some varieties of some apple rather than oranges and pineapples. In the end it was a mixture of rational and economic factors that opened the door for Europeans to come to Canada but not the rest of the world.

Even though Europe was considered a favourable continent with potential immigrants, there were certain groups that were considered undesirable. For example the Scots, the Irish and the Welsh were accepted with some reservations, other groups were on a "preferred list" or an "inner circle" of sorts. For example the Germans, the Swiss, the Dutch and the Danish were among the preferred groups. The Scandinavians also got a comfortable place in the list. Then the eastern and southern Europeans were next on the list but they were selected mainly for their skills. The Ukrainians for example were very talented farmers and were highly preferred for working on the farms particularly in the Prairie Provinces. Their migration to these parts of Canada brought tremendous progress for the nation as well as for themselves. Even today Canada has been benefiting from meeting the growing domestic needs and raising substantial revenue from exporting agricultural products.

The southern Europeans who migrated from Greece, Italy, Portugal and Spain contributed to the progress of this country in more of the non- agriculture sectors, such as mining and construction. In the city of Toronto for example the Prince Edward Viaduct was built by immigrants from these countries in the 1930's.

It is not necessarily the case that the immigration policy and the attitude of the masses go hand in hand. Historically there were sections of the Canadian population that were not pleased about accepting certain groups of people in large quantities and in some cases there were those who were prepared to accept it out of necessity. However there were times that when the economic situation in Canada changed in a negative way the first group of people to be blamed were the new immigrants. These people having left very difficult situations behind in their home countries found this hard to tolerate. It is quite interesting to witness that the trend of blaming the new comers as an economic burden, the cause of social disorder, the increasing crime rate, and how they consume undue benefits is not a new one. I have seen these types of magnified accusations particularly during the periods of economic recession in the 1980's and 1990's but not much in the 2000s. It reminds me of a time when I was travelling at the peak hours in the morning on the subway on my way to work downtown from my home in Scarborough, Ontario. The train made frequent stops for the passengers to board and leave in order to reach their destinations. The train was almost full at the third station and then the passengers who boarded at the followings stations struggled to get in and then at the next station when others were trying to board the subway, the very passengers who were accommodated at the last station were the ones who tried to block the entry of these new passengers. They seemed to have forgotten that they were all in the same boat and it would have served them to remember that this land never hesitates to accommodate strangers and offered benefits which they received. It is also a land where both the new comers and the nation are in a winning position. I do not think that immigrants have any moral right in harbouring negative attitudes towards newcomers as long as the new comers respect law and order and are loyal to this nation.

If Canada had been a country like Germany, Russia, France, England, India, China and Japan that was built by the ancestors for generation after generation and have claims not only to the land but also to all of the historical buildings, cultural and civil institutions and economic means, these would have been the determining factors if newcomers from certain ethnic groups would be allowed into the country. Furthermore, these newcomers would be expected to blend in fully; one example that comes to mind is the necessity to adopt a Japanese version of one's name should one be expected to integrate into Japanese society. I do not mean to underestimate the contributions that have been made by the new comers in those countries but the degree of their contributions did not alter the well-established norms of these societies and the structure of their systems. One example of this is the Greek influence in India. Though the Greeks made many contributions to Indian culture particularly in the realm of art, the cultural norms of India held greater sway over the Greeks especially the religion of Buddhism. The Buddhist teachings made such an impression on the Greek King Menander that he converted to Buddhism and changed his name to Milinda. In contrast to the comparison of these two groups let us look into most of the South American nations where the Spanish became the dominant culture and where the land was occupied the Spanish descendants. However these people did not exploit the natural recourses to a high degree with the help of new immigrants and their status of the economic development is still not at the same level as other developed nations with the exception of Brazil.

The approach of the Americans is quite different. The attitude of Americans from the Revolution to the present has remained unique yet peculiar. The idea of the "melting pot" though it has altered slightly still remains and the idea that one is an American regardless of where one may come from or their ancestral background is still strong. Though it was been said that the melting pot has absorbed and continues to absorb many cultural elements and ingredients, it tastes predominately Anglo-Saxon. I know that German Americans suffered in silence and that African Americans fought against discriminative measures until Barack Obama was elected as the President of America but I am sure that by watching history it will appear in another form.

The overall structure of Canada has been built, maintained and restructured with the materials and the human resources of newcomers who have migrated from across the globe.

Discriminative immigration policies have been in existence from the beginning of the first human settlements to this modern era. The native people are considered as a homo generous entity; rather they are a collection of many ethnic groups having similar patterns of life and followed a common path. It is true that there were some commonalities in their ways of living, habits and traditions and the source of economic activities. In spite of it all they preserved their own identities. Later on when met with the challenges from the Europeans and with the intent to chase them away it became important to put aside some of their differences and work towards a common goal.

As far as the unresolved disputes between the British monarchies, the government of Canada and the natives who for this piece will be considered as a unified group go, there are two views. The first is that the government has adopted a policy in that they have done economically more than the rest of the citizens of this land and therefore there is no room to complain. The other view is that many Canadians blame the government for providing the native people with more money per capita than anyone else. In contrast it seems that the natives do not much appreciate the privileges at the expense of forgone rights. My only question is how come at this time where the modernization process would bring these to the 21st century while preserving their identity seems to be impossible considering that that their population is only 1.4 million out of 35 million Canadians. It is certain that something has gone wrong somewhere and this needs to be resolved. However it is important to note that the native people are not the only ones who have faced discrimination.

It was the continuation of the discriminative actions that was held against the Scots, the Welsh and Irish by the English when they arrived in Canada as immigrants and refugees. Immigrants are mainly pulled by the attractiveness and prosperity of the new country while refugees are pushed by natural calamities or persecution, torture, or discrimination by the rulers

The Immigration act provided for greater selectivity by the admission process, in order to weed out undesirable Immigrants to some extend from the eastern and southern Europe and mainly from Asia.

32. The Third Wave of Racial Discrimination

Even at the beginning of the twentieth century racially biased Immigration policies were in existence. The Immigration Act of 1910 gave power to the cabinet to prohibit immigration on racial grounds and this continued until the implementation of the new Immigration Act of 1978. The Immigration Act of 1978 though it narrowed down the racial lines, left some room for the cabinet to impose restrictions in a very sweet coated package and this subject will be discussed in a later chapter. Some of the wording in the Act was changed to make the soup milder later on and the basics remained intact.

According to those Immigration Acts it was crystal clear that they were both targeted against non-Europeans in particular though it was not spelled out in black and white. It said that:

"Owing to their peculiar customs, habits, modes of life and methods of holding property and because of their prohibit inability to become readily assimilated" This assimilation policy is narrower than the current American melting pot theory. It focussed on prohibiting German, Austrian, Hungarian and Bulgarian immigration on 14th March 1914. It was at the time of the First World War and during that time and during the Second World War those considered "enemy aliens" were denied entry and some immigrants from the targeted groups who had arrived earlier and had been accepted were repatriated to their respective nations such as Japan. To this day, some of these Canadians are still wounded from the pain this policy caused and they have not forgiven and forgotten the actions made against them.

Asians were denied entry into Canada from 1923 to 1956 and it was targeted against certain groups such as the Japanese, Indians, Chinese and Koreans but with the exception of farm and domestic workers as well as spouses and under aged children but only if one of the parents was Canadian. Later on a quota system was introduced, after establishing governmental agreements in 1956, in which 150 Indians, 100 Pakistanis, 50 Sri Lankans, in addition to the migration of the said family members and consequently the number was increased and this remained until 1962.

The continuous passage rule was another form of discrimination. According to the Order in Council of 1914, it was prohibited for anyone to break their journey between his or her native country to Canada. It was possible to migrate from Europe to Canada and they were pretty much aware that it would be possible for Indians to travel on any ship. It was not unknowingly done; rather it was a deliberate move to prevent the Indians from migrating to Canada on a large scale. Those who came to Canada on the ship called the Komogata Maru which was owned by a Japanese shipping company and hired by Indians is a prime example of how this Order in Council was applied. On this ship there were 376 passengers in which 340 them were Sikhs who were subjects of the British Empire began their journey from Calcutta India and reached Vancouver British Colombia, Canada via Hong Kong, Shanghai and Yokohama in 1914. The ship arrived in the Canadian waters but was not allowed to dock and it was under the strict order of the Premier of B.C. The Indians in Canada organized protests and helped the passengers to disembark but it was all in vain and they had to return to Calcutta on 27 September 1914. At last on August 3rd 08 Prime Minster Stephen Harper made an apology at the 13th annual Ghandi da Mela festival in Surrey, B.C. he formally said that " on behalf of the government of Canada,I am officially conveying as Prime Minister that apology"

The head tax imposed on Chinese immigrants due to the Chinese Immigration Act of 1885 was an act of deliberate discrimination and was meant to discourage the Chinese from entering Canada. It was a pity that after extracting manual labour from Chinese workers to build the Canadian Pacific railway, this policy would have been presented to the world as a decent way of limiting immigrants from non-European ethnic groups. It is crystal clear that the Indian and Chinese labourers were conveniently allowed to migrate to Canada to work in demanding and physically dangerous jobs that the European labourers had little or no interest in. Therefore there was no choice other than to recruit the Indians and Chinese and as soon as the project was completed, there was no need for their services and thus the head tax was imposed with the intent of discouraging migration. It was evident that among the established Canadians that there was a fear that the Chinese would end up taking over in British Columbia and there was evidence that in spite of the employment opportunities that were given there was discrimination in the workplace. There were over 3,000 in the provincial population of 33,586 and that number accounts for 8.93 % and the accumulation of the Chinese was in a very short time. Chinese workers engaged in the construction sites were paid between one third and one half of the wages that their Canadian counterparts made. The hands of the Dominion of the British Empire was not opened enough to ban their immigration outright but was able to restrict them. The tax began with the price of $50.00 and rose to $500.00 in 1903. Although they collected $ 4 23 million which is almost $300.00 today from over eighty thousand Chinese immigrants the primary concern was to restrict the migration of Chinese. Another method used to prevent permanent settlement plans was to discourage the migration of whole families. This led to many Chinese families being separated for many years only to be reunified when the immigration legislation changed.

When the Canadian immigration policies were modified and welcomed new immigrants without such restrictions, the Canadian Chinese realized that they were the victims of a discriminative immigration policy. Though they became part and parcel of the Canadian culture, they felt that the fee that had been levied on their ancestors had to be redressed and an apology given from the government. Mrs. Margaret Mitchell the Member of Parliament in 1984 raised the issue in the House of Commons at the behest of her constituents. Though it did not bear any fruit spontaneously, it motivated and encouraged the Chinese community across Canada to educate the public about the Head Tax and this also opened the eyes of the Canadian politicians. The negotiations continued and in 1993 Prime Minster Brian Mulroney made an offer and it was rejected by the Chinese community council. Finally Prime Minister Stephen Harper offered an apology and compensation for the head tax paid by the Chinese immigrants on 22nd June 06 and with that the legacy of the Chinese Exclusion Act of 1923 came to an end.

The discriminative immigration policies also brought restriction for immigrants from desirable countries such as the United Kingdom, United States, France, New Zeeland and Australia with the proviso that they should have the means to support themselves in Canada without being a burden. Highly encouraged were those Europeans who were able to make positive contribution to the economic progress of the country. In spite of these demarcations the immigrants from the Middle East, although it is geographically a part of Asia could act as investors and were encouraged to migrate to Canada due to the massive amount of wealth from the petroleum industry. The continuation of economic status as one of the criteria for migration in the Immigration Act of 1906 had a mixed message and as such it was able to restrict migration from the racially undesirable ethnicities. The discrimination was very obvious as it required $25.00 for other immigrants but for Asians the fee was raised in 1914 to $200.00. In the case of Japanese and Chinese immigrants there was another set of restrictions applied.

In 1914, just after the order was passed by the cabinet, Mr. Munshi Singh, an Indian but a subject of the British colonial government arrived in Vancouver, British Colombia with less than $ 200.00 dollars and challenged the law in the Supreme court and the court of appeal and the extraction of the long verdict given by the Justice of Appeal is as follows:

As you can probably tell by the tone in the decision it was clear that it did not matter if a person from an undesirable ethnicity was educated or not or had money or not. It was simply accepted as a fact that these people would not blend into Canadian culture and would cause nothing but trouble. It was also the case that any Indians who wanted to migrate to Canada by ship had to begin their journey in India and reach Canada without any stopovers in between. All were very aware that it was impossible to sail any ship with a large capacity such a long distance without stopping for food or fuel, but that was exactly the point.

Although the government of Mr. Stephen Harper made an apology on behalf of Canada to the Indians for that historical shameful act some of the Indians were not pleased with the way it was made. He also apologized for the inappropriate treatments given to the native children and for the head tax levied against the Chinese and these two apologizes was made in parliament and documented properly. But the apology that was extended to the Indians was in a public platform outside the parliament. Some were trying to justify that other two incidents took place within Canada and that of Indian was on the ship. However the discrimination was still there.

It is also true that making the effort to balance the economic benefits with the homogeneous interests was not an easy task. At times when the advancement of the economic prosperity superseded the protection of the homogeneous interest the elasticity of migration policy was very flexible like Malaysian rubber.

The Japanese faced another form of discrimination that was based not on ethnicity but rather due to the participation in World War II. It was not targeted against common men in particular. During the Second World War Canada was in the camp of the British allies along with France and the United States against the Nazi regime in Germany and Japanese regime. The restriction was for a smaller period of time as during and just after the World War II. According to the War Measures Act of 1942 the Japanese citizens were restricted in entry from abroad. Furthermore the Canadian born citizens of Japanese descent were also subject to deportation. The British subjects of the Japanese race aged 16 and older and residents of Canada were requested to repatriate.

The Jews were also discriminated against even before the execution of six million Jews within a period of six years during the war. Though there was no such law that restricted the migration of the Asians, in practice there was an element of discriminative measures that were taken against them.

The immigration Act of 1978 almost closed the door on discrimination in immigration policies. It mentions that " " to ensure that any person who seek admission to land is subject to standards of subject to admission that do not discriminate on the grounds of race, national or ethnic origin, color, religion or sex"

The law made a tremendous change in putting a stop on discrimination in immigration but any law on immigration has some loopholes there is room for some discriminative measures which may not be obvious. The element of discrimination may be hidden and would not necessarily be easily proven in the justice system but it would linger in the nature of the execution of the laws. It would be also possible in achieving the intended targets by delaying the process, levying taxes to certain areas, imposing strict measures on issuing visas are also some of the technical ways to achieve what has to be done without having any legal challenges.

33. Anti-Discriminative Measures

It is not always true that the government dances according to the tune of the masses, there are times that the pipers of the government impiously play certain tunes and make the people dance accordingly. In certain times the voice of the government has been highly influenced by certain groups of people or regions of the country that helped them by permanently or temporarily supporting the existence of a particular party or winning the election to form the government. The right leader should not always act to satisfy what the people want, rather he should guide and direct them for the long term and it may at times be a bitter pill to swallow but in the long run the people who hate and opposed will turn back and appreciate what has been done. He has to forgo the instance benefits and take short term pain for the long term gain. The regime of a good leader will not be assessed with what he has contributed to the current benefit and wellbeing of the country, rather what kind of foundation that he laid for the future of the nation.

Immigration is one of the main organs of the Canadian government and it is a very sensitive and vital sector that should be planned and dealt with consciously. In immigration, we treat with human beings with respect, not in a manner that deals with assets or international trade of services and commodities. It is true the immigrants need to migrate into Canada more than any other nation in the world and Canada is in need of new immigrants for the purpose of maintaining the current status and economic activities and progress with abundant natural resources. We shouldn't compare the two aspects as a part of the price mechanism based on demand and supply. I am not inclined or supportive of comparing and contrasting, who needs and get more benefits from the migration, the immigrants or the receiving nations. Some have the view that new immigrants need Canada more than Canada needs them whereas others have the opinion that Canada needs them more than they need Canada. I rather consider both as two sides of the same coin. Both parties also have the tendency of achieving the best out of the deal as such the receiving nations prefer to have the potential skills or capital for investments, and are not inclined or involved in any terrorist activities or having serious criminal backgrounds. The migration of the new immigrants has various factors that pushed them to leave their native land or the habitual resident and choice the migrating country. The predominant pushing factors are as such: poverty, varieties of discrimination, persecution, low income, natural calamity, political instability and lack of employment. There are also the motivational pulling forces that encourage them to migrate to developed nations such as better standards of living with a constant supply of social amenities, better salary and employment, prosperity, safety, stable government, freedom and the ability to have a bright future for their children.

The recent Liberal Party capitalized on the Liberal immigration policy of the late Pierre Elliott Trudeau that opened the gate for unimaginable numbers of immigrants to migrate to Canada including those not having sufficient funds for the initial support or the necessary skills for meeting the scarce demands of the labour market. Even today after passing the second and third generation of those immigrants that sense of gratitude and sentiment pushed them to support the Liberal party in the political elections. In order to continue to maintain their support and their heart they are always very supportive of Liberal immigration policies. They always oppose restrictions on any immigration policies, even if the restrictions are in the best interest of the nation in the long run. Still they oppose it when it is brought forward by the Conservative government. A similar trend can also be noticed not only in Canada but in France, England, and the United States of America between the right wing and the labour or Liberal or Democratic Party in the USA.

The Citizenship and Immigration Canada works with community agencies and also funds and operates projects with the intent of eliminating racism against new comers. The month of February for example has been declared as Black history month, the month of May is Asian heritage month. Citizenship and Immigration Canada is also dedicated to building bridges between different cultures, Anti-racism and human rights Outreach Projects, racism prevention and Cultural integration training for frontline workers are some of the things that this department has taken on.

Let us have a look at some of their objectives and evaluate that how far they have been able to reduce racial discrimination after the arrival of new immigrants:

1. Reduce the impact of discrimination through the empowerment of new immigrant parents as a result of their active participation in community programs.

2. Promote a greater understanding around the concepts of oppression and strategies for stopping racism.

3. Increase the awareness of racism and discriminatory practices.

4. The development of skills in the area of public speaking and communication on issues related to racism.

5. Newcomer parents and youth are encouraged to have a dialogue about racism, diversity and human rights in a safe environment.

6. Increase youth understanding of the consequences related to prejudice, racism and discrimination in all its forms.

7. Increase awareness among Canadian born youth of issues related to racism and discriminatory practices.

These objectives prove that racism has been in existence to a certain extent and in some of the major ethnic groups racial discrimination in the schools, work places, job markets, and in some public places has been an ongoing issue. In some of the private enterprises there is discrimination against some ethnic groups and it entails more than negative attitudes, it has gone into the scale of salaries and benefits and they are paid less than their counterparts. I appreciate such positive efforts in reducing racial discrimination but we have gone only a few kilometres on a very long journey. The only consolation that I have is the image that compared with European countries; the degree of racism in Canada is minimal and is fading faster than ever before. In spite of it, it would not be naturally paralyzed and it requires constant treatment, otherwise it may wake up from a dormant state as exemplified by the revival of Anti-Semitism in Germany.

There is no harm in being proud of someone's identity, culture, economic superiority and it should be one of the motivating factors for its continuous growth. In fact anyone who forgoes his identity for the sake of a few economic or other privileges would not be trusted and he could jump from where he is now to the superior one later. A broader national outlook and inner determination is highly recommended for Canada, a nation that has been built mainly by new immigrants who migrated from all corners of the globe. The share for the building and developing of this nation by certain groups certainly are the back bone and it has to be acknowledged by the rest. No matter who has made lion share on it, it matters that basically every section of the Canadian mosaic has been recognized and has the fundamental rights in preserving and practising their root culture and traditions without the improvement of the main stream culture.

34. Canada is No Longer a Transit Lounge

On international flights from well reputed and other airlines from all over the world, many of the passengers are preparing to fill out their disembarkation cards before landing at Pearson International airport in Toronto Canada. Many are thrilled and excited about reaching their final destination after a long period of time in processing their immigration papers with a lot of patience. In contrast there are flights originating from Toronto bound for international airports carrying Canadians who want to repatriate or migrate to another country and Canada on the one hand, bids them farewell forever while keeping the door open should anyone change their mind.

Along with these two groups of people there is another section of the Canadian population who are undocumented immigrants who are not supposed to remain in the country and are expected to voluntarily depart on or before a given date.

These immigrants fall into one of the following categories:

a. Rejected refugees on a removal order or departure, deportation order or voluntarily on a return order but remain in Canada after the said dates

b. Those who legally arrived in Canada on student visas, temporary resident visas, temporary foreign contract workers, Religious workers and others whose work permits have expired

c. Naturalized citizens who have criminal convictions,

d. Those who have permanent resident status and either entered Canada as a refugee claimant or as privately sponsored refugees or who arrived as permanent residents, skilled workers, or investors and got involved in criminal activities before or after arriving in Canada

e. Those who have crossed the border into Canada inappropriately.

Countries like Canada and Australia are not only the two leading generous countries accepting new immigrants; they are highly concerned about observing and respecting human rights. I do appreciate the respect and consideration for universal human rights and their respective declarations are mostly based on the international declaration. According to these aspects of the declarations, once anyone enters into the respective country, they have many opportunities to appeal the decisions made by the Immigration and Refugee Board (in the case of Canada) and the time and resources that are consumed for this and the public expense for those concerned refugee claimants are a burden to the nation. Therefore in order to weed out the bogus refugees and claimants with economic interests, they face an initial screening process at the border and only those considered prospective refugee claimants are allowed to enter into Canada.

After entering into Canada and claiming refugee status and when the initial results were negative and after going through all possible venues and exhausting all possible options, they are given an opportunity to voluntarily depart and it may help them in their possible return to Canada if they apply in the future in another category and meet the eligible criteria. If they were to be on a departure order or a deportation order, this has more serious consequences and the chances of being able to return to Canada in the future is either totally denied or allowed with certain conditions. This being said however, there are some refugee claimants after exhausting all legal battles still want to remain in this country and do remain here as illegal immigrants and the Canadian government is taking steps to track these people down.

Canada also encourages potential international students to join our educational institutions and make positive contributions to Canada while they gain a high calibre of education and invest their resources and time. These students have a very high potential and desire a better educational experience compared with those of their own countries. They are also aware that they have to bear most of the cost for the educational services. Canada also has dual benefits in this program as it carries a portion of the educational expenditures. The cost for educational services are growing higher and higher and it has become second highest expenditure for the respective provincial governments and the federal government.

The attraction and certain privileges given to international students eventually encourage and motivate quite a number of them to remain in this country permanently. Canada would not hesitate in having them join us as a part of the Canadian family. They are educated and have gone through the Canadian system and not strangers to the Canadian way of life and it is easy for them to get absorbed into the economic sector without any hostility. They have also been given an opportunity to join certain sectors of the labour market while learning and immediately after the completion of their educational program successfully, they are able to apply for permanent residency in Canada without leaving the country. By internationalizing our post-secondary institutions, Canada has received many benefits.

Certain countries that send their children as international students are aware of this and they do not want to lose their best and brightest students to the Canadian team. For example, I am aware that China, one of the leading nations in supplying foreign students, has touched on this issue and has expressed concern.

In time, these people eventually settle down and become part of our growth in many aspects. But once they have gained experience and wealth up to certain extent, once they discover they have better chances and more recognition and a life with the flavour of their ethnic values they either repatriate to their country of origin or emigrate to the United States of America where they would be able progress better and faster.

The entry and exit of the International gates of Canada are always busy with the transportation of human capital from its beginning until today. The destinations and the socio-ethnic backgrounds and their calibers are changing all the time but the trend of immigration and emigration remains intact. The natives, the people of the First Nations migrated almost thirty thousand years ago, presumably from Mongolia without any passports or travel documents on animals and on foot.

They reached the western parts of Canada and eventually migrated to other parts of this nation internally and the process of this migration both internationally and internally takes place simultaneously. Of course they had no serious challenges from any other human beings and the only struggle that they had was the fighting with the climate and animals and they were prepared for overcoming uncertainties. Since their occupation was hunting with age old hand crafted tools and collecting fruits and vegetables, they were not stationed in particular places and established a mobilized social life and collectively progressed at a reasonable speed.

Though in the Canadian constitution there is a clause for repatriating anyone except those who have obtained citizenship by birth in Canada or were born to a Canadian parent abroad, until recently there has not been a need for the repatriation of people in high numbers. Unless someone has or had committed a serious criminal offence or was involved in any activities related to crimes against humanity, the process for revoking citizenship is also very time consuming. Since Canadian citizenship replaced the British Subject status in 1947 for Canadians, fewer than seventy citizenships were revoked. These days Citizenship and Immigration Canada has discovered another section of naturalized citizens who attained Canadian citizenship through fraudulent means and over 3100 cases have been under investigation.

Allow me to quote on the revocation of Canadian citizenship 27 July 2011 as outlined by Citizenship and Immigration Canada:

"Revocation means removing someone's citizenship. People can have their citizenship revoked if they have obtained their citizenship by fraud, false representation or knowingly concealing material circumstances (for example, knowingly concealing information that could have affected their eligibility for citizenship or permanent residence).

The Minister of Citizenship, Immigration and Multiculturalism sends a Notice of Intention to Revoke Citizenship to the person concerned, outlining the grounds for revocation. The person concerned has the right to request that the matter be referred to the Federal Court to determine whether he or she obtained Canadian citizenship by false representation or fraud or knowingly concealing material circumstances.

If the person does not refer the matter to the Federal Court within 30 days, the Minister of Citizenship, Immigration and Multiculturalism may directly proceed to submit a report to the Governor in Council (GIC) recommending that citizenship be revoked.

If the matter is referred to the Federal Court and the court finds that citizenship was not obtained by false representation, fraud or knowingly concealing material circumstances, the matter ends there. However, if the Federal Court finds that citizenship was obtained through false representation, fraud or knowingly concealing material circumstances, the Minister of Citizenship, Immigration and Multiculturalism may submit a report to the GIC recommending that citizenship is revoked.

The text of the report that the Minister presents to the GIC is disclosed to the person concerned, who has the opportunity to make written submissions. Any such submissions would be considered by the Minister and attached to the final report presented to the GIC. If the Governor in Council decides to revoke the person's citizenship, it is carried out by an Order-in-Council.

The person who is the subject of the Order-in-Council has the right to have the Federal Court judicially review the GIC's decision to revoke citizenship."

Border crossing from both sides legally and otherwise has been another issue that is widening the gap between the United States and Canada. In the early days of the European settlements, crossing the border was not a serious issue. After the American Revolution, the view of Americans towards Britain and other European countries did not go in parallel to that of the British subjects in Canada. Canada's independence evolved over time and was made official on July 1, 1867. The influx of refugees from the U.S however, continued to dominate until both the countries signed a mutual agreement based on a safe third country policy

Under this Canada – United States safe third country agreement either way anyone seeks refugee protection, the claim must be made in the first country that he or she arrives in, unless they qualify under the exceptions given on the agreements. The safe third country for Canada is a country other than the country where the alleged persecution of the refugee claimant took place.

The influx of Canadians into the U.S was closely watched after the terrorist attacks in New York and Washington D.C by four hijacked airplanes which destroyed the World Trade Center and the Pentagon. Over three thousand people, including 227 civilians and 19 hijackers aboard the four planes were killed. Since then, the U.S is very cautious about anyone crossing the border from Canada and it was discovered that some of the terrorists initially entered into Canada in some disguised manner either as refugees or otherwise.

The next important group of Canadians who leave Canada for the U.S are predominantly skilled workers and highly qualified persons.

All the contributing factors in the process of migration and emigration can be grouped into two major components. They are the pushing forces and the pulling forces and though both contribute in many cases, the proportion of the force in making the decision to migrate or emigrate varies. The following are the main factors:

Statistics

Inter-censual Net Migration Ratios, by Province			
Provinces	1901-1911	1911-1921	1921-1931
PEI	- 13.6	- 16.4	- 11.1
Nova Scotia	- 0.6	- 7.6	- 14.5
New Brunswick	- 3.8	- 7.3	- 11.5
Quebec	4.3	- 4.0	0.9
Ontario	9.3	2.3	5.1
Manitoba	41.2	5.1	- 1.7
Saskatchewan	125.6	15.1	- 0.7
Alberta	123.8	20.9	3.8
British Columbia	69.4	14.8	18.7

Source: Leroy O. Stone *Migration in Canada: Regional Aspects*. Ottawa: Government Publication, 1969. p. 138

Material and Charts

Emigration to the United States from Canada and Quebec, 1840-1940

Last revised:
23 August 2000

Period	Canadian emigration	Rate of Emigration (%)	Quebec Emigration	Rate of Emigration	Quebec as % of Canadian Emigration
1840-1850	75 000	4,3	35 000	5,4	47
1850-1860	150 000	7	70 000	7,8	47
1860-1870	300 000	10,7	100 000	10 (est.)	33
1870-1880	375 000	11	120 000	10,1	32
1880-1890	450 000	11,3	150 000	11,3	33
1890-1900	425 000	9,7	140 000	9,6	33
1900-1910	325 000	6,4	100 000	6	31
1910-1920	250 000	4	80 000	4	32
1920-1930	450 000	6	130 000	5,6	29
1930-1940	25 000	0,3	-	-	-
1840-1940	2 800 000		900 000		32

Source: Yolande Lavoie, *L'émigration des Québécois aux Etats-Unis de 1840 à 1930*, Quebec, 1981, 68p., p. 53.

Pushing Forces

1. Physical conditions – particularly extreme weather conditions
2. The uneasiness in adopting to the nature of their Socio- cultural background
3. Adjustment hardship -Migration from rural background to urban cities
4. Initial hardship for skilled works to find jobs in their own field of expertise
5. The impact of Canadian foreign policy
6. Racial discrimination
7. Expulsion

8. Natural calamities

Pulling Forces

1. Better prospective in employment
2. Family ties
3. Better investment opportunities
4. Political motivation
5. Accustomed climatic condition
6. Change in governments and its systems
7. Cultural inclination
8. Creation of a new nation
9. End of civil war

Facts and figures 2014 – Immigration overview: Permanent residents

Canada – Permanent residents by gender and category, 1989 to 2014

Total by Category 1990-2001

Category	1990	1991	1992	1993	1994	1995	1996	1997	1998	1999	2000	2001
Family class	74,664	87,944	101,102	112,636	94,185	77,377	68,316	59,925	50,864	55,261	60,613	66,794
Economic immigrants	97,921	86,494	95,786	105,644	102,304	106,622	125,367	128,349	97,909	109,241	136,281	155,707
Refugees	40,215	54,069	52,338	30,590	20,433	28,092	28,472	24,307	22,842	24,308	30,091	27,915
Other immigrants	3,601	4,248	5,543	7,751	7,453	760	3,865	3,400	2,547	1,031	460	206
Category not stated	0	0	0	0	0	0	1	0	0	0	0	1
Gender not stated	50	47	18	17	7	13	50	55	33	19	10	13
Total by Category	216,451	232,802	254,787	256,638	224,382	212,864	226,071	216,036	174,195	189,950	227,455	250,636

Total by Category 2002-2014

Category	2002	2003	2004	2005	2006	2007	2008	2009	2010	2011	2012	2013	2014
Family class	62,292	65,123	62,274	63,374	70,515	66,239	65,584	65,208	60,225	56,453	65,012	81,843	66,659
Economic immigrants	137,864	121,046	133,746	156,312	138,252	131,244	149,066	153,489	186,915	156,114	160,792	148,154	165,088
Refugees	25,110	25,982	32,686	35,774	32,499	27,954	21,859	22,849	24,697	27,873	23,079	23,831	23,286
Other immigrants	3,779	9,194	7,111	6,779	10,371	11,312	10,730	10,622	8,842	8,301	9,014	5,194	5,367
Category not stated	0	1	0	2	2	1	2	1	7	3	5	0	1
Gender not stated	4	3	5	1	1	3	3	1	1	3	1	1	3
Total by Category	229,049	221,349	235,822	262,242	251,640	236,753	247,244	252,170	280,687	248,747	257,903	259,023	260,404

Facts and figures

Facts and figures 2014 – Immigration overview: Permanent residents

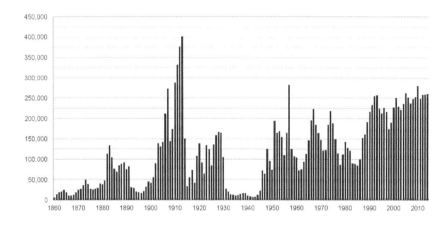

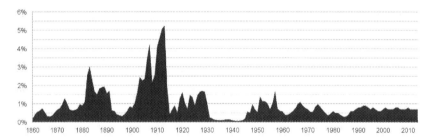

208

1860-1869

YEAR	1860	1861	1862	1863	1864	1865	1866	1867	1868	1869
Number	6,276	13,589	18,294	21,000	24,779	18,958	11,427	10,666	12,765	18,630
% of Population	0.2	0.4	0.6	0.6	0.7	0.6	0.3	0.3	0.4	0.5

1870-1879

YEAR	1870	1871	1872	1873	1874	1875	1876	1877	1878	1879
Number	24,706	27,773	36,578	50,050	39,373	27,382	25,633	27,082	29,807	40,492
% of Population	0.7	0.8	1.0	1.3	1.0	0.7	0.6	0.7	0.7	1.0

1880-1889

YEAR	1880	1881	1882	1883	1884	1885	1886	1887	1888	1889
Number	38,505	47,991	112,458	133,624	103,824	76,169	69,152	84,526	88,766	91,600
% of Population	0.9	1.1	2.6	3.0	2.3	1.7	1.5	1.8	1.9	1.9

1890-1899

YEAR	1890	1891	1892	1893	1894	1895	1896	1897	1898	1899
Number	75,067	82,165	30,996	29,633	20,829	18,790	16,835	21,716	31,900	44,543
% of Population	1.6	1.7	0.6	0.6	0.4	0.4	0.3	0.4	0.6	0.9

1900-1909

YEAR	1900	1901	1902	1903	1904	1905	1906	1907	1908	1909
Number	41,681	55,747	89,102	138,660	131,252	141,465	211,653	272,409	143,326	173,694
% of Population	0.8	1.0	1.6	2.5	2.3	2.4	3.5	4.2	2.2	2.6

1910-1919

YEAR	1910	1911	1912	1913	1914	1915	1916	1917	1918	1919
Number	286,839	331,288	375,756	400,870	150,484	33,665	55,914	72,910	41,845	107,698
% of Population	4.1	4.6	5.1	5.3	1.9	0.4	0.7	0.9	0.5	1.3

1920-1929

YEAR	1920	1921	1922	1923	1924	1925	1926	1927	1928	1929
Number	138,824	91,728	64,224	133,729	124,164	84,907	135,982	158,886	166,783	164,993
% of Population	1.6	1.0	0.7	1.5	1.4	0.9	1.4	1.6	1.7	1.6

1930-1939

YEAR	1930	1931	1932	1933	1934	1935	1936	1937	1938	1939
Number	104,806	27,530	20,591	14,382	12,476	11,277	11,643	15,101	17,244	16,994
% of Population	1.0	0.3	0.2	0.1	0.1	0.1	0.1	0.1	0.2	0.2

1940-1949

YEAR	1940	1941	1942	1943	1944	1945	1946	1947	1948	1949
Number	11,324	9,329	7,576	8,504	12,801	22,722	71,719	64,127	125,414	95,217
% of Population	0.1	0.1	0.1	0.1	0.1	0.2	0.6	0.5	1.0	0.7

1950-1959

YEAR	1950	1951	1952	1953	1954	1955	1956	1957	1958	1959
Number	73,912	194,391	164,498	168,868	154,227	109,946	164,857	282,164	124,851	106,928
% of Population	0.5	1.4	1.1	1.1	1.0	0.7	1.0	1.7	0.7	0.6

1960-1969

YEAR	1960	1961	1962	1963	1964	1965	1966	1967	1968	1969
Number	104,111	71,698	74,856	93,151	112,606	146,758	194,743	222,876	183,974	164,531
% of Population	0.6	0.4	0.4	0.5	0.6	0.7	1.0	1.1	0.9	0.8

1970-1979

YEAR	1970	1971	1972	1973	1974	1975	1976	1977	1978	1979
Number	147,713	121,900	122,006	184,200	218,465	187,881	149,429	114,914	86,313	112,093
% of Population	0.7	0.6	0.6	0.8	1.0	0.8	0.6	0.5	0.4	0.5

1980-1989

YEAR	1980	1981	1982	1983	1984	1985	1986	1987	1988	1989
Number	143,138	128,641	121,175	89,185	88,272	84,346	99,351	152,076	161,585	191,550
% of Population	0.6	0.5	0.5	0.4	0.3	0.3	0.4	0.6	0.6	0.7

1990-1999

YEAR	1990	1991	1992	1993	1994	1995	1996	1997	1998	1999
Number	216,451	232,802	254,787	256,638	224,382	212,864	226,071	216,036	174,195	189,950
% of Population	0.8	0.8	0.9	0.9	0.8	0.7	0.8	0.7	0.6	0.6

2000-2009

YEAR	2000	2001	2002	2003	2004	2005	2006	2007	2008	2009
Number	227,455	250,636	229,049	221,349	235,822	262,242	251,640	236,753	247,244	252,170
% of Population	0.7	0.8	0.7	0.7	0.7	0.8	0.8	0.7	0.7	0.7

2010-2014

YEAR	2010	2011	2012	2013	2014
Number	280,687	248,747	257,903	259,023	260,404
% of Population	0.8	0.7	0.7	0.7	0.7

CHAPTER 5

Demographic Dynamics

The dynamics of Canada in terms of the size of the estimated population of April,1,2016 is 36,155, 487 and based on the census of 2011, it is 33, 476,688 and represents 0.50 % of the total world population, in the second largest country in the world in size is insignificant and nothing much to be proud of. But the demographic composition by having citizens from all around the world speaking over 165 languages, practicing almost all major cultures freely and fairly and co-existing with unity from their diversified ethnic backgrounds in an excellent manner is unbeatable and is cited as a role model for the rest of the world.

This analysis on the dynamics of the demographics includes the following: the population policy, the size, density, geographical distribution, age distribution, fertility, abortion rate, immigration and emigration, costs and benefits, mortality and fertility, life expectancy, linguistic distribution, education and literacy, economic status, decline in natural increase in population, de-demographic, sex, over-under population, brain drain and gain, politics and population projection and focus.

The ratio of the mixture of textures in the cocktail in the policies of demographics changes due to the political, social, and up to some extent the religious historical, geographical and economic policies, therefore the policy on demographics is not an independent entity, and rather it is a part of the integrated policy pool. With these policies, the factors that directly determine the demographics are fertility, immigration and emigration and mortality rate.

The combination of the forces are from three main factors such as social, political and economic factors brought a great change in demographics. The recognition of individuals, regardless of their social status, economic class, and race and religion to greater extent in modern human history starting from the latter part of the 18th to the 21st century, human dignity and respect has been elevated. The contribution for the value of ordinary human beings by the industrial revolution that brought a brand new system into the economic structure and made major structural changes from the agrarian and trading society into manufacturing industry and also to skilled workers from traditional handcrafts and liberated many farm workers from a semi slavery status. Later on the collective force of the labourers under the trade unions brought them undisputable power and elevated their status by collective force. The First and the Second World Wars also made some positive contributions as a blessing in disguise of sorts since rival groups were united in fighting a common enemy and thus relaxed their Master- slave and aristocratic relationship to certain point and it gave opportunities in earning respect for the colonial masters. The French and American revolutions coupled with the Soviet revolution awakened the world for having due respect for mere human beings. The religious institutions, regardless of their denominations brought the institutions and leaders in society to learn, understand and respect people at the grassroots level.

There was a rapid increase in population ever since human beings were differentiated by evolution in the animal kingdom. In the 20th century, there were two significance changes. There was an explosion in population growth in the first half of the century and in the second half it was an increase in the aging population. Of course this was not uniform in all countries in the evolutionary processes. There are four main stages in the evolutionary process:

Stage 1

While having a higher rate in birth, an increase in the death rate occurs and the net remaining natural birth is low and the trend of the increase in population is too slow. Usually this stage has been experienced at the very low level in the socio-economic and education levels in a society.

In the early establishment of the European settlements in 15th and 16thcenturies the demographic polices were not that complicated. It was almost a closed door affair with the attitude of protecting the newly discovered territory for themselves from the natives and rival colonial entities of a handful of other nations. Although an Italian helped the British in settling Canada still he was a paid employee and that's all and the French and the British monopolized power in the North American territories.

The second stage came into the scene after secure the power of the land in making efforts developing it as a source of a potential supply of raw materials and also the market of their processed and finished goods. They felt that adding more manpower from their own circle would be more profitable and economic priorities penetrated into their demographic polices. Still the white sentiments and supremacy would not allow them to look for alternative sources from other sectors of human beings.

FERTILITY

Canada has been a part of the global village and somehow the demographic process is basically similar to the rest of the world with slight variations. These days reproduction has been controlled and measured by various external factors and also follows a "check and balance" formula. It has been considered that sex is primarily meant for pleasure, not necessarily always a means for reproduction. Though reproduction is a consequence of sex, it is considered a different entity and has to be treated separately. Furthermore modern medical technology has made the process of reproduction easier in some cases. But in the days when the size of the population was low and the mortality rate was very high and in the absence of modern technology sex was for pleasure and having a higher number of children.

The early inhabitants in the land of Canada over thirty thousand years ago were primarily nomads and never settled in a particular place permanently. With the available data for the pre-historic period the major three groups of nomads, hunters and food gathers, pastoral and peripatetic had a similar level of fertility of other nomads elsewhere at that time. It was in the first stage of the population growth as such high birth rate and high death rate and low rate in increase in population. The necessity of mass mobility was very low due to various factors, as such the ignorance of not being able to foresee in a broader sense and also the tools for the transportation, exploration and protection from the other groups of people who would attack them, the attachment to certain areas, the pagan's religious beliefs of moving far distances or deserting their blessed land is an evil attempt, insecure mentality and many other factors discouraged them in exploration.

In this regards, the United Nations has made a reasonability substantial contribution in advocating and assisting in family planning with the promoting of safe sex. According its recent report of March 2016, in developing countries, there tremendous progress in the use of contraceptives and the projections for global population growth could be cut by as much as one billion over the next 15 years. According to the report an estimated 64% in 2015 by married women or women living with a partner between the ages of 15 and 49 use family planning either in a modern or traditional way. It was a big jump from1970 when it was far below to 36%

"The UN projection of population growth already gives us an idea of the impact that increased access to family planning could have. If by 2030 the average family size is just one child fewer than 2030 the world population is estimated to be approximately 8 billon rather than 9 billion" said by Jagdish Upadhyay, head of reproductive health commodity security and family planning at the UN population fund.

It had some adverse effect of the demographics, as such, the natural calamity, floods, drought, prolonged ice, volcanic eruptions, tsunamis, earthquakes, and the spread of infectious disease at times pushed them to move out and it might have been one of the primary reasons for the migration for the Natives to migrate to the continent of North America from Asia.

The progress of the economic activities of human beings evolved when they were in the stage of hunters and food collectors initially using stone spears and arrows. The switch to agriculture was revolutionary as was the Industrial Revolution. In fact almost all of the world's civilizations were established only after many years of the establishment of farming and other related sectors of agriculture. The solid foundation of the kingdom of human beings on the earth was laid with when he began to sharpen his brain and settled in a particular place. It gave birth to the sense of establishment in life and social units starting from family, the smallest unit in the social fabric. The size gradually increased from the couple, siblings, and children and slowly expanded. The groups of families began to share certain responsibilities and rights and privileges within themselves and the accumulated collective forces brought in big strength and development in education, improvements in settlements, shelter, collection and preservation of food and other items

Education and training added more power to their societies and strengthen their power and helped them in terms of further improving their lives. Here the collective power and the power derived from education made a revolutionary change and the collective power gave birth to the world civilization. The base for almost all major worlds' civilizations was agriculture supported by river water. Those civilizations were the Incas in South America around Peru, Ecuador, and Chile, the Aztecs in Central America, Roman, the Greeks, Chinese, and Mayans in Central America, the Egyptians, and Indus Valley and Mesopotamian civilizations had a high rate of fertility and decreasing infant mortality and this sparked an increase in the size of population.

After a prolonged period of the predominance of agriculture in society, there developed a way for the expansion of trade by exporting the excess agricultural products and importing goods for the export value by bartering. This was due to the absence of high levels of money in circulation. It led exploration, and to the expansion of power and finally ended in colonization of weaker nations by the more powerful ones. It also brought more room for immigration and emigration.

The fourth stage was the Industrial Revolution in England which expanded all over the world but in different time frames. It left no stone untouched, the fast increase in the population, better standard of living, moving from the domination from mono cultural background to multi- cultural background, easy movements of people, high density of populations in cities, the shifting from the rural structure to urban and its complexity, the joining of more females to the work force, the formation of labour unions as collective labour modernization in agriculture, and expansion in supplying raw materials and food for the service and manufacturing industry the accommodation of more manpower in arms and emanations and mass destructions by the conflicts and war with modern weapons produced by those machineries. Building more infrastructural facilities, from transportations, roads, rail way, air, bridges and so on.

World Wars and economic depression

U.S President Ronald Reagan told the president of the Soviet Union Mikhail Gorbachev on February 10, 1989

"Here are two of us in a room and probably the only two people in the world who could start World War III, and we're also the only two people, perhaps, in the world, that could prevent World War III"

The stage of the cold war between the Soviet Union and United states of America from 1945 the post second world war till 1991 the collapse of the soviet Union had an impact on demographics all around the world directly and indirectly.

Demography

The four generations, including major events, key interests and shared beliefs, are as follows:

Second World War generation: born before 1940

- The Second World War
- Respect for hierarchy (top-down management)
- Men belong in the workplace; women at home
- Importance of the nuclear family

Baby boomers: born 1940 – 1960

- End of the Second World War
- Vietnam War
- Cold War
- Television
- Feminism and civil rights
- Casual clothing expressing individuality

Generation X: born 1960 - 1980

- Cold War
- Microwave technology
- Divorce and single-parent families are common

Echo boomers: born 1980 – 2000

- The Gulf War
- The fall of the Berlin Wall
- Business scandals, such as Enron
- The rise of multiculturalism and globalization
- Terrorism
- Rapidly expanding technology, especially the Internet
- Emphasis on multitasking
- A refocusing on family (close parent-child relations)

Echo boomers should not be perceived as lazy or demanding, but merely products of their environment. Learning to see their positive side will help you use them to their full potential as employees. Echo boomers have had many choices available to them, and they are used to being choosy about where they work. They might appear demanding and impatient but consider this: they were raised in a time where news did not take days or hours to circulate, but mere seconds, due to the immediacy of the Internet.

Their approach to authority has been influenced by the scandals affecting many political and business leaders. Having witnessed the downfall of these once reputable figureheads, their respect for authority does not come automatically from position or title alone, but from proven integrity. After having seen the toil and hard work of their parents result in layoffs or termination, echo boomers are not automatically prepared to put work first. Instead, they want a life-work balance that allows time for family, friends, volunteering, sports, social events and further skill development.

The following are some of the characteristics used in describing the Echo Boom generation:

- Technologically savvy – Born with computers, Cellphone, CD's, MP3's etc.
- Well rounded – Incorporating more of life into a work-life balance
- Optimistic – Positive view of the future, but still practical
- Civic-minded – Active in community affairs
- Inclusive – Everyone is equal regardless of superficial differences
- Ability to multitask – Capable of performing many tasks in a given time frame
- Keen and interested – They have a desire to be involved in everything

Successful businesses will grasp the characteristics of this group and not complain of its weaknesses but profit from its strengths. This group is sharp, capable, craving knowledge and success, just doing so in a different manner than was done in the past. Facilitate the positive growth of your organization and capitalize on what is being referred to as the busiest generation ever. Your challenge is to get them busy working toward your business goals and success.

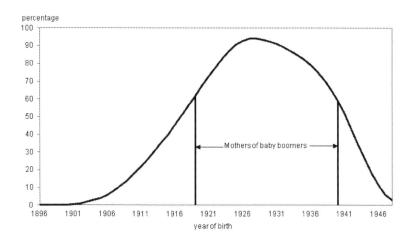

Source: Statistics Canada, Health Statistics Division, Vital Statistics

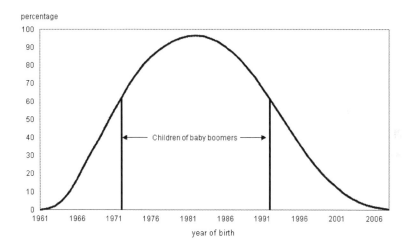

Source: Statistics Canada, Health Statistics Division, Vital Statistics.

Provinces and territories.

Main article; List of Canadian Provinces and territories by population

Province or territory	Population	Percentage	Total land area (km²)	Density (people/ km²)	House of Commons	People per seat
Ontario	12,851,821	38.39%	1,076,395	12.19	121	106,213
Quebec	7,903,001	23.61%	1,365,128	5.76	78	101,321
British Columbia	4,400,057	13.14%	925,186	4.84	42	104,763
Alberta	3,645,257	10.89%	642,317	5.77	34	107,213
Manitoba	1,208,268	3.61%	553,556	2.22	14	86,305
Saskatchewan	1,033,381	3.09%	591,670	1.75	14	73,813
Nova Scotia	921,727	2.75%	53,338	17.63	11	83,793
New Brunswick	751,171	2.24%	71,450	10.50	10	75,117
Newfoundland and Labrador	514,536	1.54%	373,872	1.36	7	73,505
Prince Edward Island	140,204	0.42%	5,660	24.98	4	35,051
Northwest Territories	41,462	0.12%	1,183,085	0.04	1	41,462
Yukon	33,897	0.10%	474,391	0.07	1	33,897
Nunavut	31,906	0.09%	1,936,113	0.02	1	31,906
Canada	**33,476,688**	**100%**	**9,252,161**	**3.73**	**338**	**99,043**

Sources: Statistics Canada

224

Population 65 years and over, Canada, Historical (1971-2011) and Projected (2012-2061)
(percent)

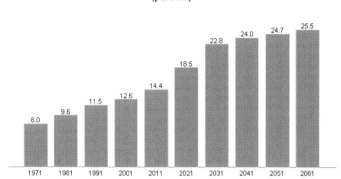

Note: Population projections use a medium-growth scenario (M1) based on interprovincial migration trends from 1981 to 2008. For further information see: Statistics Canada. *Population Projections for Canada, Provinces and Territories (2009-2036)*. (Cat. No. 91-520 XIE).

Source: HRSDC calculations based on Statistics Canada. *Estimates of population, by age group and sex for July 1, Canada, provinces and territories, annual* (CANSIM Table 051-0001); and Statistics Canada. *Projected population, by projection scenario, sex and age group as of July 1, Canada, provinces and territories, annual* (CANSIM table 052-0005). Ottawa: Statistics Canada, 2011.

Canadian trend

The natural growth of population in Canada declines in recent consecutive years and there is no indication that it will reverse. The decline in the birth rate while the death rate continues to rise and may go for another three decades of having a substantial of so called baby boomers. Within the decades of 2020-2030 the growth rate of the population reaches to zero and then move on to the negative side. At this junction the focus will be more emphasized on immigration.

The recent trend reveals that the contribution made by immigrants supersedes the natural growth.

The Canadian population is aging. In 2011, the median age in Canada was 39.9 years, meaning that half of the population was older than that and half was younger. In 1971, the median age was 26.2 years. [1]

Seniors make up the fastest-growing age group. This trend is expected to continue for the next several decades due mainly to a below replacement fertility rate (i.e. average number of children per woman), an increase in life expectancy, and the aging of the baby boom generation. In 2011, an estimated 5.0 million Canadians were 65 years of age or older, a number that is expected to double in the next 25 years to reach 10.4 million seniors by 2036. By 2051, about one in four Canadians is expected to be age 65 or over.

Generations in Canada, 2011

Generations in Canada, 2011 Description. This table displays the results of generations in Canada. The information is grouped by generation (appearing as row headers), age and population, calculated using number and percentage units of measure (appearing as column headers).

Generation	Age	Population	
		number	percentage
Source: Statistics Canada, Census of Population, 2011.			
1918 and before	93 years and over	91,195	0.3
Parents of baby boomers (1919 to 1940)	71 to 92 years	3,074,045	9.2
World War II generation (1941 to 1945)	66 to 70 years	1,444,035	4.3
Baby boomers (1946 to 1965)	46 to 65 years	9,564,210	28.6
Baby busters (1966 to 1971)	40 to 45 years	2,823,840	8.4
Children of baby boomers (1972 to 1992)	19 to 39 years	9,142,005	27.3
Generation Z (1993 to 2011)	18 years and less	7,337,350	21.9

The demographic policies are based on the distribution of population by age, economy, religions, race, geography, and other factors in a particular time and considers the high rate of increase in population and its investment is currently a burden, whereas in the other corner the low rate of natural increase in population while having high rate of Senior citizens itself is also a burden. In the developed nations the structure of the demographic nature has low fertility, high life expectancy, higher productivity of man power, increasing seniors and in the developing countries it is vice versa. If the current trend continues before the end of this century if not all then most the countries will reach the stage where the developed nations have attained the current stage. The 21st century is a very significant year in human history due to the fact that in the early second half, it will have the peak of the human population ever since man was differentiated as a new creature with six senses and also the beginning of the decline in population increase. The speed of increase rate has been so high within the last two decades and the world's population has increased by two billion. The reduction in fertility is going to be the main factor for the decline in population, not the mass destruction of human beings by the most powerful atomic, biological or chemical weapons the every end of the 21st century. Humans have two faces in the economy as such the capital for production and consumers on marketing sectors

China has relaxed its one child only policy that was implemented starting from 1978 till 2015 and according to the government of China it prevented the birth of 400 billion babies. According to certain probability theories towards the end of this century people in many parts of the world practise one child policy voluntarily without inserting any external power.

Population Decline in Percent by Country (from various sources)

Country	Year	Population	Rate of natural decrease in percent (2007)	Notes
Albania	2014	2,893,000	0.456	low birth rate, emigration
Belarus	2014	9,469,000	0.362	low birth rate, population increased in 2014 due to positive **net migration rate**
Bosnia-Herzegovina	2013	3,792,000	0.003	low birth rate, emigration, Bosnian War
Bulgaria	2014	7,202,000	0.796	Low birth rate, high death rate, high rate of abortions, a relatively high level of emigration of young people and a low level of immigration.
Cook Islands	2013	10,447	3.136	emigration of the 20 - 34 age group due to the restructure of the public service starting in the 1990s
Croatia	2014	4,284,889	0.092	low birth rate, emigration, War in Croatia, difference in Statistical methods
Czech Republic	2015	10,537,800	0.134	low birth rate
Cuba	2012	11,075,244	0.115	emigration, low birth rate
Estonia	2014	1,314,000	0.65	low birth rate
Germany	2014	81,174,000	0.2	low birth rate, population increased in 2012, 2013, and 2014 due to positive net migration rate
Greece	2014	10,992,000	0.16	low birth rate, economic crisis
Hungary	2014	9,848,000	0.184	low birth rate
Italy	2014	60, 808, 000	0.09	low birth rate
Japan	2015	126,880,000	0.077	low birth rate and a low level of immigration
Latvia	2014	1,995,000	0.598	low birth rate, emigration
Lithuania	2014	2,907,000	0.278	low birth rate, emigration
Niue	2011	1,446	2.308	Emigration
Northern Mariana Islands	2012	44,582	2.449	Emigration

Population Decline in Percent by Country (from various sources)

Country	Year	Population	Rate of natural decrease in percent (2007)	Notes
Federated States of Micronesia	2012	106,487	0.343	Emigration
Moldova	2013	3,559,000	1.014	low birth rate
Poland	2014	38,484,000	0.075	low birth rate, emigration
Portugal	2014	10,401,000	0.07	low birth rate, economic crisis, emigration
Puerto Rico	2013	3,598,357	3.136	low birth rate, economic crisis
Romania	2014	19,897,000	0.26	low birth rate, high death rate, high rate of abortion, emigration
Russia	2014	146,090,613	0.48	high death rate, low birth rate, high rate of abortions, and a low level of immigration Population increased in 2014 due to positive natural change and positive net migration rate
Serbia	2014	7,132,000	0.464	low birth rate, high death rate, high rate of abortion, emigration
Ukraine	2014	43,001,000	0.625	declining births

Population: Past/Future-**World 1950-2050 by continent**

Historic, current and future population of

Population mid-year	Africa	Americas	Asia	Europe	Oceania	World
1950	228,826,701	339,484,233	1,395,749,366	549,043,373	12,674,996	2,525,778,669
1960	285,270,283	424,790,595	1,694,649,832	605,516,913	15,775,319	3,026,002,942
1970	366,474,876	519,017,284	2,128,630,599	657,369,142	19,680,715	3,691,172,616
1980	478,459,469	618,950,076	2,634,161,250	694,510,142	22,967,861	4,449,048,798
1990	629,986,978	727,488,767	3,213,123,453	723,248,103	26,969,366	5,320,816,667
2000	808,304,337	841,695,330	3,717,371,723	729,105,436	31,223,602	6,127,700,428
2010	1,031,083,666	942,692,345	4,165,440,162	740,308,364	36,658,945	6,916,183,482
2020	1,312,142,128	1,037,448,638	4,581,523,062	743,569,194	42,066,020	7,716,749,042
2030	1,634,366,269	1,120,044,329	4,886,846,140	736,363,555	47,317,181	8,424,937,474
2040	1,998,821,019	1,183,328,314	5,080,418,644	723,887,158	52,232,016	9,038,687,151
2050	2,393,174,892	1,227,766,905	5,164,061,493	709,067,211	56,874,390	9,550,944,891
2060	2,797,337,341	1,256,295,770	5,152,203,354	690,622,327	60,939,796	9,957,398,588
2070	3,195,254,409	1,270,521,911	5,074,752,919	672,504,684	64,305,306	10,277,339,229
2080	3,569,536,916	1,271,719,302	4,957,153,827	658,811,548	66,939,412	10,524,161,005
2090	3,903,238,814	1,263,337,367	4,833,369,114	648,740,397	68,715,329	10,717,401,021
2100	4,184,577,429	1,249,292,969	4,711,514,029	638,815,665	69,648,478	10,853,848,570

United Nations, Department of Economic and Social Affairs, Population Division (2013). World Population Prospects: The 2012 Revision. Projected populations based on the medium-fertility variant.

230

CHAPTER 6

Cultural evolution
An Evolving Vision for
Our Third Generation

The hidden aim for the multicultural mosaic is to have the third generation of any ethnic minority become fundamentally assimilated within the mainstream culture. The third generation has been conceived and raised in the well-established Canadian cultural mosaic and their interaction with the rest of the community also has a common platform that has been designed to keep them within its limits without any force. Currently approximately 41% of Canadians are first or second generation and one fifth of today's Canadians were born outside of Canada and according to the Statistics Canada projects that by 2031, nearly one half of Canadians above the age of 15 will be foreign-born have one foreign – born parent. The generation averages about 25 years from the birth of a parent to the birth of a child. After taking into consideration that the older generations had their marriages early and gave birth at an early age and these days in the urban cities it has reached to late twenties and early thirties the First Europeans who settled down in Canada almost four hundred years ago and their current generations have been accounted for the twelfth generation.

Although Canada designed the Multiculturalism Act based on both bicultural and bilingual polices and has given ample opportunities for many groups to promote and protect their respective heritage values while at the same time integrating with the mainstream; the hidden truth is that when the third generation is growing, they are empowered more by the mainstream culture. Their way of thinking, conception of social ideas and interaction with parents, senior citizens, teachers and so forth are far more inclined towards mainstream cultural values. In fact the core values of any culture, regardless of its nature and origin, evolve around the formation of individual thoughts starting from the interaction from within the family which is the smallest unit of society to national level.

Let us examine the impact of symbolic cultural exhibits such as folk aesthetic arts in community life. It has taken a prominent role in promoting the status of heritage values by the expressing the dynamics of the values through the performing arts in which the direct role of the expression through its language does not monopolize and those who do not understand the language or who are illiterate in the said language are entertained and this in turn helps us keep the identity alive. These types of activities supplement the deficiency in learning heritage language or languages in question.

Many are not highly impressed with the learning of the heritage languages by the third generation in terms of enrolment and the cultural performances are not matching the expectations sought. Who is to blame for this however? Is it the teachers? Is it the students, or is it the parents or the influence of the heavy workload the mainstream curriculum at school?

I have done a comparative study with other ethnic groups, regarding this issue and it reveals that there is only a small fraction of variation among these ethnic groups. First of all in many ethnic groups not more than thirty percent of the children in the third generation learn their heritage languages at least up to the functional literacy level and complete both primary and secondary levels. Language is one of the most powerful tools in the promotion of heritage values and maintains the identity and passes it to the forthcoming generations. However with the environment that the third generation is functioning in, communicating the mainstream first language is faster and easier. There is research which reveals that anyone who can speak more than one language has better communication skills than those who speak only one language. This means that learning a heritage language is an asset. My main concern is that the skills acquired in learning to speak the first language has an impact on second or third language learning; Therefore it would be better for the teachers in the heritage language classes to have a sound knowledge of the first language of the students. Furthermore, the teachers also need to be familiar with the teaching methodology for the second or third language in the environment of the first language for it is important to remember that the students were born in Canada and are more comfortable with the mainstream style of learning.

When it comes to the arts, we have to find ways to collaborate and include those who are able to function in the heritage languages and those who are not. Those who have the various artistic skills and are interested in developing them further need to be encouraged even if they are literate in their heritage language. Those who are illiterate in their heritage language should not be ignored however; rather they should be directed and guided in promoting our heritage values in their first language. Of course we highly appreciate and are grateful to those who value and engage themselves in learning their heritage language, but learning a heritage language is not easy for some and we must be open to compromise.

Our primary goal and concern is to keep our identity strong while promoting ourselves in the international arena. We must be clear in our vision and without any further delay we have to expend much effort in this without undermining one another and we need to allocate a portion of our time and resources to these goals. This is not confined to the intellectual circles, we must all be involved. Tamils was forced by the war to flee and migrate to almost seventy countries within last three decades and this is a blessing in disguise. We should make optimal use of this to help benefit people in these countries while taking into consideration that there are those who may have a biased opinion about Tamils. This is a very large task and must be handled with grace and care. My sincere request to the third generation is this: Please be proud of who you are and what you have inherited from your forefathers and carry the beauty and richness of this culture forward in the best way that you can.

Apples with Oranges

"Mom, this is Canada. I am eighteen years old; I know what I am doing and please stop advising me in a commanding manner because it is interfering in my personal life. If you continue behaving in this way, I may have to find my own way and get prepared for the consequences and mind you, the ball is in your court"

I have heard such heated conversations between the first generation of Canadians and their second generation who have been residing under the same roof. I am very certain that the wide range of this generation-gap among the new immigrants in Canada and probably in other receiving countries in the west and Australia from the source countries is not peculiar or remote or exceptional to a particular ethnic group. Rather, this has been a battle that has been ongoing between the two generations in many families, regardless of their color, religious and regional backgrounds.

The children of this new generation in the cosmopolitan cities aggressively demand better and more self centered freedom for themselves. They create their own world and live the way they want and then look for justifications for their contrary behaviour and attitudes from their parents. The modern cosmopolitan cities have moulded their own culture which deviates from any single heritage cultural values. It is as if the process of the cultural melting pot with its many cultures and all of its roots with their own flavour got lost in the melting process and the flavour that results is an unrecognizable combination for it has its own unique qualities. The interesting part of this culture is that it is foreign to the cultures of the hinterland and its surroundings, but closer to other urban cities located in other places around the world as such. Torontonian culture is closer to that of Paris, London in the United Kingdom, New York, and Tokyo than its hinterlands.

The complexity of the nature of urban regions in all aspects has directly or indirectly impacted everyone and for an example, let me begin with the demographic composition. The density of the population itself is high in the history of human beings. The method of calculating the density of the population by area is divided by the total population per square kilometre; however this does not reflect the true nature of the demographic pattern. Furthermore, this calculation does not determine the relationship between the economies and whether or not it can sustain the population, nor does it determine if a country is over or under populated. For example, two cites may have almost equal density in population but there may be variations regarding the economic strength and the distribution of wealth. There will be different impacts on life patterns such as communication, interaction, hospitality, unemployment, crime rates, law and order, and moral values. Although the nature of urban cultures have similar roots, still each and every one has its own variation and therefore its analysis has two sides and has to be dealt in terms of micro and macro.

The structure of urban economic activities are in most cases based on free enterprise where an individual has, if not absolute freedom, more freedom than ever before in human history. In the old days, under the divine rights of the Monarchy, the feudal system of government was the main source of wealth and the bulk of the economic activities were controlled by a handful of so-called higher ranking and well positioned people. It was also a closed system whereby any skilful or capable person on the grass root level would not be able to take over for advancement was confined to the higher ranking family circle who had in turn inherited it from their ancestors. There was a steady and stable life for almost all citizens in certain designated areas and the mobility of the inhabitants was highly restricted and there was less hope for change in their economic sector. The two main sources of income were agriculture and trade and both of these fields did not accommodate large numbers of people and the density of the population was very sparse.

The turning point in the global economy which made a huge impact on the most number of lives was the introduction of the industrial revolution in the United Kingdom in the later part of the eighteenth and early nineteenth centuries. Since then, industrialization has been in a continuous process around the world and has deeply penetrated into the developing nations even in this twenty- first century. The manufacturing industry brought mass scale production of goods directly and widened the service industry rapidly and also improved agriculture. There also began widespread settlement into the urban areas as opposed to the nomadic lifestyle.

The modern industrial sector has four main factors involved in production and they are: the land and buildings, capital, entrepreneurs and labour and the rewards from the gains of production respectively rent, interest, profit and wages. Since the entrepreneur is the only part of the entire process which bears the risk, they are rewarded with a high percentage of the income. The labourers are more in numbers and gain a comparatively low share from the income as their wages. However, the structure of modern society has given birth into three main classes; the rich who control a major share of the wealth, the low income class living at the grass roots level mainly the labourers living hand to mouth and the middle class who are neither rich nor struggling for their survival. The reflection of these economic classes fundamentally changed life and culture accordingly.

Let us also into the socio-economic background of the new comers in the developed nations. Most of the new immigrants can be categorized into three groups and they are: the independent class immigrants which include skilled workers and investors. The second group is the family class immigrants which mainly includes members of the family who have been sponsored by permanent residents or citizens of the country from where they have been residing. The third group is the refugees who seek asylum as victims of war or natural calamities.

Those who have fled as refugees with their children have brought a lot of pain, emotional and psychological depression and their behaviour at times are deemed unacceptable even by their own community. There is also the difficulty in that some experiences are so upsetting that for some refugees, recovery is very difficult.

The geographical distribution of the majority of recent new immigrants to Canada is mostly concentrated in the cities. Most of them came from rural areas of the sources countries such as Asia, the Middle East and Africa. Their cultures and languages are not close as compared to the Europeans and Australians when contrasted with the mainstream Canadians. Most of these new immigrants undergo two main cultural shocks; the first one being that the mainstream culture and their languages are not similar to theirs and the second is that their status and the occupations back in their respective countries are not comparable to what they get in Canada though eventually some of these new immigrants do become qualified and acquire jobs in their field. For some however, due to economic necessity get jobs outside their fields and for a small percentage, this continues for the rest of their lives.

In spite, of these two components there is another factor that affects their life and that is the global revolution in technology which began in the 1990s which has affected not only new immigrants but also the rest of the population. The technological revolution has made the global village into a global family with the ability to share many things faster, easier, and more cheaply. The internet, e-mail, cell phones and electronic media have made the quality of life better. These items, such as the cell phone, were once considered a luxury but today they have become essential commodities. It has improved the standard of living but it never came free of charge. Rather, the cost of living increased and pushed many immigrants to search for other venues in finding second jobs or to improve their skills by retraining or changing their profession. Its negative impact in their life is that they spend less, and in some cases the husband works the evening shift while his spouse is engaged in a day time job and the cell phone and the door of the refrigerator is the venue for passing information to each other. They hardly spend time together with their children and share their family values and this pushes the children to seek companionship elsewhere.

However, I do not want to give the impression that economic and technological developments are the only reasons for the structural changes in people's lives. The structural changes in the political system have also made a tremendous contribution. The decolonization process and the introduction of democracy have brought a new strength and importance to the masses even at the grass roots level. In countries where the principal of "one man one vote" has been in practice such as in Canada, politics has uplifted our moral status and has given a psychological boost. An ordinary citizen feels that he or she can make a change in politics by simple casting their vote in the three levels of government.

The politicians explored new views from some sectors of the population and brought awareness of suppressed or underserved communities and granted new waves of rights and privileges. I could pick a few main areas where this has occurred; the areas of women's rights, the fight against racial discrimination, concerns for the First Nations and recognition of same sex rights.

The role of multiculturalism in the life of new immigrants has certainly had some positive impacts on the first generation but its influence begins to fade in the following two generations. The second and the third generation get absorbed into the powerful mainstream culture. The exception of preserving and maintaining their root cultural values is one of the primary concerns for the first generation of Canadians but for their children who are either born in Canada or migrated on sponsorship are more inclined with the mainstream culture and following it is more natural and comfortable. They believe that following the root culture of their parents is like planting orange tree in a zone that is suite for apples. I am sure that the designers of the multiculturalism policy were aware of this process down. I know that it is a tug- of-war between the two generations and in most of the cases the second generation wins the battle.

In light of this, I would like to discuss a few examples. The honour killing of their own children by parents who have migrated mainly from the Arab nations and Asia is a very real and recent issue in this country. It has become an unacceptable issue for the western world including Canada. These children want to be like any other age group in their circle with whom they are learning from in school and outside. When they become involved in a dating relationship, they do not feel like they are engaging in any sort of sin or bad behaviour.

For their parents, particularly maintaining the virginity of the girls until their marriage t and ensuring their modesty after marriage by not getting involved in adultery is one of the most important parts of their life and the violation of this is a very serious offence. The parents must be made aware that according to Canadian law, a girl at the age of fourteen is allowed to have sex with a girl or boy of the same age or up to the age of sixteen. Western governments are set against honour killing. The relationship between the boy and the girl is more one of companionship and I do not deny the involvement in sex and in most cases it is unavoidable.

These days, if the marriage of a second generation Canadian does not work out due to obvious reasons, the next step that they take is to file for divorce and they do not consider it an act of shame or failure in life. In fact another major issue is the postponement of marriage due to long years of education, other commitments and other economic reasons and these appear to be down to earth reasons. Some may consider it would be hard or impossible to abstain from sex for an average person for such a long period of time. Though it is not common in the Middle East and Asian cultures of having sex before marriage, still the rigidity of the practice has somewhat relaxed in some cases.

Marriage is only a social function and recognition and legally binding but love is a more personal and psychological aspect. The tendency of making commitments in a married life is slowly fading in the cities around the world and living with common law partner is becoming more common. However, let me say that common law partners can and are just as committed to each other as conventionally married couples.

The computer industry both the hardware and software has brought the investment operation function so close and it also encourages the mobility of Capital and migrants from north to south and east to west and vice versa.

The multi-dimensionality of global migration is complex and its dynamics are very unique and is confined within a unified frame work and its distinctive look and migratory process varies from time to time and country to country and the level of migrants starting from manual labour to the skilled worker and also from refugees to illegal immigrants.

But the recent Immigration changes in Canada in this regard starting from the first of January 2015, the system of recruiting skilled workers under the system of "express entry" that does not allow the first come first processed and grants permanent residency status. Rather the companies and economic sectors as a first have to have taken all reasonable and possible steps in recruiting such employees locally and other reasons then they have to apply through job banks and then on the other hand the potential foreign workers either within Canada or outside workers who got themselves registered under this system will be pulled out and invited to apply for the permanent resident status under the skilled worker category on Independent class and then if they meet all other requirements they will be granted the status and after migrating into Canada they do not have to look for in any available sectors and job in their field of expertise and also in order of the chosen the province on their priority basis. It is a brand new system as far as Canadian Immigration policy is concerned and it is too early to judge the effectiveness and it sound more benefited by the new Immigration who will have the job satisfaction on continuing in the field where he has the exercise and skills and also for the country in utilizing their expertise skills for the best interest for the economy and optimum level of utilizing his /her potentiality and what is the point of allowing them to migrant and grab the jobs of those who are local and unemployed. It is a winning situation for both sides.

There is a new trend of a wave of immigrants for migrating not for the benefit of their personal or family life rather utilizing every possible means for a designated common cause at any cost even against the interests of the nation that had given them privileges and rights and accommodated them. The terrorists from South America, the Middle East, Europe and Asia are operating quietly in the USA, Canada and in most of the western countries in Europe and countries that are merging into world super power nations like India and China. They are determined to be a part of their groups or organizations that plan and execute their agenda at any cost and do not hesitate in making use of every available resource and do not mind sacrificing their personal benefits and comforts even at the cost of their valuable lives in the capacity of suicide bombers without hesitation and without even expecting a reward in this world or in heaven.

I have personally had some opportunities in terms of associating with some of these groups in Ethiopia at the time when the Ethiopians were fighting for an Independent nation during and after Emperor Haile Selassie's regime, under the rule of Mengistu Haile Mariam's ruthless rule. Though I was not a supporter for either of them, I was working in a mighty secondary school and spoke Amharic fluently and had integrated with the locals very well. Because of these things, I was able to understand the situation and sensed certain political motives. I was able to notice that some of my teachers and ordinary citizens were engaged in some anti-governmental activities aimed at over throwing the emperor and conducting secret meeting in the jungles during most of their the weekends and holidays, but managed their duties perfectly well. I being a foreign contract worker carried out my assignments as guided and left the activities of the teachers during their off time alone as it was none of my concern. I also noticed that the security agents were rampant everywhere and they were vigilantly monitoring at all levels and took action ruthlessly like most of the tranny monarchies.

The Eritrean independence network was also very effective and those who were working for their movements outside of the Eritrean territory but within Ethiopia were almost doing the same things as the anti-Emperor movements but these ones were well organized and better equipped. But when came to sacrificing their lives, it was not to the same degree.

During the regime of Mengistu Haile Mariam though he was ruthless in not only eliminating all opponents but also the potential rivals who were right hand personnel and in a high ranking position in the forces were eliminated. Their tactics were such that once someone had to be eliminated when she or he was a potential treat for their power struggle, they prepare a fabricated list of false accusations and then assassinated them and blamed them by accusing them of treason, misuse of public properties, money, abusing human rights, working in collaboration with anti-national and government forces, the Central Intelligent agent and so on. He did it twice by assassinating two of the leaders. Even after the dedicated sacrifices that were made by the Eritreans and Ethiopians, Magistua made use of the people and the country at large for his own fame and finally when the crisis and opposition mounted he deserted the nation and escaped from the situation to Tanzania for asylum, like Idi Amin from Uganda, and Marcos from the Philippines to USA.

Humanity beyond Boundaries

A typical city man's heart would not feel comfortable opening his mail box on a Friday evening just after completing his forty hours for the week and about begin his lovely weekend with a long list of entertaining programs because the mail man certainly would not have delivered any cheques or vouchers; rather what would likely await him would be the utility, credit card and telephone bills along with a bunch of flyers that tempt him into buying more and emptying the wallet.

Let's move on a few hours' drive to the agrarian society and meet with the traditional farmers and converse about their expectations and achievements in their lives. They start their conversation after taking a deep breath empowered with gloomy emotion. Their conversation reveals that they see those who live in the city as the blessed ones who have a well-protected, established and secure life and the bottom line is their life is like a boat sailing in uncertain waters. They always say that the lifeline of their occupation is the weather and in most cases it is unpredictable and the consequences of crop failure or a less than bountiful yield are negative due to the structure of the market and the determination of the pricing is mostly controlled by the buyers and the middle men who are on the other side of the economic coin.

Where do we go from here? From the highly sophisticated modern man to the primitive man, humanity has been struggling to meet the needs in their life by various means. No matter what their level of progress and achievement, their objectives in life have not been altered nor has it deviated or changed. The only objective for all seven billion human beings and those passed through this life circle from the first man who evolved from the modern monkey almost four hundred thousand years ago is to be happy.

It is impossible to define happiness in a way that can be accepted by all for as the saying goes, one man's food is another man's poison. For a person who has become influenced or has gone up to the level of addiction to alcohol, the means of happiness can be only derived through it where as another person who is so interested in sex would not mind forgoing alcohol. I can cite a long list of other examples but the bottom line is how do we make ourselves happy for a longer period of time, if not for ever, with limited resources and the limited time of one's life expectancy. At this junction we shouldn't forget that once a need or want is satisfied, it does not reduce from the scale of preference, rather another need conveniently replaces it. Lord Buddha emphasised that the root cause of suffering in human beings is desire and the higher the degree of desire, the higher the level of dissatisfaction and suffering that we earn and therefore handling the desire with wisdom is the only means for the reduction of suffering and thus elevates the level of happiness.

We could certainly acknowledge that human beings in due course of his evolution and revolution in many aspects of his life have reached a level higher than ever before. The progress in terms of reaching higher levels of material wealth or higher levels in education has made a tremendous impact in the quality of human life. But have these things lead to a greater sense of happiness? If so, than a wealthy person is happier than a less privileged one or the educated person would be happier than a less educated person or an illiterate one. There is no positive correlation between the two. Humanity has been searching for a solution, but cannot find it. This could be a simple task if you know the right path. It is not necessary to accumulate abundant wealth or reach a higher level of education, but I do not want to underestimate the contribution made by these elements in advocating for it in the global family.

We are people of two worlds. The material world which is full of materialistic desires is one that we must function in while at the same time, we must be aware of the fact that this world allows for some to unduly take more than give and denies many their fair share. We have to remind ourselves that the material world has limits and that the only way we can achieve any sort of balance is within the spiritual world. Indeed, such a balance is not impossible to achieve and here are some basic ways to do it:

a. Love every living thing as you love yourself
b. Make use of your time and resources in the pursuit of self-realization
c. Eliminate the contradictions between thoughts and actions.
d. Care for humanity and make positive contributions
e. Cross all manmade barriers and eliminate hatred

I am proud to be a member and hold the position of one of the presidents and I am also happy to be working together with others in the World Shiva Mission. I am very certain that this mission with the young, educated and committed second generation of Canadians, in the well protected and promoted multi-cultural environment that we can do much for Canada and for humanity as a whole.

Canadian Values

"We experience Canadian niceness as soon as we reach customs. The US border guards are gruff and all business. The Canadians by contrast are unfailingly polite, even as they grill us about the number of wine bottles we're bringing into the country. One year, we had failed to notice that our 9- year old daughter's passport had expired. They nicely, let us enter anyway. The niceness continues for our entire trip, as we encounter nice waiters, nice hotel clerks, and nice strangers." Said by George Rose/ Getty

"Canadian niceness is pure and untainted by the passive- aggressive undertones found in American niceness" said by Said by George Rose/ Getty"

"We we're a small group of people, spread across the second-largest national territory in the world.....

We have known that, in order to survive- or just stay sane- we had to watch out for one another; from the old lady down the street, the teenager at the bus stops who forget to bring a scarf when it's 5 below. Hence our general willingness is to proffer assistance rather than aggression." Said by Tara Gresacore, Canadian writer

Working in Pyjamas

Recently, a young and educated lady named Melissa Johnson in Scarborough, Ontario, Canada had exhausted all venues in gaining employment in the traditional way and ended up with no positive results. She was desperate to find job after losing her job due to the adverse effects of the current recession. Though, the need for a job was a burning issue at that time, still she was not inclined to make quick money in an inappropriate way and stayed far away from scams. Finally, she took an adventurous step finding employment online and her efforts brought great success.

It is a job that does not require rising at 5 am, dressing up formally and starting her car in the morning, ignoring the challenges of the weather and getting into traffic jams, paying high fees for parking and reporting for work only to return home exhausted and then prepare dinner and watch television for a while and retire to bed and repeat the same cycle to following day.

She is free to work as she likes and forget about the alarm clock. She does not have to rush into the closet to look for a matching dress for the office and start her car in the morning. All she has to do is stay in her pyjamas with her morning cup of coffee and begin to work. The schedule is not bound by the traditional 9-5, Monday to Friday atmosphere and she makes $ 7000.00 - $8000.00 a month working for companies that are worth billions of dollars.

At the consumer's end, this connectivity has penetrated all corners of life starting from work to the bed room. Photographing sleeping public employees in transit stations, footage from war zones, watching movies, listening to music, check the weather and traffic exchange ratoo, paying bills, depositing cheese at the financial institutions, doing online courses, on-line shopping, and communicating on Face book. Email communication has become a controversial issue for former US secretary of State Ms. Hilary Clinton who used her personal email address in her official communication with foreign leaders. It also entered into the modern wars and has played a vital role in America with NATO allies against Iraq, and during the Afghanistan war. Mr. Edward Joseph Snowden, a computer professional, former CIA employee and former US government contractor, leaked millions of world governments and corporate sectors confidential secrets in 2013 and the effects are still felt by many governments to this very day.

Online shopping is another aspect of the modern technological transformation and the investor Michael Aldrich, a successful English entrepreneur in 1979 never thought it would change the nature of global commerce. Online commerce and e-shopping now moves billions of dollars all over the world from e-shopping to the purchase of millions of dollars' worth of machinery.

The mobile devices as such the iPhone, smart phones, tablets, lap tops and smart watches have also allowed for a greater state of monitoring. These new devices have turned the concept of "the global family "into reality and have made revolutionary changes in the day-today lives of global citizens.

It also encouraged entrepreneurs to explore new venues, conduct research and invest billions of dollars for the building of the information super highway. Numerous firms around the world, particularly fast developing countries, like China, India and Brazil, coupled with the western nations moving in this highway from hardware to software. The speed of communication is faster than any other man made device and it is very high bandwidth rate, greater than a billion bits per second and China is taking steps to develop an even higher speed to help carry out interactive multi- media transactions. These costs of computations are also affordable and becoming cheaper. There is a substantial reduction in production and coordination costs and also due to the high volume of supply in the market and cut throat competition the profit margin levels have also declined. The short life span of the software industry, due to its improvements and the invention of ultra-modern devices, also contributes to the cheaper prices for these products.

Social media particularly 24/7 on line world of interconnectedness has entered the core of family and social life deeply and its contribution in creating, updating, sharing, and exchanging information, ideas, feelings, and personal data along with dating, marriage and many other family aspects by computer-mediated means is accessible and very inexpensive. These days it has taken the lions share in the time of usage of other electronic devices. Although social media strengthens the relationship with friends and family relations and other concerned persons, the absence of the face to – face communication is a missing link.

The baby of technology was born from the mother of Industrial Revolution in England and it was one of the milestones in the modern life of human beings. The effects of the Industrial revolution (1760-1820) were a turning point not only in the transition to new manufacturing processes in the economy, but also in every aspect of daily life. Though it has penetrated in the developing reigns later and brought in a meaningful life in the late 19th and 20th century, still its positive impact cannot be under estimated.

By requiring and having employees working from home is a cheaper, more productive and more cost effective option for the employers. Some the well reputed and multi bullion financial institutions conveniently get much of the daily work completed through the internet

This is the outcome of modern fast growing formal educational techniques in an informal way by propositionally replacing `` the chalk and talk `method of learning and teaching. The transformation of the overall life patterns around the world starting from the personal life to international socio-economic and political life the revolutionary penetration by modern technologies such as information technology has left no stone untouched, including the learning and teaching process.

Labour mobility internationally and internally has become an adventure in not only among the youths and early middle-aged workers in almost all categories of trades but also those who are well educated, reputably positioned and reasonably settled and having financial means for the next generation, still got motivated by finding his junior positioned staff abandon his job and settled in a developed country and doing well and occasionally visit back so off in their children's weddings and birthday parties by having expensive dress, music band, jewellery, in a high class party hall and touring around and it irritates the spouse of him and somehow motivate him to leave his position and migrate abroad. After migrating to a developed country only he realizes the naked truth that there is no red carpet treatment, he is unable to find a job in his field of expertise instantly and has to undergo certain courses and get license in praising. His thoughts have come down to earth and he finally has to seek help from his junior for initial employment for immediate means for his bread and butter.

Unskilled and semi-skilled workers are also flooded with dispirited and are uprooted for the transnational workers market pool. The developed countries also relay on menial labourers from the developing nations to do the jobs that their own citizens at times prefer not to do. Even in Canada in the 1970s after the shift of many economic sources from the province of Quebec due to the uncertainty of the ethnic and socio- political climate and then most of the moved entities uprooted to Ontario, particularly to Toronto and its surroundings. It was a peak time in mass construction of new high rise buildings, roads, bridges, condominiums and other infrastructure. There was a high demand for workers for construction and the interest shown by the locals was not sufficient enough and a large number of them have to be recruited mainly from southern European countries, such as Portugal, Spain, Italy and Greece. There were Chinese recruited in working in the mines recently, and most of the nature of washing dishes and kitchen help jobs in restaurants and demanding jobs in the manufacturing industries, seasonal jobs on farms, and live in caregivers, are mostly done by the either new immigrants or illegal immigrants. But the interesting part of the low skilled labour from the poor nations, the poorest who were desperate to migrate but could not because of the expenses that occur to pay the employment agents, as it was in the case of most of the hardly victimized poorest refugees as well.

There are another group of workers who don't want to leave their countries of origin but are not satisfied with the resources that are available to meet their target of having employment locally and internally move from one region or state, provinces that are designated politically and move out get settled and they are accounted for 740 million and its four times the number who migrate internationally

The radical change in climatology and the geological changes is another factor for the high level of migration both internally both internal and internationally.

Canadians from the eastern provinces were seeking employment in the provinces of Alberta and Ontario. Where there are ongoing economic activities in higher volumes in Ontario and in the province of Alberta the nature of the economic activities has made a tremendous "u" turn in shifting the main forces to extraction of crude oil sands, a single commodity business and related activities and development of high volume of infrastructure.

Among the international mobility of labour around 40% of settled down where their culturally different environments.

An Evolving trend on human resources

Maria is beautiful and wonderful lady who has been born and brought up in a suburban area in the United States of America after completing her college studies spent a short while in looking for a job in her field of accounting and business management and restricted her job search within the field of specialization and it was very demanding and time consuming; even to get an interview she had to climb up many steps in the high rise buildings in Toronto. Her charming and beautiful physique is added a little bit to her scores in the interviews. Her effortless attempts finally got her a position as a financial analyst in a multilevel enterprise. She's highly pleased with her working environment and accommodative colleagues and understandable boss made her to carry her assignments within enthusiasm. It so happens that her association with Mr. John Smith one of the co-workers gradually made the relationship more intimate and highly attached and in turned the new type of relationship as of boyfriend-girlfriend. In eighteen months period of time they couldn't resist the type of relationship as boyfriend and girlfriend and they wanted to be the life partners for each other and finally they got married. Their relationship as husband and wife went on very well without any mayor misunderstanding or disputes. Maria by nature loves birds and highly attached with reproduction of lovely birds. Since they have been residing in semi luxury condominium having pets being prohibited and somehow it was a thorn in the flesh for Maria. Those she was sharing everything without editing whatever she has in her mind with John still she was hesitating her desire to have a baby of their owe so that she can deviate her thirst for pouring her affection with the love birds.

She and her spouse were invited to spend their Christmas holidays with her mother who has been living in a small conservative town located two hours' drive from Sudbury, Ontario. She was so glad to spend the holidays with her mother in very relaxed and conducive environment from highly pressurised cosmopolitan city life. While in enjoying the Christmas holidays Maria was able to closely interact with the members of the extended family. John also felt closely accommodated and like a member of the family who has been sharing the family values with them for years. Mrs. Marie Johnson the beloved aunty of Maria had long conservations in the late night and it was so happen in one of those conservations they talked about the comfort and pressure of having children of their own and the only thing in a family life that cannot be substituted

Somehow both of them agreed to have a baby of their own and continued in doing their assignments at work and leading a normal life. In addition to their daily routine they also engaged in taking extra efforts in having sex primarily for the purpose of conception of a child. She realized that marriage is a social function between two human beings, love is a psychological ensign and sex is a human urge more of physical need and the combination is the most successful life and the reproduction is a gift of the union.

Maria was born in a practising Catholic family and is neither firm and blind believer nor a non- believer and at times only visit church for prayers. She is like any other urban citizens who are children in two worlds. While engaged in the urban social life and getting adjusted to it and facing challenges from various corners they have to take a bold decision and at times the religious indoctrinations contradict. Whenever John travel out for the business purposes, she rent out family movies and watch and also listen to music. While engaging her with these entertainments her mind travels out of the living environment and searches for answers to pressing questions. At times some portions of the movie do not attract her then her mind travels back to her teenage memories.

She was dating David Thompson who was her school mate and he was in grade 11 while she was in grade 10. After having a couple dates, a superb mutual understanding developed between the two. It was so happened that they have to attend a birthday party of their classmate in their condominium in one of the Islands in Caribbean on a Friday evening in the mid-summer. There was nice food and drink, excellent music and the party mood was elevated so high up to the sky. A slow song was played and Maria could not resist her feelings and slowly exchanged kisses with David and took him to a corner and opened a small package that was received from a male friend and she took the condom and handed to David and they had sex. Now she entered into her the other world of with full of religious preaching and seen a red light flashing for it is immoral to have sex before marriage and she begged for forgiveness.

She came down to the earth and went into kitchen and prepared a cup of coffee and brought it with her and continued to watch the movie. While watching, the cell phone went off with the display the name of John. She had a brief conversation and bid good bye and continued watching the movie.

It did not occur to her that those days of having sex before marriage with someone who may not be her would be spouse is a sin and also using preventive measures such as condoms, contraceptives, sterilization, withdrawal by the male partner by the time elongation, or avoiding sex during the unsaved period between the period cycle is also a sin according catholic faith and practice.

She recollected that Pope Francis had given some consideration for people who could be protected from HIV by allowing them to use condoms while having sex but not with the intention or motive of interfering in fertility with sex.

In 2010 Pope Benedict XV1 categorically mentioned that using a condom is not a real moral solution to the spread of AIDS but as a first step with the intention of reducing the risk of infection. It does not mean that extra matrimonial relationship is accepted.

Furthermore, Pope Francis while on a visit in February 2016 in Mexico he was cautious and made comments on the preventive side from the Zika virus, he said it might be okay for women exposed to the Zika virus to use contraceptives to avoid pregnancy. His Holiness also reiterated the Vatican's stance on abortion, which he described as an "absolute evil."

He further mentioned how earlier situations where the Popes how they handle it as such Pope Paul VI who granted exceptional dispensation to Catholic nuns in Africa, where they were permitted to take birth control pills in the face of potential rape. It referred to the conflict in the Belgian Congo during the 1960s and 70s.

He further said that Vatican's position on abortion is unacceptable in all circumstances, including cases involving Zika and the potential onset of birth defects. Abortion is a crime and killing a person to safe another. It is what the mafia does"

John arrived Sunday afternoon from the U.S.A and after having dinner together with her and went to bed and tried their best to conceive. It was a pleasant effort and she did not have her regular monthly period. And they were so trilled and celebrated their victory and the period came in and they were disappointed.

However Maria did manage to conceive again and the pregnancy was normal for a few months. On one fine morning she was about to attend a medical appointment for a periodical test. She was bleeding and almost fainted. Her husband started his car and allowed it to warm up in the cold weather and came back inside the home to remain until the car got warmed up. By that time he could hear screaming from the bedroom. He saw that Maria was almost unconscious and he rushed her to the hospital. She was admitted immediately and John waited anxiously. He noticed two nurses running up and down the room where she was admitted and a few hours later the doctor who treated Maria told John that once again, it was a miscarriage. This was a thorough disappointment and again the couple searched for some alternative ways of conceiving a child. One of John's friends had told him an encouraging success story of how he underwent a similar experience and how he and his own wife were finally able to have a biological baby of their own but in a slightly different way; that is nothing other than having a third person involved in carrying the egg of Maria and sperm of her spouse through a surrogate mother.

Maria was having a tug of war between her religious faith and the anxiety of having a baby. John was well aware of this and was able to read her sensitive mind in this regard and he had already decided that he was ready to have a baby by surrogacy. He was sitting beside her having a couple of coffee and mentioned to her that while he was going through some chapters in the Old Testament of the Bible in it was mentioned that Abraham's wife Sarah was barren until a miracle son Isaac was born and he told Maria that having a baby by the surrogate method did contradict religious traditions and beliefs. At the time Maria's mind was puzzled with what had been going on. There are almost a million women that have been suffering from the miscarriages and most of them are so interested in having a baby of their own by any means. Maria was wondering why the government should legalized abortion, but she also looked at the other side of the issue where due to certain avoidable circumstances almost eleven million women around the world conceive by having unprotected sex purely for the purpose of pleasure in having sex and this resulted in the birth of unwanted babies. Though Maria was confused, she finally decided to have a baby of hers by any means.

Maria then wondered about the actual process of using a surrogate. Historically if a woman couldn't conceive the entire blame was passed onto the woman without considering her medical history or that of her partner. But medical research in this sector shows that the inability to conceive could be on the part of the woman, her partner, or both.

Finally, Maria and her husband went to a clinic that specialized in the investor fertilization process. The processes is done very carefully by removing ovum from woman's ovaries and fertilized by the sperm in a fluid medium in the laboratory. In the laboratory the process takes two to six days and then the fertilized eggs are planted in the woman's uterus then the growth of the baby proceeds as normal. If the woman who brought her eggs to the laboratory is able to carry out the pregnancy she receives the fertilized eggs. If not, then the woman who agrees to be the surrogate receives them. This procedure is a relatively recent development in human history. The first baby born in this way successfully was Louise Brown in 1978 and the process was introduced by the Physiologist Robert G. Edwards.

Maria also looked into the economic and social factors that are involved in its process. There are in some parts of countries such as in India, women who live below the property line and struggle to meet with their daily needs with related income. There living conditions are not acceptable or at the basic level of human survival. Their shelters are made of tiny plastic sheets and are roughly the size of ten square feet with a corner to cook another corner to sleep and the other corner to keep their belongings. These shelters have no running water and no proper toilets. The volume of the water is so limited that any available water quickly becomes contaminated. Maria was worried about where to find an appropriate surrogate mother. In certain Latin American countries surrogacy has become a business and the unfortunate part is that these business enterprises exploit the surrogate mothers by paying them only a small portion of what the potential parents paid and deceive potential parents by cheating them out of their money and giving their much longed for child to parents who can pay more.

In the end, though Maria and her husband had all of the information regarding surrogacy and their questions were answered, ultimately they ended up adopting two children. Maria's family was actually very supportive of the couple's decision because they did not want Maria to undergo any more medical hardship for they knew that miscarriages were physically and emotionally taxing.

The intention of telling you the story of this couple (albeit a fictional one) is to discuss a very important issue that many people in Canada face—the inability to have children. Many believe that in this country having children is a right and any attempt on the part of the Federal or Provincial governments to implement any sort of restriction is wrong.

I am not trying to say that surrogate motherhood or invitro fertilization methods are wrong; what I am saying is that we need to have a mature discussion on this topic without trying to shut out the opinions of anyone who may have opposing views. Like many issues facing this country, there are no right or wrong answers and the answers that we develop now, can change any time.

Chapter 7

Canadians at War

Canada hardly engaged in any war and if there is involvement at all it is not in the direct interest for Canada, rather it is for global peace and harmony.

Title	Location	Period	Purpose	Lost
South Africa war *a.	South Africa	1899-1902	Supportive British against Boers	300
First World war	Europe	1914-1918	In support of Aliens	66,665
Second world war *b	Europe	1939-1945	In support of Aliens	46,998
Korea	Korea	1950-1953	Civil war	516
Peace Keepers*c	Around the world	1947-2003	Peace keeping	121
Afghanistan	Afghanistan	2001-2014	War against terrorism	158
Canada *d	, Ottawa Quebec	2014	In support of radicalization	2
Us coalition	Syria	2015	In support of de-radicalization	1
Total				114, 761

*a was the first time in Canadian military **history** that Canada dispatched troops to overseas war

*b over one million Canadians served during the Second World War.
*c. Over 125,000 Canadian men –in-uniform served in more than 35 countries over the past six decades.
*d. Cpl. Cirillo Nathan on 22October 2014 the National War Memorial Warrant Officer Patrice Vincent, 53Saint-Jean-sur-Richelieu, Quebec

Radicalization has been the modern global threat for

Pre-1956 UN Observer Missions

1947-48: UNTCOK—United Nations Temporary Commission on Korea. Canada sends a contingent to Korea to supervise elections and withdrawal of USSR and US from Korea.

1948-ongoing: UNTSO—United Nations Truce Supervision Organization. Canada contributes a contingent to the 1st peacekeeping type operation operated by UN observer groups in Palestine. Today, military observer groups (including 7 Canadian military observers) continue to supervise and monitor the ceasefire.

1949-ongoing: UNMOGIP—United Nations Military Observer Group in India and Pakistan (Kashmir). Canada contributes a contingent to the mission in Pakistan to supervise ceasefire between India and Pakistan.

1950-53: UNSK—United Nations Service in Korea. Canada sends the 3rd largest contingent to UN mission in Korea.

1953-ongoing: UNCMAC—United Nations Command Military Armistice Commission. Canada sends a contingent as part of UNCMAC to supervise the implementation of the armistice, putting an end to the Korean War. Although UNCMAC is still ongoing today, in 1978, the responsibilities of the Canadian contingent were transferred to the Canadian military attaché in Seoul, whose purpose is to serve on the UNMAC Advisory Group.

1956: Canada's Minister for External Affairs, Lester B. Pearson proposes to the UN General Assembly to send a multinational contingent to the Middle East, in response to the Suez Crisis. This culminated in the first designated UN "peacekeeping" mission— UNEF I.

Post-1956 UN Peacekeeping Missions

1956-67: UNEF 1—United Nations Emergency Force I. Canada sends a contingent to the UN mission in Egypt to supervise the withdrawal of French, Israeli and British troops from Egypt.

1957: Lester B. Pearson is awarded the Nobel Peace Prize for his remarkable diplomatic achievements and his innovative thinking in resolving the Suez Crisis through the establishment of a UN Emergency Force.

1958: UNOGIL—United Nations Observer Group in Lebanon. Canada sends a contingent to the UN mission in Lebanon.

1960-64: ONUC—United Nations Operation in the Congo. A Canadian contingent is sent to the Congo. The mission's purpose is to restore order in the African nation while assisting in the removal of Belgium troops.

1962-63: UNSF—United Nations Security Force in West New Guinea. Canada sends a contingent to monitor the ceasefire between Indonesia and the Netherlands, and help ensure peaceful transition of the territory to Indonesia. The purpose of UNSF was to assist the United Nations Temporary Executive Authority (UNTEA) in administering the territory, maintaining the rule of law, and protecting human rights.

1963-64: UNYOM—United Nations Yemen Observer Mission. Canada sends a contingent to Yemen.

1964-ongoing: UNIFICYP—United Nations Forces in Cyprus. UNIFICYP is Canada's longest UN peacekeeping mission. The purpose was to maintain balance between the Greek and Turkish Cypriots in their newly created island.

1965-66: DOMREP—Mission of the Representative of the SG in the Dominican Republic. Canada contributes to the observation of the ceasefire and to the withdrawal of OAS forces.

1965-66: UNIPOM—United Nations India-Pakistan Observer Mission. Canada sends contingent to the border between India and Pakistan to supervise ceasefire.

1973-79: UNEF II—United Nations Emergency Force II. Canada sends a contingent to Egypt to supervise the ceasefire between Egyptian and Israeli forces. The greatest loss of Canadians lives on a peacekeeping mission occurred when nine Canadian peacekeeping soldiers serving as part of UNEF II were killed when the plane they were traveling in was shot down.

1974-ongoing: UNDOF—United Nations Disengagement Observer Force. Canada sends a contingent to the buffer zone between Israel and Syria, and provides communication, logistics and technical support for the UN force.

1978-ongoing: UNIFIL—United Nations Force in Lebanon. Canada sends contingent to Lebanon to support security to the government.

1981: UN establishes September 21st as the annual International Day of Peace, celebrating a global ceasefire and non-violence.

1988-90: UNGOMAP—United Nations Good Offices Mission in Afghanistan and Pakistan. Canada sends contingent to Afghanistan.

1988-91: UNIIMOG—United Nations Iran-Iraq Military Observer Group. Canada sends a contingent to the borders of Iran-Iraq.

1988: UN Peacekeeping Forces are recognized and win the Nobel Peace Prize for their contribution to reducing tensions around the world under extremely difficult conditions.

1989-91: UNAVEM I—United Nations Angola Verification Missions I. Canada sends contingent to Angola to monitor the withdrawal of Cuban troops.

1989-90: UNTAG—UN Transition Assistance Group in Namibia. Canada sends contingent to Namibia to assist in the transition to independence.

1989-92: ONUCA—United Nations Observer Group in Central America. Canada sends contingent to Central America to monitor compliance with the ceasefire.

1990-91: ONUVEH—United Nations Observer Group for the Verification of the Elections in Haiti. Canada sends contingent to Haiti to observe electoral process.

1991-95: UNAVEM II— United Nations Angola Verification Missions II. Canada assists in monitoring the ceasefire. Subsequent missions in Angola (in which Canada did not take part) are: UNAVEM III from 1995 to 1997 and MONUA from 1997 to 1999.

1991-2003: UNIKOM—United Nations Iraq-Kuwait Observer Mission. Canada sends contingent to monitor the Noor Abdullah waterway between Iraq and Kuwait. Canada provides mine clearance and unexploded ordnance disposal duties.

1991-ongoing: MINURSO—United Nations Mission for the Referendum in Western Sahara. Canada sends contingent to Western Sahara to monitor ceasefire.

1991-95: ONUSAL—United Nations Observer Mission in El Salvador. Canada sends contingent to observer mission to monitor ceasefire following El Salvador's 12 year civil war.

1991-92: UNAMIC—United Nations Advance Mission in Cambodia. Canada assists in monitoring the ceasefire and establishes mine awareness.

1991-99: UNSCOM—United Nations Special Commission on Iraq. Canada sends contingent to supervise commission in Iraq.

1992-95: UNPROFOR—United Nations Protection Force. Canada sends a contingent to Croatia to monitor demilitarization of designated areas. The mandate was later extended to Macedonia to monitor border areas.

1992-93: UNTAC—United Nations Transitional Authority in Cambodia. Canada sends contingent to Cambodia to monitor ceasefire.

1992-95: UNOSOM I and UNOSOM II—United Nations Operations in Somalia I and II. Canada sends contingent to UN mission in Somalia. This mission produces no political success. As well, the mission gains attention and becomes a national scandal referred to as "the Somalia Affair" after Canadian soldiers is convicted of torture, assault and murder of Somali civilians.

1992: Creation of DPKO (Department of Peacekeeping Operations) to provide support to field missions.

1992-94: ONUMOZ—United Nations Operation in Mozambique. Canada sends contingent to Mozambique to monitor the elections in 1993.

1993-94: UNOMUR—United Nations Observer Mission in Uganda-Rwanda. Canada assists in verifying that military supplies do not cross the border into Rwanda

1993-96: UNAMIR—United Nations Assistance Mission for Rwanda. Canada sends contingent to the mission in Rwanda. Canadian Lt.-Gen. Roméo Dallaire led this mission to supervise the warring Tutsi and Hutu population. This mission meets significant hurdles as UN troop's witness the slaughter of nearly 800,000 Rwandans in what will later be identified as genocide. Despite specific plans by Lt. General Dallaire to retaliate upon growing violence, the UN does not agree. This mission is viewed as a significant failure, resulting in not only the loss of hundreds of thousand Rwandans but also a significant loss of UN lives.

1995-2002: UNPREDEP—United Nations Preventive Deployment Force to the Balkans.

1995-2002: UNMIBH—United Nations Mission in Bosnia and Herzegovina. Canada contributes 30 civilian police.

1993-96 UNMIH—United Nations Mission in Haiti. Canada contributes 750 military personnel and 100 civilian police.

1994: Operation Forward Action. Canada sends contingent to UN blockade of Haiti.

1996-2002: UNMOP—United Nations Mission of Observers in Prevlaka.

1996-97: UNSMIH—United Nations Support Mission in Haiti. Canada contributes 752 military personnel and 100 civilian police.

1997: SHIRBRIG is officially established. SHIRBRIG is a multinational Stand-by High Readiness Brigade created to rapidly deploy at any given time by the UN.

1997: UNTMIH—United Nations Transition Mission in Haiti. Canada contributes a contingent of 650 military personnel and 60 civilian police.

1997: MINUGHA—United Nations Verification Mission in Guatemala. Canada assists in monitoring the ceasefire agreement.

1997-2000: MIPONUH—United Nations Civilian Police Mission in Haiti. Canada contributes 22 civilian police and police trainers.

1999: UNAMET—United Nations Mission in East Timor. Canada sends a contingent to assist in East Timor's democratic independence from Indonesia.

1999-ongoing: MONUC—United Nations Organization Mission in the Democratic Republic of Congo. Canada is contributing 9 military observers.

2000-ongoing: UNMEE—United Nations Mission in Ethiopia and Eritrea. Canada sends 450 military personnel between 2000 and 2002.

2000: Creation of mandate by the UN Security Council (Resolution 1325) for mainstreaming gender perspectives in peacekeeping operations and to identify the importance and significance of women's roles in peace and security.

2003: On October 24th, the 1st annual International Day of United Nations Peacekeepers pays tribute to all men and women who have, and continue to, serve in UN peacekeeping missions. The UN invites all peoples and nations to celebrate the global day of ceasefire.

2003: Retired Lt.-Gen. Roméo Dallaire releases his influential book, Shake Hands with the Devil, recounting the mission he led in Rwanda and identifying its failures, such as the international community's reluctance to commit further troops to stop the violence. Dallaire's book becomes a significant contribution to the obstacles that peacekeeping missions are facing. His book identifies the failure of the international community to stop the genocide, despite the UN's involvement.

2004-ongoing: UNOCI—United Nations Operation in Côte d'Ivoire. Canada is contributing 2 civilian police.

2004-ongoing: MINUSTAH—United Nations Stabilization Mission in Haiti. Canada is contributing 66 civilian police and 5 military personnel.

2005-ongoing: UNMIS—United Nations Mission in the Sudan. Canada is contributing a total of 31 troops, police and military observers. In 2006, the mandate of UNMIS was expanded to include its deployment to Darfur in support of the implementation of the Darfur Peace Agreement.

2005: Member states approve a standing civilian police capacity and military strategic reserve force to make peacekeeping missions more efficient and effective.

2006: The Canadian Association of Veterans in United Nations Peacekeeping name August 9th as Peacekeeping Day to recognize the service and dedication of Canadians who served and continue to serve in the name of peace and security. On August 9th, 1974, Canada suffered the greatest single loss of Canadian lives on a peacekeeping mission; 9 Canadian peacekeepers died while serving with UNEF I.

2006: Canada ranks 55th (out of 108) as a UN peacekeeping nation based on its commitment of military and police personnel. Over the years, Canada has sent over 120,000 troops as part of UN peacekeeping missions, and it has the 2nd highest peacekeeping fatality with 114 fatalities.

CHAPTER 8

Radicalization

"The Criminal code is not a holy book. It's just written by a set of creations they're not perfect because only the creator is perfect. So if we are basing our judgment... we cannot rely on the conclusions taken out from these judgements". These words were spoken by Chiheb Esseghaier, on Wednesday April 23rd, in Toronto. I believe that these words were well chosen and were derived from his religious convictions and did not come out of the blue and they certainly carry a very strong message for all of us. Certainly there some truth in his words in the assertion point that no person is perfect in thoughts and actions and that true perfection is with god. But why was this statement made during a sensitive time in the judicial process and procedures. The suspect, Mr. Chiheb Esseghaier was arrested by both uniformed and plain clothed RCMP officers on Monday 20TH April 13 at about 12.20 pm at a McDonald's restaurant inside Montreal's busy Central Station, a Via Rail hub and almost a half hour later Mr. Raed Jaser was arrested in Toronto.

The accused men have been charged under sections 248, 235 (1) 83.2, 83.18, 83.21 of the Criminal Code.

Mr. Chiheb Esseghaier,

- Conspiracy to interfere with transportation facilities for the benefit of a terrorist group
  (April 01- September 2012)
- Conspiracy to commit murder for the benefit of a terrorist group (April 01- September 25, 2020)
- Participation in a terrorist group (September 25, 2012 – February 14, 2013)
- Instructing someone to carry out an activity for the benefit of a terrorist group
- (September 7 – December 20, 2013)
  Mr. Raed Jaser has been charged with the following:
- Conspiracy to interfere with transportation facilities for the benefit of a terrorist group
- (April 01- September 2012)
- Participation in a terrorist group (April 01- September 25, 2012)

It was a coincidence that two deadly bombs exploded near the Boston Marathon finish line on Monday April 5rd 2013, killing at least three, injuring more than 140 and is alleged to have been planted by Starwave,Dzhokhar, 19, and his brother, 26-year-old Tamerlan Tsarnaev, and legal action is being taken against the younger suspect. The twin explosions killed three people and injured 180 others and within a short period of time these two arrests were made on April 19, 13. The terrorism suspects related to the Via Rail conspiracy were arrested in Canada on 22 April 13. It is believed that there is no direct link between these two incidents but the root causes and whether they are identical or not have yet to be determined.

"We have to look at the root causes. Now, we don't know if it was terrorism or a single crazy or a domestic issue or a foreign issue. But there is no question that this happened because there is someone who feels completely excluded. And our approach has to be, okay, where do those tensions come from?" said by Mr. Justin Trudeau, the newly elected leader of the Liberal party, in an interview just hours after the bombings simultaneously occurred.

Tamerlan Tsarnaev was killed early Friday in a fierce firefight with police in Watertown, a Boston suburb and Dzhokhar was captured 19 hours later while hiding inside a boat in the backyard of a Watertown home. That is where he surrendered Friday evening after reportedly exchanging more gunfire with the police. Dzhokhar and Tamerlane Tsarnaev are brothers who were born in the former Russian territory known as Kyrgyzstan and are of Chechen descent and had lived in Cambridge for several years. Dzhokhar became a naturalized American citizen in 2012.

The reaction by Prime Minister Stephen Harper on the comment made by Justin Trudeau was as follows:

"When you see this type of violent act, you do not sit around trying to rationalize it or make excuses for it or figure out its root causes. You condemn it categorically, and to the extent you can deal with the perpetrators, you deal with them as harshly as possible"

Before I analyse these comments based on two different schools of thought I would like to bring another prominent politician Mr. Jean Chrétien for example reacted very strongly against the invasion against terrorism in Iraq during a very critical and sensitive moment faced by America after the 9/11 terrorist attacks in Washington and New York.

Of course any sort of terrorist act for any reason has to be condemned and we must give in the very least our moral support to the victims of these attacks. It does not matter if the victims are citizens of a friendly or rival nation because we are all living on this earth and we share global resources, knowledge and respect each other's rights as fellow human beings.

The Indian Prime Minister Manmohan Singh expressed his concern by saying "Solidarity with the American people in the struggle against terrorism "The Somali President called it "the most depraved and vicious act of cowardice" The UN Secretary General Ban Ki Moon condemned it seriously. The Foreign minister for Pakistan expressed concern by saying that "the government of Pakistan and the Pakistani people are deeply shocked and saddened by the despicable act".

The spontaneous reaction expressed by world's nations on the September 11, 2001 attack was very touching. Canadian Prime Minister Jean Chretien ordered all Canadian flags to be flown at half- staff for a month of mourning and expressed our support for the victims. The North Atlantic Treaty Organization pledged that those responsible would not get away with it. The European Union extended their solidarity with the United States of America. Australia expressed its concern as such " Australia's steadfast commitment is to work with the United States " The French President Jacques Chirac made a very sensitive statement " It is with great emotion that France has learned of these monstrous attacks- there is no other word- that have recently hit the United States of America. And in these monstrous appalling circumstances, the whole French people, I want to say here is beside the American people. France expresses its friendship and solidarity in this tragedy. Of, course, I assure President George Bush of my total support. France, you know, has always condemned and unreservedly condemns terrorism, and considers that we must fight against terrorism by all means"

The world's nations are worried about terrorist attacks more than ever before and many fear that these poisonous plants are growing in their backyards and will eventually threaten the peaceful execution of the government and existence of their people. Furthermore in many cases the fear against home grown terrorism will lead nations to report suspected home grown terrorists out of fear of getting blamed for not trying to stop them.

For example, both the United States of America and Russia are rivals even after the Cold War and now they help each other when it comes to mutual interests. In most cases the enemy of my enemy is considered my friend in politics. It applies in this case too. The Russian intelligence services contacted the American security services almost a decade ago about the suspected involvement in terrorist activities by the brother of Tamerlane Tsarnaev. The Tsarnaev brothers were accepted into the United States in 2002 and 2004. Both of them were born and brought up in Russia before migrating to America from the Southern Russian Republic of Chechnya. The State Department realized the danger in the activities of the Islamic Caucasus Emirate of Chechnya and placed it on the list of terrorist organizations.

China also has been under the threat of terrorist organizations, such as the Eastern Turkestan Islamic Movement, The East Turkestan Liberation Organization, The World Uyghur Congress and The East Turkistan Information Center. Likewise, the Philippines, India, Indonesia, Malaysia, Somalia, Nigeria, Afghanistan and many other countries around the world.

Of course, it is hard to define or have a globally accepted definition of terrorism and at this time there are over one hundred and ten definitions. None of the terrorist organizations has accepted that they are involved in terrorist activities and they proclaim that they are fighting for justice, freedom, and are against oppression, inequality, discrimination, segregation, aggression and invasion. Many of the leaders of these organizations who were condemned are now accepted as heroes or recognised leaders as such Nelson Mandela, Jomo Kenyatta, Julius Nyerere, and Kenneth Kaunda

There is other interpretation of the same actions and viewed not as terrorism, rather radical actions, actions based on fundamentalists, war against foreign oppression, struggle for freedom and nothing more than a holy war, a Jihad.

Mullah Abdul Salam Zaeef, former ambassador of Afghanistan to Pakistan, before the US invasion, once said that

"I wrote to president Obama last year, and to your Gordon Brown. I explained that it wasn't arms that defeated the Soviets, it was the people's sense of foreign oppression- and it will be the same for you." The message is clear that the war against the US by the Taliban had the primary purpose of eliminating undue foreign influences, interference, infiltration, domination, and invasion and they claimed that it wasn't a new phenomenon in their history, and it has been a part of their struggle."

Jihad is a very sensitive and commonly used term these days on the world stage. It is an Arabic term meaning "struggle" and it appears over forty times on the holy book Quran. It has been interpreted in many ways and "holy war" is one amongst them. The radicals somehow, want to justify their motives and actions in many ways. They say that they want to reinstate the Islamic way of life for the Muslims as they have interpreted the core of it by removing any obstacles. Some may have the conviction that engaging in violent means to achieve the goal is justified and that the ends will justify the means. Some might have considered that engaging in a holy war and sacrificing his life is their obligation. Those radicals are convinced of what they are doing and intend to do it and are in no way going to be compromised.

I have met some Islamic leaders and asked their opinions and some of them totally disagree with any sort of violent actions and they do have their own interpretation which is far away from that of the radicals.

There are over 1.2 billon people who follow the Islamic faith in all six continents and I do not think there is any umbrella organization that acts as a centralized organization which can monitor and direct them. Islam consists of a number of denominations that are essentially similar in belief, but have some differences in their interpretations. They do have some conflicts and confrontations within themselves and the two main denominations are Shi'a and Sunni and others such as Sufis and so on.

Mr. Muhammad Robert Heft one of the Toronto based Muslim community leaders disagreed with the actions of the radical's. In an interview with the Sun News Network, he said that "I think we have our idiots like any community, so it's not one or two. It won't be the first, won't be the last' (The Toronto Sun, Thursday April, 26, 2013). Some of the Muslim leaders don't feel comfortable in portraying any of these conspiratorial actions as the work of certain persons or groups. Instead they have generalized this as an Islamic action which gives a negative image of the entire Islamic community. There are patriotic Muslims in the western world who are thankful to their respective nations for providing an equal opportunity and they live their lives as peaceful, law abiding citizens.

Anti-Americanism is the one of the core reasons for radical attacks. However, it must be noted that it is not only America that is targeted but their allies as well. Many of these plots were discovered in the early stages such as the members of the Toronto 18 and the conspirators captured and charged. Many of those radicals believe that the American foreign policies either from the Republicans or Democrats are oppressive and harm the Muslims, particularly in the Middle East especially after the creation of Israel. Over sixty such terrorist attacks and attempts have taken place in America within last thirty five years.

On an international level, it is believed that the bombing in Mumbai, India on March 13th, 1993 killed 257 and injured 713, the hijacked Air France flight 8969 on December 24th 1994 killed everyone on board, bombing in Coimbatore, Tamil Nadu, India on February 14th 1998, and the bombing and killing of 224 in Kenya and Tanzania in August 1998 show us that acts of terror do not recognize borders and that to use an old expression, one man's food is another man's poison.

The Boston bombing and especially the foiled Via Rail plot tell us that we in Canada should not be complacent when it comes to terrorism for Canada is just as ripe a target as anywhere else. That being said, we must not live our lives in fear, for if we do, the terrorists win.

The best thing for us to do is take the advice "Keep Calm and Carry On" to heart.

Are We at War or Not and is Canada a Safe Haven?

We are not at war, but we are in a fight with ISIL according to Prime Minster Justin Trudeau and Stephan Dion, the Foreign Minister for Canada in an interview with CBC Radio on Wednesday March 23, 2016 in the House of Commons foyer when the entire western world was in shock after the terrorist attack in Brussels on March 22, 2016 that took the lives of 34 people and injured around two hundred innocent civilians.

This was one of the worst terrorist attacks which were also somehow linked to the mass shootings and bombings in Paris and the suburb of Saint Denis on the evening of Friday the 13th of November 2015 which killed 130 people 89 of whom were at the Bataclan Theatre and wounded 368. The Islamic State of Iraq and the Levant claimed responsibility and mentioned that it was retaliation for the French airstrikes on ISIL targets in Syria and Iraq. Though it was planned in Syria, it was organized in Belgium and the attackers had already attained European Union Citizenship, so they were technically Europeans. The immediate cause for the attack was the arrest of the suspect Mr. Salah Abeslam on March 16, 2016 for the Paris attack and the attack in Brussels was form of retaliation and the Islamic State claimed responsibility for the blood bath. This operation was carried out on a fine morning on March 16, 2016 with the blue sky kissed by the golden rays of the sun as the people were preparing for their daily routine and the time was around eight o'clock. It was at the Zawentem Airport in Brussels where as usual the passengers, their visitors, airport employees, airline workers, air crew and others were busy. Suddenly an explosion of a bomb at the baggage area in the departure terminal brought the normal routine to a stop and everyone began to panic and run for their lives. Another bomb blast took place inside the Starbucks cafe in the same area and altogether 34 people were killed and over 200 were wounded.

The Prime Minister of Belgium Charles Michel stated "What we feared has happened. In this time of tragedy, this black moment for our country, I appeal to everyone to remain calm but also to show solidarity"

The reaction of the French Prime Minister Manuel Valls was "We are at war". The French President Francois Hollande remarked "Terrorists struck Brussels, but it was Europe that was targeted, and it is the world which is concerned by this".

Both are recent victims of terrorist attacks and Canada recently had an attack by Montreal born Ayanle Hassan Ali at the Military recruitment center on 4900 Yonge Street in Toronto on Monday March 14, 2016 and was charged with attempted murder, two charges of aggravated assault, three charges of assault with a weapon and one count of carrying a weapon dangerous to the public. According to Toronto Police Chief Mark Saunders, Ali said "Allah told me to do this, Allah told me to come here and kill people," during the attack.

During the Harper regime on October 20, 2014 in a parking lot in Saint-Jean-sur-Richelieu, located approximately 50 kilometres southeast of Montreal Quebec, Warrant Officer Patrice Vincent was attacked by Martin Couture Rouleau who was killed and two days later at the Canadian National War Memorial on Parliament Hill, Michael Zehaf-Bibeau shot Corporal Nathan Cirillo who was on ceremonial sentry duty. These attackers are to be believed to be sympathizers of ISIS.

The Toronto -18 prepared for a series of attacks primarily targeting Southern Ontario and on June 02, 2006 it was uncovered through counter- terrorism raids and 14 men and 4 youths were arrested and these individuals were inspired by Al-Qaeda.

The nature and operation of these terrorist plans and attacks have their basis in radicalization. I can appreciate the fact that these people have a deep love for god and a strong commitment to religious devotion. But when it comes to unlawful activities, dealing with the laws of the land and protecting the citizens in and outside of the country, the behaviour of such individuals is not acceptable and our law enforcement and intelligence agencies must step in to protect us all. The actions of these individuals and groups should be dealt with vigorously. When the former Canadian Prime Minister Stephen Harper, traveled to Australia to attend the G20 summit in Australia, he was expected to focus in part on the crisis in Syria and Iraq, he said Canada does not support war on the Syrian government or any Middle Eastern nation — only war against the Islamic State of Iraq and Syria (ISIS).

The Obama administration said for the first time in March 2016 that the United States was "at war" with ISIS militants. The White House press secretary Josh Earnest said that " the US is at war with ISIL in the same way the U.S is at war with al Qaeda" The Pentagon spokesman, John Kirby expressed similar views regarding this battle.

The State Secretary of the U.S Kerry said "I believe what we're engaged in is not a full-fledged war like we were in before. It's a heightened level of counterterrorism campaign, and it will have its own pace, its own dynamic, but its counterterrorism."

"A war is something that can be won by one side or the other and there is no path for ISIL to actually win against the West," Trudeau said..."They want to destabilize, they want to strike fear. They need to be stamped out."

Dion suggested that the notion of labelling the fight against extremists as an actual war might simply be out-dated." If you use the terminology 'war,' in international law it will mean two armies with respecting rules and it's not the case at all, "Dion said." You have terrorist groups that respect nothing. So we prefer to say that it's a fight. "A fight, Dion added that the West is determined to win. "Each of the attacks will only strengthen our resolve."

He further said in a one on one interview with CP 24 on March 24, 2016 " The government will work to defend against extremists at home without sacrificing personal freedom.' "Here at home we have to be extremely vigilant and make sure we're keeping people safe, while at the same time demonstrate the kind of openness and values that ISIS finds such a threat to their narrow exclusionary vision".

Prime Minister Justin Trudeau is very smart in moving his knights and others on the chess board carefully. By inviting Syrian refugees starting in November 2015 to the middle of February, 2016 and separating the non-radicals from the radicals won sympathy and support before withdrawing from the air strikes. Then, the number of Canadian Special Forces trainers in Iraq who are highly involved in intelligence gathering, was increased and more money and resources for displaced civilians was allocated. After that we accepted the invitation to the state dinner and expressed cordiality with U.S President Obama and the Americans. After the unexpected terrorist attack took place in Belgium, he boldly mentioned that we were not at war which means that he kept Canada out of the US coalition in the war against ISIS, ISIL and al-Qaida. Though he committed during his election period of 2015 that Harper was not closer to the U.S president, he has now created an image of being closer to the U.S but when it comes to actions, he takes his own stand.

When he said that we are not at war it is necessary to point out that we aren't unwilling, unsupportive or against war nor are we wanting to isolate ourselves. We are willing to take part should the need arise.

U.S president Obama mentioned in the same text that both "war" and fight for the same mission is concerned.

"Finally, if Congress believes, as I do, that we are at **war** with ISIL, it should go ahead and vote to authorize the continued use of military force against these terrorists.

For over a year, I have ordered our military to take thousands of air strikes against ISIL targets. I think it's time for Congress to vote to demonstrate that the American people are united and committed to this **fight.**"

Among the western nations, Canada has been maintaining its unique foreign relationship and policies, regardless of whom the Prime Minister is and the dominant political party. Throughout the course of tie this country has fundamentally stayed on a similar track, except for a few rare occasions. As one of the U.S presidents said, the U.S does consider Canada like any other foreign county and it has a special place in their relationship, likewise Canada has such a relationship with the U.S, Britain and France. Though Australia has similar roots in terms of settlement, their political system and has the Queen of England as the head of state, it is also a member of the British Commonwealth organization; its relationship to Canada is like that of any other foreign country.

Canada is a young nation among most of the leading western nations with a history of only one and a half centuries of independent status is unbeatable and very inclusive in minding its own affairs without having any undue interference in the internal affairs of other nations. Canada never got involved and does not have any age-old or current accounts of disturbing other nations and facing the consequences. Nations like Great Britain, France, Holland, Germany, Italy, Spain, and Portugal colonized many nations around the world in all continents. It was between the 15th century and the middle of the 20th century that those nations were exploited to a great extent and used many techniques to achieve their goal in accumulating wealth such as creating and fuelling disputes among local ethnic groups with the motive of weakening their potential so that the anti-colonial forces were brought under control. For example in India the majority of the Indians are Hindus and some of them were converted during the Islamic rule during the 12th and 13th centuries and they somewhat coexisted in peace. But there were radicals in both communities and during the British Empire at times they capitalized on those feelings of enmity and secretly with the help of some loyal citizens slaughtered cows, the sacred animal, in the night and throw them in front of Hindu temples, and did the same with pigs in front of the Mosques. The innocent people woke up in the morning on the following day and someone who visited those holy places of worship saw the corpses of these dead animals and the respective communities were understandably outraged and the emotions reached a feverish pitch. Though they could not find out who had really slaughtered these animals, the Hindus suspected the

Muslims and vice versa. Both groups took revenge on each other so often that the strength of both these religious groups was weakened and the Colonial powers had to step in. Even today, seven decades after gaining independence from Britain, some of the Indians and Pakistanis claim that the Koh-I-Noor diamond weighing 793 carats on the crown of the British Queen is theirs and was unduly taken from Punjab during the regime of Queen Victoria in 1849.

I had been working as a school principal, and as an instructor in both high schools and college for eighteen years and due to my interest in exploring and learning about other cultures, I spend most of my spare time intermingling with local people and gathering valuable information. I have seen three sets of interpretation about colonial rule in their respective countries. A small group who are mostly practicing Christians are very loyal to not only Christianity, but also to the former colonial rulers for the reason that they have not only converted them into a new religion but also enlightened them and brought them to the modern world. Missionaries had built schools and taught them how to read, write and listen. Furthermore, not all of the developments established by the colonial rulers were terrible. For example many of the world's languages that were only oral (spoken) became languages that had a written script using a Latin alphabet due to the colonial rulers and Missionaries.

The second group has very negative feelings about the colonial rulers. According to some, their grievances are based on the fact that the colonial rulers robbed them of their valuable wealth and taken it to their respective countries. They too at times blame their former leaders who were in cooperation with this so that they would be able to receive some personal gains such as an elevation to the better position in the local administration, recognition and the accumulation of wealth.

I personally listened to a conversation with some educated elites in Ethiopia during the overthrowing of Emperor Haile Selassie in a coup on the 28th June 1974. They criticized the western world and exaggerated some of the adverse effects of western influence. They said that they were brain washed, and demoralized and that their culture, tradition, and customs were inferior, uncivilized, out dated and destroyed their overall values. The anti-western, anti-American sentiments were slowly growing in Africa, the Middle East and other areas around the world. One of them spoke in a mass gathering in a revolutionary meeting in Amharic, a language, which I was able to understand and speak, that "we are engaged in dirty washing from the baring washing made by the westerners."

The third group is the bulk of the population that is neutral and neither praises nor condemns the westerners for their past; rather, they are worried about their corrupted power hungry politicians and local chiefs and headmen who have great control in their respective communities. I give my thanks to Canada for being part of the few drops of praise in an ocean full of critical opinions and a few bitter condemnations.

We should not forget the atrocities and contributions made by the expansion of ancient empires such as the Greeks, Romans, Babylonians, and Ottomans the remains of which still contribute to current power struggles and radicalization in some pockets of the globe. The current cold war among the super powers of Russia, the U.S and China has been creating a lot of impact in positive and negative ways. They have earned solid support from some corners and nasty and negative reactions and both are fighting in direct war, cold war, psychological war, economic war, diplomatic war, propaganda wars, under cutting actions war, immigration and emigration war, ideological war, political war and many more.

Canada is totally free from all of these dramas, though this does not that we do not pay any attention to them. Rather, we watch quietly and see if our presence is needed.

Prime Minister Justin Trudeau must have a master plan in inviting more and more Syrian refugees starting from 2015 till 2017 and it must have some hidden political motives for the best interests of Canada. Though outwardly it appears that humanitarian sympathy, love, and affection for the victimized fellow global citizens are taking centre stage; internally there are other motives behind these types of plans and its fast execution. Though the main motive may be to take advantage of having primarily middle-aged man power in order to solve the shortage in the active population for economic reasons, political interests are still a major factor. Canada has been maintaining its unique quality in international affairs and this has resulted in having good friends and silent supporters. It is a political manoeuvre to drum up sympathetic feelings and win support. It will certainly create a gap between the radicals and its hinterland support. Usually in any war, the support is for the warriors. They are needed as a shield for them in fighting against their enemy in their own land or in targeted zones. By reducing such support, the strength of the enemy is reduced and psychologically weakens their power. By accepting Syrian refugees at the critical time, Canada will certainly uplift its reputation among the fellow refugees and the displaced sixty million people around the world and also win the hearts of people who have the same faith, and ethnic relationship. It may not pay back instantly and also it is very hard to access the success rate against the economic strain in having them.

The Prime minster has a clear vision for Canada in line with Canadian conservative traditions. It does not mean that he has undervalued the strength and motives behind the terrorist attacks in the Middle East. He made it clear to the world when he was in attending the International Nuclear Security Summit in Washington DC, with a dozens of international leaders by saying "There is no question that ISIS are not a state". The so-called Islamic State is terrorists, criminals, thugs, murderers of innocents and children and there are a lot of labels for them"

But he continued to say that Canada is not at war with the Islamic State. He further said that "what matters to me is that we are doing everything we can to contribute to the global fight against them and by stepping up our involvement in training in empowering local people to actually be able to hold against ISIL to be able to take back their homes and their land- that's how Canada can best help them"

He also expressed his concern on the gravity of the war on terror and at the end the summit on Friday April 1st 2016 he mentioned that

"We are all vulnerable in very similar ways to terrorists using extremely lethal materials, and therefore need to do a better job of sharing and co-ordinating, collaborating in our approach if we are to successfully keep our citizens safe from an increasingly sophisticated network of terrorists." We should also remember that during the Second World War, Canada was historically one of the original countries involved in the Manhattan Project to produce the first nuclear bombs. But when he did not hesitate to attend an Islamic Spirit conference in Toronto in December 2012 mainly sponsored by an outlawed terrorist organization, it was his bold step in his interaction.

We should neither overlook nor under estimate the threat for Canada by the terrorist. Even before the active involvement by the ISIS and ISIL, Al-Qaida had an intention of attacking Canada. According to documents obtained by the U.S Navy SEALS from the raid on Osman bin Laden in the compound in Abbottabad, Pakistan in May 2011, confirmed beyond doubt that Canada was one among the targeted countries like the U.S, Britain, France, Israel, Germany and Spain.

The recent influx of Syrian refugees

"Water, Water, everywhere,
And all the boards did shrink
Water water, everywhere,
Nor any drop to drink'
By Poet Samuel Taylor Coleridge

Canada sheds its blood around the world for world peace and harmony, protecting democracy, fighting against human rights violations by engaging as combat, peace keepers, military trainers, advices, humanitarian service providers from our Nobel, beloved sons and daughters who were primarily soldiers and civilians so far 114,761 and among them two of them as two became veterans on Canadian soil.

The western world has accepted the Syrian refugees for the most part with a warm heart and with the intention of sharing common human values and extending help rather than furthering some inner agenda. In fact, this is the highest number of refugees the western world has accepted after the influx of refugees after World War II. The majority of these refugees have certain socio- religious and geographic links and similarities and the ground in which they became refugees are also similar.

After having them for a short while the conflict of interest dropped as a bomb shell and citizens of the countries that accepted them such as Germany, France, Finland, Sweden, Norway, Denmark, Greece, Spain, Italy, Holland, England are very furious at their governments for doing so without anticipating the negative or uncomfortable consequences. The leaders of the concerned countries began to dance to the tune of the disappointed respective subjects.

President Sauli Niinisto of Finland remarked at Finlandia Hall (parliament building is under renovation) on Wednesday 03rd February2016 by saying that to criticize the international agreement on asylum. According to him the current international rules on helping refugees are out-dated and the right to seek asylum has become a subjective right to come to Europe even without grounds to receive asylum."

While he was making the opening speech of the Legislative's Spring term, he clearly said that if the Geneva Conventions were written now they had be significantly stricter but would still offer help to those in genuine need of assistance. He also mentioned that the current migration to Europe threatens European values. Migration is a serious problem. The western way of thinking and our values have all been challenged. This is a stark transformation, just few years ago we were exporting our values and regarded them as unquestionable, now we are having to consider whether even we ourselves can preserve them' The flow of immigration into Europe and Finland is largely a case of migration rather than a flight from immediate danger

"The flow of immigration into Europe and Finland is largely a case of migration rather than a flight from immediate danger," said Niinistö, who had been practicing law and has sound knowledge behind what he was saying and commenting. He further said "All estimates that the flow of people will increase this year. This is challenging the ability of western democracies to help and also challenging the very structures underlying the idea of Europe.'

He also said that The Geneva Conventions, upon which modern, western states base their approach to refugees, are out dated and states will need to be creative in how they apply them. Otherwise anyone who can say the word asylum will have the right to cross the border and enter Europe. He further said that the international rules were drawn up and their interpretation evolved quite differently.

"The international rules were drawn up and their interpretation evolved under quite different circumstances," said Niinistö. "I feel sure that if these international regulations, and the national regulations based on them, were drawn up now, their content would be fundamentally more stringent, while still taking account of human rights and helping those in need."

"There are therefore no good options. We have to ask ourselves whether we aim to protect Europe's values and people, and those who are truly in acute danger, or inflexibly stick to the letter of our international obligations with no regard for the consequences."

The president outlined what he feels must be done, saying that in order to protect European values, Finland and other countries will have to take a harder line on immigration and asylum.

"First of all, we must safeguard our foundation of European values – there should be no confusion about this," said Niinistö. "Secondly, we must help those who are in distress or being persecuted. At the moment, however, we cannot help those who are merely seeking a better life or feel that their circumstances and future are difficult in their home countries."

His speech was welcomed by Finns Party MPs, who said it aligned with their party's immigration policy. Sources

Sources; Yle, Suomen Uutiset

The assimilation of the new comers from these refugee claimants in the view of westerners feel that it is up to some extent inflexible. For example according to the Norwegian authorities that among the asylum seekers at least 61 of them were married minors at the time they sought asylum in Norway in 2015 and the youngest one was only 11 years old and 10 of them are under the age of 16. And two of them are expecting their second child. According to the law consent for sex is 16 years of age. Most of those married minors came from Syria, Afghanistan or Iraq.

The assimilation of the newcomers from these refugee claimants in the view of the westerners feel, It is up to some extend inflexible. For example according to the Norwegian authorities that among the asylum seekers at least 61 of them were married minors at the time they sought asylum in Norway in 2015 and the youngest one was only 11 years old and 10 of them are under the age of 16. And two of them are expecting their second child. According to the consent for sex is 16 years of age. Most of those married minors came from Syria, Afghanistan or Iraq.

"It's not good for our people, not for our culture, not for our life," said one protester at a recent rally in Dresden, Germany.

The Pegida (Patriotic Europeans Against the Islamisation of the Occident) a right wing German political movement aggravated the anti-Islamic sentiments and opposed Islamisation of the western world and also demanded the government to be vigilant and very restrictive in accommodating even the refugees and people who pretend as refugees but other elements who disguise themselves as refugees.

Influx of refugees and asylum applications in the Western Europe in 2015

Country	refugees	Source country
Germany	1.1 Million	Syria, Iraq, Afghanistan, Morocco, Algeria, Eretria, Tunisia
Sweden	156,120	Syria, Iraq, Afghanistan, Morocco, Algeria, Eretria, Tunisia
Denmark	18,160	Syria, Iraq, Afghanistan, Morocco, Algeria, Eretria, Tunisia
Norway	30,460	Syria, Iraq, Afghanistan, Morocco, Algeria, Eretria, Tunisia
Brittan	35,075	Syria, Iraq, Afghanistan, Morocco, Algeria, Eretria, Tunisia
Greece	10,200	Syria, Iraq, Afghanistan, Morocco, Algeria, Eretria, Tunisia
Hungary	174, 425	Syria, Iraq, Afghanistan, Morocco, Algeria, Eretria, Tunisia
European Union (28)	1,211,830	Syria, Iraq, Afghanistan, Morocco, Algeria, Eretria, Tunisia
Czech republic	1,120	Syria, Iraq, Afghanistan, Morocco, Algeria, Eretria, Tunisia
Serbia	N/A	Syria, Iraq, Afghanistan, Morocco, Algeria, Eretria, Tunisia

Linguistic nature and distribution

The deep rooted sense of languages a recent and most powerful component, the internet followed by computer technology, science and the traditional expressed 3Rs, reading writing and arithmetic in the evolution of human communication and expression on the human beings that has superior sixth sense, among the other over 8-7 million of spices has entered into the bedroom, classroom, office, transportation centers, hospitals, and beyond the gravity forces on the space. Although plants and animals communicate within and beyond their spices, still it is restricted with shorter distance and memory and its evolution is very limited. But the revolution in the evolution of the Human tools of expression of ideas, feelings, emotion, thoughts, and communication is phenomenal. The technological revolution brought global family closer than ever before and penetrated and changed the family structure, of the system of economic activities, pattern of war, within the last six decades is a technological development and in fact it is next to the Industrial Revolution in England.

Verbal communication with sign language before birth of the spoken language and then pre development of written languages was very slow. As far as the Native Americans are concerned still quite a number of those modes of communication in the form of language was still only at the level of spoken languages and not reached the next step of a written script. It is also unfortunate that some of those languages are almost dying and spoken by a handful of natives. Anyhow, even the languages that were flourishing and rich and in high command like Latin, Sanskrit, and ancient Egyptian are almost considered dead languages. One of the recent linguistic researchers says 90% of the world languages will disappear almost at the end of this century.

CHAPTER 9

Challenged Economy

The economic freedoms for production, investment, capital accumulation, distribution, consumption and accumulation of wealth for everyone is equally granted and the doors are wide open theoretically in Canada and most other countries around the world. But the gap between the reality and theory is millions of kilometres wide and it is getting bigger rather than smaller. The distribution of national wealth among individual households and the equity in business, financial assets, industrial and agricultural and service sectors is not justified in front of economic equality. Economic inequality is a serious issue rather than the issue of increasing the volume of income generated. The rapid changes in the wealth to income ratio is another serious concern in the economy and the ratio between the two and the changes towards increasing income from wealth is another area where income inequality has an impact. The distribution of income that is generated from the production from the four main sectors such as land, labour, capital and entrepreneurship is expected to be fair enough.

Before I go any further, let me analyze the basic structure of the fabric of the Canadian economy. The following are some the key areas in which the current and future Canadian economy will be influenced and allow the nation to determine the direction where we are to be headed, at what speed the mechanism will run and how to share the national wealth.

1. The maintenance and modification of the three main sectors of the economy, natural resources and agriculture, the manufacturing industry and the service industry.
2. Capital formation and financial sector.
3. The role of the Bank of Canada and its economic guidance and direction with maintaining the interest rate and Canadian exchange rates against foreign currency, particularly the U.S.A
4. Man power and immigration in relation to education and human resources.
5. Brain drain and gain and immigration and emigration.
6. Government economic plans and other development plans and allocation of wealth.
7. Welfare Capitalism and other public sectors.
8. Government debts, reserve funds.
9. The sharing of national wealth between the public and private sectors.
10. Globalization and the impact of the technological revolution.
11. Sources of renewable and non-renewable energy sectors.
12. Balance of trade and international trade and partnership with free trade organizations.

To start, the Canadian economy did not pass through the system of feudalism where the common people were treated as slaves. In many nations in their early historical stages passed through this; they kingdoms with rulers that claimed divine right and protected their accumulation of unquestionable rights by exploiting the strong religious conviction and unshakeable beliefs of the common people. As one can imagine, this is a very difficult system to live under and for example, in 1789 the citizens of France incited a revolution in order to change the status quo.

The Canadian and the American economies had been pressured into satisfying the interests of the colonial rulers as such the **British** for the Unites States and the French and the British for Canada. Most of the potential resources were directed and deviated in producing the cash crops that would enrich the colonial rulers. The Americans deeply resented this and were somewhat annoyed for the reason that the primary cause for leaving their beloved United Kingdom was not for an adventure trip; rather they had been deprived of fair treatment and were made to suffer whereas some of the subjects accumulated abundant wealth and enjoyed their life so well. The second reason for this is that they risked their lives in their passage on the ocean on vessels that were not well equipped with navigational facilities, and also a lack of medicine. The third factor is that they entered into a strange land with only high hopes and perseverance, courage and determination with very little knowledge of the inhabitants and the physical features of the land. It was not an easy task. There were conflicts the natives of the land where they had been living for thousands of years and modern weapons such as gun and so on superseded the low profiled weapons of the natives; still there was uncertainty. The fourth reason was they realized how they suffered in clearing the bush, constructed homes, built bridges, roads and also cleared the forest and levelled the lands for cultivation.

They felt that they were able to make some gains with all of these hardships, and only when they made some gain, the colonial rulers demanded the lion's share without expending any effort. There is no gain without pain. For these colonial rulers, the North American territories were significant but a fraction of their globally extended colonies, but for these people it is the only land with hope. I think the Canadians did realize this but the sentiments over the economic justification superseded everything else and they swallowed the bitter pill.

Canada is not only one of the wealthiest nations in the world, but also has a very stable, unshakable and well balanced economy and over the last 150 years, even during several recessions and the global economic depression of 1929 and the unpredictable and prolonged recession of 2008 Canada comparatively among the G7 nations is in a better position internationally.

The natural resources and related industries such as the arable farming, livestock and forest industry continued to be one of the strongest sources of income and engaged a large proportion of man power and also made both foreign and local commodities and service supplies. Mostly the primary source of income generated and accommodated substantial number of workers in the labour markets in the prairies regions from this sector of economy. Furthermore it contributes raw materials and a food supply for the urban and industrial areas and makes their life comfortable and also reduces their cost of living and also helps the government in reducing the import expenses and general export income. The subsidies for fertilizer and equipment are another way that helps the government make money. But the international trade agreements such as the free trade agreement with the European Union if it is accepted by both the parties and implemented the extra exports of meat will boost the meat industry whereas the expected additional imports of dairy products harms them. Anyhow when we look into the overall mutual benefits the nation as a whole will be benefited. The direct and indirect restrictions by the importing countries are another challenge that this sector faces from time to time. I would cite an example of an indirect challenge in that Mexico, Canada and the USA are the only members in the North American Free Trade Agreement but in practise it does not work as any of the free trade agreements and each country has its own export and import decisions without giving due concern for the member nations. Obama's protectionist policy on economics openly hurt the Canadian economy. For example, in some of the major supermarkets in the USA some the meat packages have Canada as the producer of the particular meat. The intention was not to promote Canadian meat rather it was to tell consumers to watch out as there had been an outbreak of mad cow disease in Canada. It is a simple act but it has a serious message and impact.

The urbanization and conversion of the arable land into settlements and city dwellings, the construction of roads, bridges and other infrastructure and mining and drilling are some of the challenges for the farmers. In spite of it Canada is blessed with abundant land with natural resources and still there are untouched virgin arable lands in almost all provinces. In the northern territories new minerals have been discovered and new mining and drilling projects have been proposed its expansion wouldn't affect farming due to the cold climate, such activities are at the lower level and the effect is insignificant.

The adverse effects of global warming has left no stone unturned. The low levels of snowfall for the winter wheat and the decrease in annual rainfall that causes drought and also dries up and lowers the water level in the lakes and rivers, not only for the purpose of irrigation, but also fish farms, hydroelectric power, recreation, navigation. In spite of all these disadvantages, still in the northern parts of Canada where the low temperature is the cause for the low level growth of plants and crops and this global warming in a way helps in an increase in growing seasons and better yields. But compared with both the effects the adverse effects contribute more harm.

Canada will continue to have a growing potential world market for its agricultural products due to various reasons such as the world's population has been increasing particularly in the developing countries in South America, the Middle East, Africa, and many parts of Asia and the increase will continue according to certain demographic reports till 2080 and then the global population will slowly start to decrease. The rapid increase in urbanization and the uncertainty of continuous income from farming is one of the pushing forces and the attraction of the urban life is a pulling factor. Another important factor is that when the economy and population increase simultaneously with the better standard of living and better financial resources also contributes to the access of more nutritious food. For example, this has been noticed in India and these days India has made a couple of restrictions on the export of rice in particular and some other products.

Although Canada is bordered with three oceans, the Atlantic, the Pacific and the Artic and excellent fishing grounds in the Atlantic Ocean where the Mexican warm ocean current mixes with cold ocean current from the north; still there is not a sufficient supply of fish for fish farmers. Interior fresh water fishing has contributed to the economy but at a low level.

The demand for agricultural products including leather, paper, textile, housing and some other constructions, for raw materials for the manufacturing industry has not been diminished; rather it remains in a substantially sound position. The agricultural sector also opened many other industries in processing, preservation, and other finished products.

Another pillar in the Canadian economy is the manufacturing industry that entered only after the industrial revolution in England and spread around the world and made a very significant impact and Canada is no exception. The mass scale production of machinery, spare parts for other industrial sectors including the automobile industry has made significant contributions to government revenue and wages for the large scale labour markets. It has provided a steady source of employment and revenue for the government directly as corporate taxes and income taxes from the workers. Canada fortunately has a revolving but solid market both internally and externally. Canada is blessed with sixty minerals and they are the source for providing raw materials as such iron ore, copper, platinum, sulphur, gold, diamonds, and also uranium, natural gas and abundant crude oil and its extraction and supply for the manufacturing will certainly make this industrial sector strong for another five decades.

The production of arms and sales is very profitable but somewhat controversial. The reason for that is there are no guarantees and one is not obliged to use the weapons for defensive purposes only. Canada like many other developed nations made serious commitments to the United Nations and some other international organizations in not participating indirectly or directly in any form of human rights violations. Canada had made sales of such materials to the Apartheid regime in South Africa, and for a while to some of the Middle Eastern countries. There is the controversial issue in selling arms to Saudi Arabia and the Canadian government under Justin Trudeau still wishes to maintain the commitments made on the sale in spite of criticism internally and externally.

Technology such as computers, internet, cell phones, and related software starting from 1990s has penetrated all corners of the world. These days it has changed nature of family life into international affairs including modern wars. It is brought people from the grass roots level to the cream of society. It is also highly profitable. Canada has a very potential capability in competing with China, Japan and the United States, but unfortunately does not have a substantially great market like China, India and the United States of America.

The labour shortage, by having the increase in the number and proportion of natural increase in population by baby boomers, is another challenge that modern technology and robots began to supplement and its penetration is also increasing faster than anticipated. In countries like Japan they have been very successful not only in the manufacturing industries; they have also entered into arable intensive farming. In Canada, particularly in Ontario it has swallowed jobs in the manufacturing industries and prompted the companies to lay off substantial numbers of workers in which there were some well experienced workers included. In fact, robots are doing the job efficiently, reliably, maintaining the speed, quality and quality with accountability as human labourers and at times are greater than them. Of course there are some occasions where errors occur and it can be mined when it becomes a substantial source of labour.

The final but the most important pillar is the service industry that accommodates more of the so called white collar workers than the other two. More professionals are accommodated in this sectors starting from the transportation, education, nursing, insurance, financial sectors, medical, corporate sector, government agencies and so on. It is the fastest growing sector and it is able to accommodate and also lay off a significant number. Modern technology has swallowed many jobs in this sector than in the other two. It has three levels of workers such as top level executives, middle level technicians and similar semi-skilled workers and the low level workers.

The role of the government is another area that we cannot ignore and plays a major role in policy making and implementing and its effects both in the public and private sectors is inevitable. There is always a tendency in sharing the wealth in production between the government sector and that of private one.

Gender Equality and Equity

The independence of Canada was granted by Queen Victoria, one of the most powerful monarchs and her intelligence, multitalented personality and courage brought glory to the British empire and she has an unbeatable place in British history though our Queen Elizabeth has over taken the regime in terms of length, (The length of rule by Queen Victoria was June 20,1837- January 22,1901, Queen Elizabeth II, February 6,1952 – today) and she has the same calibre of power and responsibilities as Queen Victoria had. Gender equality in the highest ranks of power such as a monarchy is not a pressing issue, but, at the grass roots level, it is a very different story and Britain and Canada are like any other developed nations were women have been and still are supressed, oppressed, and psychologically demoralized and many suffer in silence. There is also a kind inferiority complex implanted in the unconscious and subconscious mind and at times it gets aggravated and erupts like a volcano.

Thanks to the introduction of the industrial revolution that uplifted the masses from the feudalistic system of economy where both men and women were enslaved and hardly had any room for mass mobility.

When both members of the family become the bread winners it slowly put pressure on the women to claim their rights and privileges. In the industrial working environment large numbers of people worked in a small warehouses or offices where there was wider room for socialization. The exchange of ideas, innovation, discussions, and all sorts of socialization brought to them the realization that they have been exploited by the men.

The men noticed changes in their attitudes and behaviour pattern and somehow their efforts in maintaining their status became harder and they had to bend reluctantly.

It is the time that democratic rule determined by the one man one vote and every single vote counting equally, regardless of their education, wealth, and position elevated among others the women.

Fahima Osman received her Doctor of Medicine at McMaster University's Faculty of Health Sciences convocation on May 14, 2004. Research indicates the gap between women's and men's pay grows among higher-earning, higher-achieving groups.

Ms. Fatima Osman clearly brought forward the issue of gender inequality in the employment sector in Canada and addressed the gravity of the issue well. It is also very clear in both the unskilled level of jobs to the higher paying professions, including manufacturing, mining, and service industry, and in some other professions the degree of the variation is higher. She mentioned the medical field with a wider range of research.

The Canadian Centre for Policy Alternatives study published a comprehensive report on gender inequality in 2016. Here are some of those charts that exhibit the true nature of the inequality in income that is earned by men and women with differences in having similar education, experiences, age, and the level of productivity and carrying out the same assignments. Study author Mary Cornish clearly mentioned in her study that overall there is a 14% gap between the men and women who make the same number of contributions with same calibre in their qualifications and other criteria. It charts are given below to have a better and clearer view.

Average annual income for Ontario men and women, by decile

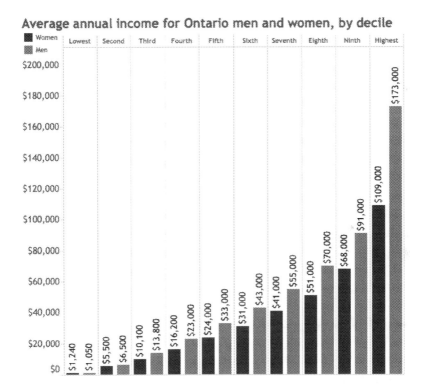

Men in the second grouping earn 18 per cent more than women in the same group; in the fourth grouping, 42 per cent more.

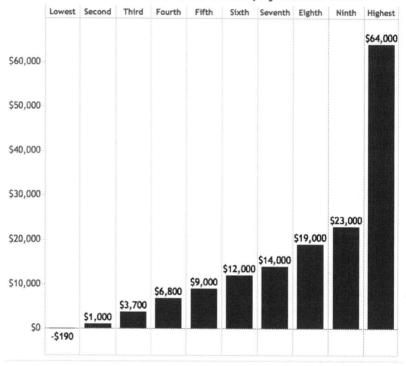

How much more men make than women, by income decile

Lowest	Second	Third	Fourth	Fifth	Sixth	Seventh	Eighth	Ninth	Highest
-$190	$1,000	$3,700	$6,800	$9,000	$12,000	$14,000	$19,000	$23,000	$64,000

The highest-earning men earn almost 60 per cent more than the highest-earning women.

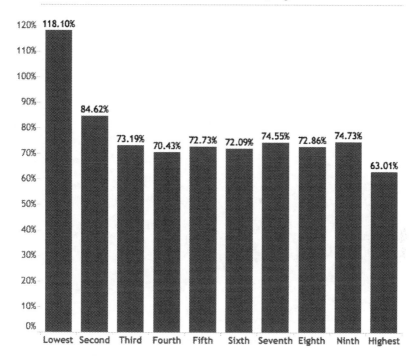

Women's income as a share of men's, by income decile

Lowest	118.10%
Second	84.62%
Third	73.19%
Fourth	70.43%
Fifth	72.73%
Sixth	72.09%
Seventh	74.55%
Eighth	72.86%
Ninth	74.73%
Highest	63.01%

These gaps persist in prestigious occupations: Women who work in health and government make less than two-thirds what their male counterparts make.

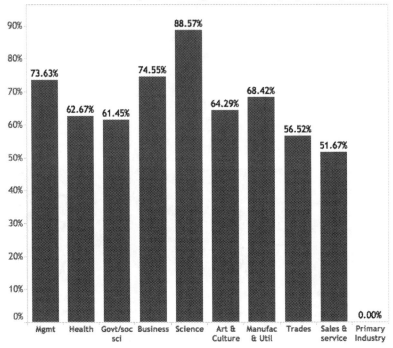

Women's income as percentage of men's, by occupation

73.63% Mgmt
62.67% Health
61.45% Govt/soc sci
74.55% Business
88.57% Science
64.29% Art & Culture
68.42% Manufac & Util
56.52% Trades
51.67% Sales & service
0.00% Primary Industry

The disparity persists no matter how much education you have.

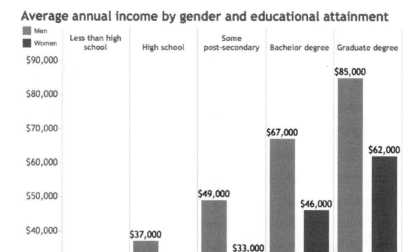

Average annual income by gender and educational attainment

- Men
- Women

Less than high school: Men $24,000, Women $14,700
High school: Men $37,000, Women $24,000
Some post-secondary: Men $49,000, Women $33,000
Bachelor degree: Men $67,000, Women $46,000
Graduate degree: Men $85,000, Women $62,000

In this case, however, the additional education pays off. Even though women earn less than men regardless of their credentials, that gap shrinks the more educated they are.

Women's income as percentage of men's, by education level

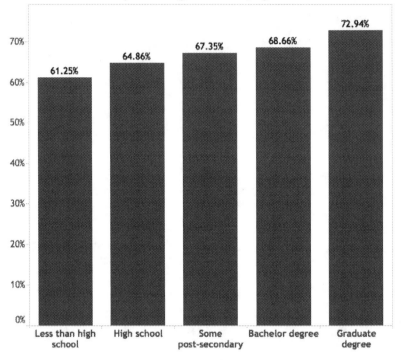

Average annual income by gender and occupation

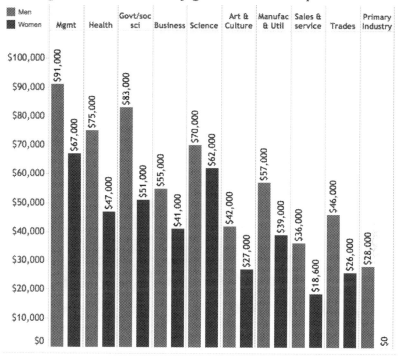

Men
Women

	Mgmt	Health	Govt/soc sci	Business	Science	Art & Culture	Manufac & Util	Sales & service	Trades	Primary Industry
Men	$91,000	$75,000	$83,000	$55,000	$70,000	$42,000	$57,000	$36,000	$46,000	$28,000
Women	$67,000	$47,000	$51,000	$41,000	$62,000	$27,000	$39,000	$18,600	$26,000	$0

$100,000
$90,000
$80,000
$70,000
$60,000
$50,000
$40,000
$30,000
$20,000
$10,000
$0

CHAPTER 10

Vision for Canada by Justin Trudeau

"We're more like siblings, really. We have shared parentage, but we took different paths in our later years. We became the stay-at-home type, you grew up to be a little more rebellious"

So said Justin Trudeau, the Prime Minister of Canada at the state dinner in Washington hosted by US President Barack Obama on March, 10, 2016.

U.S President Richard Nixon, had been prophetic with his remarks in 1972 when he met with Justin Trudeau, when he was only a few months old at a state dinner in Ottawa and said during a toast that Pierre Trudeau's son would himself become Prime Minister someday and what he said came true and he had the privilege in attending as a guest at the White House.

Let us look back to the regime of Pierre Elliott Trudeau and what was the view of him regarding the level and nature of the relationship with America.

"Americans should never underestimate the constant pressure on Canada which the mere presence of the United State has produced. We're different people from you and we're different people because of you. Living next to you is in some ways like sleeping with an elephant. No matter how friendly and even-tempered is the beast, if I can call it that, one is affected by every twitch and grunt, it should not therefore be expected that this kind of nation, this Canada, should project itself as a mirror image of the United States."

Let us now look at what was said by U.S President Harry S. Truman:

"For Canada is enriched by the heritage of France as well as of Britain, and Quebec has imparted the vitality and spirit of France itself to Canada. Canada's notable achievement of national unity and progress through accommodation, moderation, and forbearance can be studied with profit by her sister nations."

"Perhaps I should say "your foreign relations with the United States." But the word "foreign" seems strangely out of place. Canada and the United States have reached the point where we no longer think of each other as "foreign" countries. We think of each other as friends, as peaceful and cooperative neighbours on a spacious and fruitful continent."

Our Prime Minister recognizes that our relationship with the United States is between two countries, whereas U.S President Harry S Truman viewed the relationship as one between two entities even though the relationship was an exclusive one. This is quite a contrast in gauging the relationship between these two nations by two Canadian Prime Ministers who so happened to be father and son in their blood relationship but politically have independent views. The overall relationship with the United States is multi-dimensional and less complicated when it comes to fundamental structural changes. America is like an elephant in strength but it is a lion in terms of its power and it has many faces.

At this junction, up to what extent we are willing to extend our hand for a handshake is a very sensitive matter for us in Canada while it is insignificant for the almighty United States. The U.S knows very well that the nature of Canadians is such that it cannot leave its relationship with the United States completely and survive. Other than international political reasons such as the protection from air strikes from Russia and China, the U.S will have to have permission to use our air space. It has also been proposed several times by Canadian Prime Ministers Jean Chretien, Paul Martin and Harper claimed that the U.S does not need anything that can be received exclusively from Canada. Canada depends on various aspect of export income. Superficially on the surface, all nations are equal and have their own sovereignty, no matter how rich or powerful but in fact it is not the case. This reminds me of what Justin Trudeau once recollected in his book entitled "Common Ground" which recounts his past memories and mentioned an observation he made when traveling with his father at the age of twelve to India to attend the Commonwealth Heads of Government Meeting in New Delhi. He visited Dhaka the capital of Bangladesh to inspect a dam project being built mainly with Canadian aid.

"On the way in from the airport with the Canadian delegation, we drove through the Bangladeshi capital city of Dhaka, where we became hopelessly snarled in traffic. I was in the back of the government car that was frozen, like the rest of the motorcade, on a main road outside one of Asia's largest and most bustling cities. Everything and everyone around us had to wait until the traffic could move again. I looked out the side window of the car to see an older man standing with his bicycle waiting for the motorcade to move so he could cross the street. His face lined with age, he wore the weary expression of someone resigned to this kind of disruption. I remember watching him for those seconds that our paths intersected, and feeling an odd pang to realize that I would never know his story-where he had come from, where he was going, what his life was, with all the events, dreams and anxieties that made him every bit as real and as important as I was to myself. **And it struck me suddenly that he and I were just two among billions of people on this planet. Every one of us deserved to be seen as an individual, and every one of us had a story to tell."**

My point of view is that America values the concept of equality and openness and pays this back accordingly and I do not doubt this. Of course in the speech that Prime Minister Justin Trudeau made at the state dinner had re-imposed our special kind of relationship with the U.S which will make our relationship with them more cordial and in some areas the Americans would be even more cordial. But when it comes to major issues where bold steps have to be taken such as the pipeline, honouring the North American Free Trade Agreement and relaxing barriers in trade such as custom duties, quota system, having free trade agreement with countries like China, relaxing the economic protectionism policy or giving exception or consideration for Canada and Mexico, the United States might not be in such a cordial mood. I do not mean to say that the green light shown by my Prime Minister will not any serious impact, but we have to get into the bargaining aspect of our relationship.

We Canadians are very passive in international politics and do not take firm sides on many occasions. At times many of the decisions made by world leaders including the U.S are very contradictory in their own policies compared with the past. For example the relationship with Iran now is one of mixed feelings. Having relaxed the embargo and lifted the sanctions against Iran and the re-establishing a diplomatic relationship by America, Canada and many other western nations does not mean that there is a radical change in Iranian government policies on domestic and foreign affairs. But in order to punish the radical Islamic groups such as ISIS, having a better relationship with Iran will leave it in a better position to fight against a common enemy. An enemy of an enemy has become friend. In a similar manner, Canada and America resisted local and international criticism on selling arms and ammunition to Saudi Arabia, a government that violates human rights rampantly. Political manoeuvring and manipulations more the any other facts dominated the deal. Saudi Arabia somewhat unilaterally declared a war against ISIS and Al-Qaida for the survival of the monarchy and to keep the holy places out of the terrorist's hands and this has become the responsibility of the government of Saudi and a moral obligation of over 1.4 billion of Muslims around the world. Saudi has initiated a coalition with 33 countries and began to fight against the terrorists. This will give a big boost and relief for the American coalition fighters, and reduce their burden and losses. Furthermore, it also earns a huge sum of money and it will facilitate the expansion for the arms production industry and give some relief from the current economic recession.

At this junction the US, France and Canada put aside the human rights violation in many ways within its own people by Saudi Arabia, and selling arms and ammunition in billions of dollars' worth. The interesting part of it is in March 2016, Mr. Al- Mouallimi, of the permanent Representative of Saudi Arabia to the United Nations, at an interview for Al Jazeera said "Elections are unnecessary in Saudi Arabia because its people are happier with the current system of government than almost any other country in the world." At the time of Saudi Arabia advocating for an election in Syria advocating for removing Assad from the regime. Anyhow certain interest at times pushes the items on the top most agenda.

As Prime Minister Pierre Elliott Trudeau said "Americans should never underestimate the constant pressure on Canada which the mere presence of the United State has produced" we have to play our cards well and soundly.

The U.S did not comment highly on Canada when our government accepted the Syrian refugees; rather, it worried about potential radicals and terrorists that may pretend to be refugees and arrive in Canada and slowly and conveniently make use of our resources and make effective and efficient contributions to the international terrorist networks and by any means necessary enter into the U.S and continue their activities. I do understand the gravity of their concerns, but one has to look into its own interests as well. Though U.S has pledged to have 10,000 refugees, due to their state of high alert regarding terrorist activities, this would not allow them to make a more enthusiastic commitment.

America has a wide range of involvement in fighting against other superpowers such as Russia China and their allies from the supplying of arms and ammunition for ideological war, aid for allied countries like Pakistan, Egypt, and Israel, contributions to international aid, and space research. All of these assignments are complex in terms of investment, expenses, and then earning and maintaining the positive relationship. However, should anything in the relationship go astray, the United States government will react swiftly:

"Let every nation know, whether it wishes us well or ill, that we shall pay any price, bear any burden, meet any hardship, support any friend, oppose any foe to assure the survival and the success of liberty."
John F. Kennedy

Two examples that illustrate this point are as follows. The first one is the direct and indirect involvement in Syria and Iraq beginning in 2011.On September 22, 2014, the United States joined with some of the Arab coalition countries and Bahrain, Jordan, Qatar, Saudi Arabia, and the United Arab Emirates began to strike targets of the Islamic State of Iraq and the Levant (ISIL) in Syria and its membership expanded to fifty nine countries. In South America, the U.S has been fighting against the infiltration of communist ideology and the influences from former Soviet Union, today's Russia, and recently by China in Nicaragua, Guatemala, El Salvador, Honduras, Bolivia, Ecuador, Chile, Cuba, **Uruguay, the** Dominican Republic and Mexico. This has drained a substantial amount of manpower including the Central Intelligence Agency (CIA) and huge sums of money and other resources.

In a speech to the United Nations General Assembly in September 2011:

"America's commitment to Israel's security is unshakeable, and our friendship with Israel is deep and enduring. And so we believe that any lasting peace must acknowledge the very real security concerns that Israel faces every single day. Let us be honest with ourselves: Israel is surrounded by neighbours that have waged repeated wars against it.... Those are facts. They cannot be denied. The Jewish people have forged a successful state in their historic homeland. Israel deserves recognition. It deserves normal relations with its neighbours. And friends of the Palestinians do them no favours by ignoring this truth."
Obama

"[The] United States is proud to stand with you as your strongest ally and greatest friend. I see this visit as an opportunity to reaffirm the unbreakable bond between our nations, to restate America's unwavering commitment to Israel's security, and to speak directly to Israel and to your neighbours."

During a March 2013 visit to Israel; it was Obama's first trip to Israel and the Middle East was the gate way for the spread of communist ideology to the middle east and Africa from the former Soviet Union and recently both China and Russia have established a strong hold in the Middle East. The U.S has a long way to go in preventing the expansion of the rival superpowers. The U.S also has committed to a moral obligation in providing constant financial, military and other support for Israel and another cost of supporting Israel is the negative reaction from Islamic terrorist groups. In the Middle East the war in Kuwait, Libya, Iraq, Iran, and other countries has placed U.S in a difficult position.

The political manoeuvres and manipulations of the U.S Central Intelligence Agency around the world are like a world police service and to some extent the judiciary organ and it cannot be easily exposed and proven because of most of its operations are secretin nature, and in spite of this, much progress has been made. One example is Panama where the U.S was behind setting up the Panama Canal which is 77km. in length and links the Atlantic Ocean with Pacific ocean.

Today, Cuba has become a recognized nation and accepted, and is beginning to have a normalized relationship after living under a trade embargo, and a broken diplomatic relationship with the U.S over six decades. The Cuban revolution with the Missile Crisis of 1962 in which the Soviet Union targeted the U.S via Cuba, was as frightening as the terrorist attacks on 9/11. In fact Cuba though culturally a nation of Latin America, it is geographically a part of North America and this is why the Cuban Missile Crisis struck fear into the hearts of many. Obama is the first U.S President in 88 years to visit for reconciliation between Cuba and the U.S. The initiation and mediation for this event was held in back room discussions by Canada, Pope Francis, and Cuban counterparts.

The speech by U.S President Obama on Tuesday March22, 16 at Gran Teatro Alicia Alonso was like welcoming the spring of 2016 from decades of a bitter relationship between the two nations.

Let us now move on with the French leaders view between Canada with Quebec and France. When the President of France de Gaulle visited on July 24, 1967 to participate the centennial celebration with the world's fair, Expo 67 he uttered "vive le Quebec (Long live Quebec) then added "Vive le Quebec libre (Long live free Quebec)". Here the relationship with another founding member nation is bilateral and views on Canada, and claimed Quebec as an entity by itself while accepting the sovereignty which appears that it is conditional.

Let me quote from my book "Canada, the Meat of the World Sandwich" that Nicolas Sarkozy, the President of France and the Chairman of the European Union while in attendance at the summit of the Francophone in Quebec City paid an official visit to the Governor General and stated that the relationship between France and Quebec is like that of brothers while the relationship with Canada is between friends". It was said in October 2008 in the city of Quebec.

Anyhow, let me go back to the vision for Prime Minister Justine Trudeau. Just after having a landslide victory in the parliamentary election on October 19, 2015, Justin Trudeau, Prime Minister of Canada, expressed the nature of his vision for Canada.

"Canadians have spoken. You want a government with a vision and an agenda for this country that is positive and ambitious and hopeful. I promise you that I will lead that government."

His vision expressed in both words and actions with his personal approach has made a very positive impact among the middle-aged urban citizens. His appearance in public is at times very simple and informal without neck tie, and rolled up sleeves. He intermingles with Canadians in every nook and corner and this has earned him a kind of closeness and has narrowed the gap between the high profile leader and common people.

Western Canadians have not forgotten nor wiped out a comment on comparing the conservative politicians of the west with Quebecers that was made by Prime Minister Justin Trudeau in 2010 when he was preparing for the parliamentary election October 2015. This comment was made on November 2010 in French on the Tele-Quebec program Les Francs-Tireurs (The straight Shooters) He mentioned that Canada was better off in the hands of leaders from Quebec.

The Liberal leadership candidate Justin Trudeau has to explain comments he made about Albertans in 2010, one day after fellow Liberal MP David McGuinty resigned his critic role over pointed comments about Alberta Conservative MPs.

Sun Media published comments on Thursday that Trudeau made in a November 2010 interview in French on the Télé-Québec program *Les Francs-Tireurs* (The Straight Shooters). In the interview, Trudeau seemed to take aim at Alberta politicians, and argued Canada was better off in the hands of leaders from Quebec. He further told interviewer Patrick Lagacé. That "Canada isn't doing well right now because it's Albertans who control our community and socio-democratic agenda. It doesn't work," He was clear in what he said that the great contributions made by prime ministers from Quebec is significant and he also further mentioned about it mentioning some of the recent prime ministers to back up his comments He said that there was Trudeau, there was Mulroney, there was Chrétien, there was Paul Martin. We have a role. This country, Canada, it belongs to us." If he would have compared with Alberta and singled out Quebec, it would not have narrowed his vision.

The hard reaction from the Conservatives reflected and it was heard from Immigration Minister and Alberta MP Jason Kenney said Trudeau's comments were "the worst kind of divisiveness, the worst kind of arrogance of the Liberal Party, and it brings back for many Westerners the kind of arrogance of the National Energy Program, which of course devastated the Western economy. "Though the Conservatives were trying to magnify it and capitalizing for the election victory although some sections of Albertans were very furious, the flame was brought under control to some extent. The Albertans did not forget Pierre Trudeau was instrumental in bringing forward the National Energy Program in the 1980's.

On CBC News Network's *Power & Politics,* Alberta Conservative MP Michelle Rempel called the younger Trudeau's comments "ridiculous" and "insulting

CHAPTER 11

Actualization of Our Vision.

Canada is neither a super power, though if it had the ambition, it certainly could be, nor is Canada in a state of dancing to the tune of another super power. Canada is a well-balanced and enviable nation in the world. It has a stable democratic government, it has one of the best free health services, qualitative education, there is peaceful co-existence between various multicultural groups, low crime rate, a minimum level of biased foreign policy, a high degree of religious and cultural tolerance and appreciation for their contribution for the Canadian mosaic. I have penetrated to some extent into the core of some ethnic groups and visited four out of five continents and intermingled up to a certain extent with them through my personal experiences.

The vision of a nation is not stagnant water; it is like our Lake Ontario continuously flowing. How will the vision for Canada in the near future be shaped and what will be altered, adjusted, deleted, encouraged, supressed, included, excluded, welcomed, blocked, compromised, condemned, restricted, increased or decreased? Major issues such as immigration and emigration, demography, economic activities, political structure, foreign policy, rights and freedom, radicalization, and social services will also adjust and change according to time and circumstances

There are certain prolonged issues that have not been totally addressed and resolved and some of them need to be given priority; meanwhile, there are new challenges unexpectedly arising within Canada in terms of internal matters and ones imported from international issues. Let me summarize the vital ones.

The inclusion of the First Nations in a more efficient and effective way and ensuring their full level of participation by addressing their grievances and fostering reconciliation between the First Nations and non-First Nations people is paramount.

The Indian Act was in effect for the last 140 years and still some of the fundamental issues have not been addressed. Though the Indian Act has undergone numerous amendments since it was first passed in 1876, today it largely retains its original form. As it was mentioned about it on its introduction as such

"To be federally recognized as an Indian either in Canada or the United States, an individual must be able to comply with very distinct standards of government regulation… The *Indian Act* in Canada, in this respect, is much more than a body of laws that for over a century have controlled every aspect of Indian life. As a regulatory regime, the *Indian Act* provides ways of understanding Native identity, organizing a conceptual framework that has shaped contemporary Native life in ways that are now so familiar as to almost seem "natural." Bonita Lawrence.

Again, it is vitally important that the issues facing the First Nations, Metis, and Inuit peoples of this country be addressed properly so that true and meaningful reconciliation can take place and I appreciate to some extent the small contributions made by former Prime Ministers starting from Sir John A MacDonald, Paul Martin, Jean Chrétien as a Minister for Indian Affairs and Pierre Trudeau, former Premier Bob Rae and Justin Trudeau regarding First Nations issues.

The issue of Quebec sovereignty is neither dying nor growing and time will decide how this issue will resolve itself.

I hope that Quebecers, Acadians and the rest of the Canadians, both within the province and in the rest of and Quebecers in other provinces look at this issue broadly and objectively. Canada without Quebec and Quebec without Canada is unimaginable and **Canadians in Quebec** and the rest of Canadians should be considered siblings, not just friends.

In these two respects, First Nations issues are based on cultural identity with our designated provinces and partially by the reserves, but the Quebec nation is bound by a province and is not inclusive of Quebecers and Acadians.

Politically Canada has been one of the few nations in the world practising democracy without any major interruptions, and has a greater power for the people in exercising their rights and freedoms in a somewhat out dated structure of government in which is need of structural changes and it is overdue.

The Senate is one among them and it has not been serving and fulfilling the expectation of being an impartial, patriotic, non-politically biased, chamber of sober second thought. The father of this nation Sir A. John MacDonald clearly mentioned the mandatory functions of the Senate as:

"It must be an independent house, having a free action of its own, for it is only valuable as being a regulating body, calmly considering the legislation initiated by the popular branch and preventing any hasty or ill-considered legislation which may come from that body, but it will never set itself in opposition against the deliberate and understood wishes of the people."

The Senate is a democracy with an unelected second chamber appointed by the Prime Minister who does not provide an independent contribution. Their loyalty might be shared with that of the national interest with the leader of the political party that appointed them. The Senate costs taxpayers about $106,264,100 a year, and each senator makes $132,300 per year and also takes substantial time in passing bills, with the expectation of having its own out put on the basis of the best interest of the nation and it has been met not frequently. I do not mean to say that they have totally ignored their mandate; rather its overall performance could be better, if it would have been elected by the citizens directly or in another form of their participation. The extreme opinion of the late Jack Layton, the former Leader for the New Democratic Party, was clearly expressed in 2007 among the party members in Winnipeg as:

"It's a 19th-century institution that has no place in a modern democracy in the 21st century," and ``out dated and obsolete. ""It's undemocratic because (senators) are appointed by Prime Ministers who then are turfed out of office. But these senators end up leaving a long shadow of their continued presence in the legislative context."

The reformation of the senate based on the constitution of Canada is complicated but it is not impossible and it should take one of the prioritised items on the agenda. Only Parliament and the provincial legislatures can amend the Constitution and Parliament includes the House of Commons with 338 members of parliament and 102 senators and we cannot expect them to axe their position. To make matters more complicated, five of the 10 provinces are so vastly over-represented in the Senate they would hardly agree to get rid of it.

Canadians do not make changes for the sake of change and are also very conservative in their attitudes and love to preserve their treasures of historical wealth such as the political structure and having a positive link with Britain and France from where their forefathers came to this new land. The interesting part is that Americans have a contrasting attitude in these matters. The question of having an elected president instead of a British Royal as the head of state is lingering in some corners but has not erupted as it has in New Zealand. The majority of the Canadians are of the opinion is that it is an honour to have Queen Elizabeth as our head of State and after her reign we will then reconsider whether or not to continue. The pressing need is that in the three main organs of the government, The Queen, the House of the Senate and the House of Commons in a parliamentary system. Only the House of Commons has been elected by the people and expresses the voice of the people and the rest are appointed and it does not give sufficient room for the people to have direct input.

Canada, like many of the developed nations has a trend in the increasing percentage of baby boomers while decreasing in the natural increase in population and this is going to be a serious concern and will have a negative impact in the overall economy. The death rate is going to supersede the birth rate in a few decades. There is no significant means in increasing the natural increase in population substantially, but there is room for some ways to improve it. In a free society it is in the hands of the individuals and their social consciousness rather than the government.

The continuous inflow of new immigrants is unavoidable for having a strong local market on the consumption side and the need for manpower in the production corner. It has come to the point where the priority is that Canada needs them more than they need us. There are some developed nations like Germany and Japan where the total population has been decreasing due to the low natural increase and restrictive migration policies. Canada has to have a strong and suitable immigration policy that should help mitigate the concerns over the brain gain and brain drain.

Freedoms and fundamental rights at times may be restricted when the national security is being challenged particularly by the radicalization from within and outside of Canada. Global radicalization and its increasing challenges towards Canada and making use of Canada for their global network is a serious concern. As far as the government is concerned, their actions must be based on diplomatic moves in preventing attacks. It is very true that Canada as a nation and its internal and international policy, involvements has earned no small degree of enmity, but alliances and commitments with some other nations cannot be stopped.

The U.S flexibility when it comes to keeping a cordial or an arm's length relationship or in between is like the pendulum of a clock in the past years, particularly since the Second World War, when Canada came out of the strong grip of the relationship with the United Kingdom.

Mutual recognition, harmonization, consideration and rationalization of each other are the four main pillars of our relationship in all aspects.

Our relationship with the United States has multiple dimensions, such as the vital position in the sector of the Canadian economy in relation to investments and bilateral trade. Canada is in need of the States more than the States for Canada. Our export market or the US and their investment and technology in Canada are seriously important to us. Around 70% of our exports are constituently and promptly bought by the States and it would not be possible by a single reliable country or trade union like the European Union; therefore we are somewhat obliged or must consider other expectations from the States and how far and long it has to be flexible cannot be written in stone. Sometimes our relationship lies between the mouse and elephant.

Politically and ideologically Canada has no intention in shifting from the current pre enterprise economy and the democratic system of government and in no way is it inclined to consider the next alternative system of government such as the state monopoly by socialist system. Furthermore, it would not move to only a namesake democratic system of government like Mexico. Here there is no room or conflict of interest between the two nations.

Canada is privileged in reaping the fruits from the mass Medias, literature, Hollywood cinema, educational materials and intellectual products. America has made a heavy investment and a lot of research work and time and other resources available to have such colourful and tangible progress. The drawback is that literature; movies and some other products do not get into the core of Canadian life and do not reflect the true value of us. Although fundamentally these products have a similar base, still neither the British nor such products totally reflect Canadian values.

The evolving Canadian foreign policy, so far remains more of a western inclination with slight variations periodically. It is crystal clear as one of the U.S Presidents said their relationship Canada is not like with that of foreign nation, rather it is unique. However, are we going to depend and rely on our defence resources from the US at a higher degree, if not how far we are going to establish our own defence resources to the extend to stand up on our feet when a reign attack occurs or is intended.

The Canadian foreign policy is based on pluralism with willingness to embrace differences with dignity and respect and work closer in a globalized village. Canada is very smart in accommodating people belonging at different levels and backgrounds and still maintains its core values without any major interference or interruptions. In 2015 and 2016 Canada accepted many refugees and then in a short while countries like Germany, Holland, Denmark and Sweden could not handle the situation and got frustrated; in those countries refugees and immigrants were not ready or not willing to become integrated with the mainstream way of life and also proposed to take alternative measures in getting rid of a portion of them and pressuring them in their integration.

Gender inequality is another cloud in the blue sky of Canada. From the United Nations to the corner store, many government and non-government organizations have been making every possible effort if not to bridge, to at least reduce the gap to a minimal level. However, it is fair to say that changes still have to be made. According to recent reports women who have similar or the same qualifications, numbers of years of experiences, skills, age, linguistic skills, hours of working, commitments and all other criteria for the job, in almost all sectors and all level of professions there is a significant gap with income and other promotions. Prime Minister Justin Trudeau has made some symbolic attempts in having gender balance in his cabinet by appointing fifteen women out of thirty one Cabinet positions. When he was addressing a meeting at a women's conference in March 2016 at the United Nations convention hall, he expressed his interest and intentions on gender equality.

"I'm going to keep saying loud and clearly, that I am a feminist. Until it is met with a shrug"

Although in the census, our overall population has slightly higher number of women than men in some ethnic communities like the Indian and Chinese the ratio of males is higher and it was not a relaxation of the natural tendency in birth, rather the intentional terminating of female pregnancies. However, there are nationwide efforts advocating for the elimination of gender biased attitudes, and discrimination in both family and public life.

Multiculturalism is successful in Canada due to I wouldn't say tolerance, but rather our accommodating attitude. We welcome new immigrants, regardless of their entry status, as such refugee claimants, convention refugees, economic class immigrants, investors and do not mind having them in our midst. Since I have been intermingling and participating in multi-ethnic activities, I am able to understand their heart beats on this aspect. There was a degree of intolerance on Asian Immigrants, preferential treatments on western European Immigrants than eastern and Southern Europeans, but today, if is not totally wiped out, it is to a great extent gone. On the other side of the scenes, it is also the responsibly and somewhat an obligation to bend to a reasonable extent and accept the norms of the society of Canada and it is not a matter of a unilateral choice rather a bilateral interaction. We also acknowledge that multiculturalism is fading and is on the verge of dyeing in many parts of Europe. Since the investment on the new Immigrants compared with their output is less, and their presence is vital for the economy, such open door policies and providing warm welcome in the future is unshakable.

I would summarize that the vision for Canada is built from its own foundation with internal and global changes in its own path. Canada having its certain draw backs is still certainly a unique nation. A big thank you goes to the forefathers of Canada for laying a solid and strong foundation for unique, and incomparable values, and also guided the following generations in maintaining and developing this country while overcoming the challenges, internally and globally. The great success for a leader is to have its goal being achieved even after his regime is over and their deeds continued to live. This is what I have witnessed like many others including our forefathers.

I am proud of being a Canadian and having a vision for my beloved nation. I would cite the great vision for Canada by former Prime Minister Pierre Trudeau: "Our hopes are high. Our faith in the people is great. Our courage is strong. And our dreams for this beautiful country will never die."

CHARTS AND STATISTIC S

The Population growth of Canada

	1867 3,463,000	1868 3,511,000	1869 3,565,000	1870 3,625,000
1871 3,689,000	1872 3,754,000	1873 3,826,000	1874 3,895,000	1875 3,954,000
1876 4,009,000	1877 4,064,000	1878 4,120,000	1879 4,185,000	1880 4,255,000
1881 4,325,000	1882 4,375,000	1883 4,430,000	1884 4,487,000	1885 4,537,000
1886 4,580,000	1887 4,626,000	1888 4,678,000	1889 4,729,000	1890 4,779,000
1891 4,833,000	1892 4,883,000	1893 4,931,000	1894 4,979,000	1895 5,026,000
1896 5,074,000	1897 5,122,000	1898 5,175,000	1899 5,235,000	1900 5,301,000
1901 5,371,000	1902 5,494,00051	1903 5,651,000	1904 5,827,000	1905 6,002,000
1906 6,097,000	1907 6,411,000	1908 6,625,000	1909 6,800,000	1910 6,988,000
1911 7,207,000	1912 7,389,000	1913 7,632,000	1914 7,879,000	1915 7,981,000
1916 8,001,000	1917 8,060,000	1918 8,148,000	1919 8,311,000	1920 8,556,000
1921 8,788,000	1922 8,919,000	1923 9,010,000	1924 9,143,000	1925 9,294,000
1926 9,451,000	1927 9,637,000	1928 9,835,000	1929 10,029,000	1930 10,208,000
1931 10,377,000	1932 10,510,000	1933 10,633,000	1934 10,741,000	1935 10,845,000
1936 10,950,000	1937 11,045,000	1938 11,152,000	1939 11,267,000	1940 11,381,000
1941 11,507,000	1942 11,654,000	1943 11,795,000	1944 11,946,000	1945 12,072,000

1946	1947	1948	1949	1950
12,292,000	12,551,000	12,823,000	13,447,000<u>52</u>	13,712,000
1951	**1952**	**1953**	**1954**	**1955**
14,009,000	14,459,000	14,845,000	15,287,000	15,698,000
1956	**1957**	**1958**	**1959**	**1960**
16,081,000	16,610,000	17,080,000	17,483,000	17,870,000
1961	**1962**	**1963**	**1964**	**1965**
18,238,000	18,583,000	18,931,000	19,291,000	19,644,000
1966	**1967**	**1968**	**1969**	**1970**
20,015,000	20,378,000	20,701,000	21,001,000	21,297,000

1971	1972	1973	1974	1975
21,961,999 <u>53</u>	22,218,475	22,491,757	22,807,918	23,143,192
1976	**1977**	**1978**	**1979**	**1980**
23,449,791	23,725,921	23,963,370	24,201,801	24,516,071
1981	**1982**	**1983**	**1984**	**1985**
24,820,393	25,117,442	25,366,969	25,607,651	25,842,736
1986	**1987**	**1988**	**1989**	**1990**
26,101,155	26,448,855	26,795,383	27,281,795	27,697,530
1991	**1992**	**1993**	**1994**	**1995**
28,031,394	28,366,737	28,681,676	28,999,006	29,302,091
1996	**1997**	**1998**	**1999**	**2000**
29,610,757	29,907,172	30,157,082	30,403,878	30,689,035
2001	**2002**	**2003**	**2004**	**2005**
31,021,251	31,372,587	31,676,077	31,989,454	32,299,496
2006	**2007**	**2011**	**2012**	**2013**
32,623,490	32,976,026	33, 476,688	34,880,500	**35,158,300**
2014	2015	**2016 ***		
35,540,400	**34,749,600**	**36,048,500**		

- **Estimated population other than the five years of census**
- *** It is not based on the Census -2016**

<u>1867-1970</u>

Source: CANSIM, table 075-0001 (persons)[i]

1971 to present

Source: CANSIM, United Nations Population Fund has calculated.

Population of the world's countries. These figures can easily change as events such as wars, diseases, breakthroughs in life extension technologies, or dramatic demographic changes would all greatly affect the results. The study projected the world population in 2030 to be 8.321 billion.[1]

Projected rank 2030	Current rank 2014	Change	Country	Projected population (2030)	Population (2010)	Population change (percent)
—	—	—	World	8,321,380,000	6,895,889,000	+20.7%
01	02	+1	India (demographics)	1,523,482,000	1,224,614,000	+24.4%
02	01	−1	China (demographics)	1,393,076,000	1,341,335,000	+3.9%
03	03	=	United States (demographics)	361,680,000	310,384,000	+16.5%
04	04	=	Indonesia (demographics)	279,659,000	239,871,000	+16.6%
05	07	+2	Nigeria (demographics)	257,815,000	158,423,000	+62.7%
06	06	=	Pakistan (demographics)	234,432,000	173,593,000	+35.0%
07	05	−2	Brazil (demographics)	220,492,000	194,946,000	+13.1%
08	08	=	Bangladesh (demographics)	181,863,000	148,692,000	+22.3%
09	09	=	Russia (demographics)	136,429,000	142,958,000	−4.6%
10	11	+1	Mexico (demographics)	135,398,000	113,423,011	+19.4%

Population 65 years and over, Canada, Historical (1971-2011) and Projected (2012-2061)

(percent)

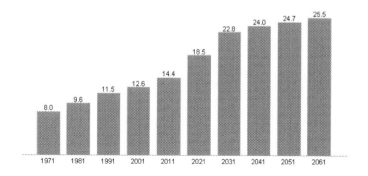

Note: Population projections use a medium-growth scenario (M1) based on interprovincial migration trends from 1981 to 2008. : Statistics Canada *Population Projections for Canada, Provinces and Territories (2009-2036)*. (Cat. No. 91-520 XIE).

Source: HRSDC calculations based on Statistics Canada. *Estimates of population, by age group and sex for July 1, Canada, provinces and territories, annual* (CANSIM Table 051-0001); and Statistics Canada. *Projected population, by projection scenario, sex and age group as of July 1, Canada, provinces and territories, annual* (CANSIM table 052-0005). Ottawa: Statistics Canada, 2011.

Population: Past/Future/World 1950-2050 by continent

Historic, current and future population of

population mid-year	Africa	Americas	Asia	Europe	Oceania	World
1950	228,826,701	339,484,233	1,395,749,366	549,043,373	12,674,996	2,525,778,669
1960	285,270,283	424,790,595	1,694,649,832	605,516,913	15,775,319	3,026,002,942
1970	366,474,876	519,017,284	2,128,630,599	657,369,142	19,680,715	3,691,172,616
1980	478,459,469	618,950,076	2,634,161,250	694,510,142	22,967,861	4,449,048,798
1990	629,986,978	727,488,767	3,213,123,453	723,248,103	26,969,366	5,320,816,667
2000	808,304,337	841,695,330	3,717,371,723	729,105,436	31,223,602	6,127,700,428
2010	1,031,083,666	942,692,345	4,165,440,162	740,308,364	36,658,945	6,916,183,482
2020	1,312,142,128	1,037,448,638	4,581,523,062	743,569,194	42,066,020	7,716,749,042
2030	1,634,366,269	1,120,044,329	4,886,846,140	736,363,555	47,317,181	8,424,937,474
2040	1,998,821,019	1,183,328,314	5,080,418,644	723,887,158	52,232,016	9,038,687,151
2050	2,393,174,892	1,227,766,905	5,164,061,493	709,067,211	56,874,390	9,550,944,891
2060	2,797,337,341	1,256,295,770	5,152,203,354	690,622,327	60,939,796	9,957,398,588
2070	3,195,254,409	1,270,521,911	5,074,752,919	672,504,684	64,305,306	10,277,339,229
2080	3,569,536,916	1,271,719,302	4,957,153,827	658,811,548	66,939,412	10,524,161,005
2090	3,903,238,814	1,263,337,367	4,833,369,114	648,740,397	68,715,329	10,717,401,021
2100	4,184,577,429	1,249,292,969	4,711,514,029	638,815,665	69,648,478	10,853,848,570

United Nations, Department of Economic and Social Affairs, Population Division (2013). World Population Prospects: The 2012 Revision projected populations based on the medium-fertility variant.

Continental Population Shift

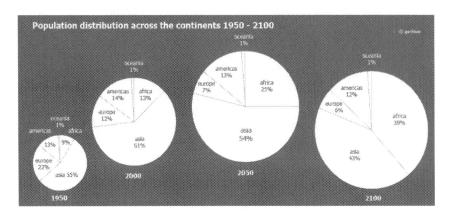

Population distribution across the continents 1950 - 2100

© genhave

1950
oceania 1%
americas 13%
africa 9%
europe 22%
asia 55%

2000
oceania 1%
americas 14%
africa 13%
europe 12%
asia 61%

2050
oceania 1%
americas 13%
europe 7%
africa 25%
asia 54%

2100
oceania 1%
americas 12%
europe 6%
africa 39%
asia 43%

340

Facts and figures

Facts and figures 2013 – Immigration overview: Permanent residents

Canada – Permanent residents by gender and category, 1989 to 2013

Number

Category	1989	1990	1991	1992	1993	1994	1995	1996	1997	1998	1999
Males											
Family class	26,669	33,664	38,780	43,391	47,266	40,021	32,256	28,121	24,079	19,894	21,456
Economic immigrants	45,732	49,931	43,137	47,813	51,005	50,613	53,720	64,496	66,829	51,401	57,833
Refugees	21,745	24,027	33,300	32,091	17,556	11,286	15,436	15,449	13,487	12,332	13,202
Other immigrants	1,671	1,733	2,013	2,719	3,850	3,657	477	2,318	1,900	1,353	539
Category not stated	1	0	0	0	0	0	0	1	0	0	0
Total - Males	95,818	109,355	117,230	126,014	119,677	105,577	101,889	110,385	106,295	84,980	93,030
Females											
Family class	34,275	41,002	49,170	57,718	65,374	54,165	45,122	40,194	35,847	30,970	33,804
Economic immigrants	44,400	47,993	43,357	47,973	54,639	51,692	52,903	60,870	61,520	46,508	51,410
Refugees	15,112	16,191	20,773	20,246	13,035	9,147	12,656	13,025	10,820	10,510	11,196
Other immigrants	1,896	1,868	2,235	2,825	3,901	3,796	283	1,547	1,500	1,194	492
Category not stated	1	0	0	0	0	0	0	0	0	0	0
Total - Females	95,684	107,054	115,535	128,762	136,949	118,800	110,964	115,636	109,687	89,182	96,902
Total males and females											
Family class	60,944	74,666	87,950	101,109	112,640	94,186	77,378	68,315	59,926	50,864	55,260
Economic immigrants	90,132	97,924	86,494	95,786	105,644	102,305	106,623	125,366	128,349	97,909	109,243
Refugees	36,857	40,218	54,073	52,337	30,591	20,433	28,092	28,474	24,307	22,842	24,398
Other immigrants	3,567	3,601	4,248	5,544	7,751	7,453	760	3,865	3,400	2,547	1,031
Category not stated	2	0	0	0	0	0	0	1	0	0	0
Gender not stated	54	46	44	13	12	7	13	49	54	33	19
Grand total	191,556	216,455	232,809	254,789	256,638	224,384	212,866	226,070	216,036	174,195	189,951

Number Category	2000	2001	2002	2003	2004	2005	2006	2007	2008	2009	2010	2011	2012	2013
Males														
Family class	23,290	26,042	24,292	24,867	23,731	25,049	28,521	26,460	26,710	26,979	24,946	23,762	27,541	33,738
Economic immigrants	72,669	82,542	73,666	63,953	70,081	80,900	71,890	67,850	75,750	78,211	94,948	80,013	82,773	75,613
Refugees	16,124	14,922	13,229	13,791	16,972	18,557	16,686	14,286	11,003	11,596	12,608	13,967	11,545	12,124
Other immigrants	260	107	1,561	3,885	3,382	3,256	5,030	5,377	5,145	5,183	4,497	4,037	4,605	3,401
Category not stated	0	1	0	0	0	1	1	1	0	1	3	1	5	0
Total - Males	112,343	123,614	112,748	106,496	114,166	127,763	122,128	113,974	118,608	121,970	137,002	121,780	126,469	124,876
Females														
Family class	37,323	40,743	37,998	40,253	38,541	38,325	41,994	39,780	38,873	38,228	35,278	32,687	37,469	45,946
Economic immigrants	63,613	73,174	64,197	57,093	63,665	75,413	66,358	63,394	73,317	75,280	91,967	76,105	78,048	72,568
Refugees	13,967	12,995	11,881	12,192	15,714	17,217	15,813	13,668	10,856	11,254	12,089	13,906	11,554	11,925
Other immigrants	200	99	2,221	5,311	3,733	3,523	5,345	5,935	5,588	5,440	4,348	4,268	4,355	3,638
Category not stated	0	0	0	1	0	1	1	0	2	0	4	2	0	0
Total - Females	115,103	127,011	116,297	114,850	121,653	134,479	129,511	122,777	128,636	130,202	143,686	126,968	131,426	134,077
Total males and females														
Family class	60,613	66,785	62,290	65,120	62,272	63,374	70,515	66,240	65,583	65,207	60,224	56,449	65,010	79,684
Economic immigrants	136,282	155,716	137,863	121,046	133,746	156,313	138,248	131,244	149,067	153,491	186,915	156,118	160,821	148,181
Refugees	30,091	27,917	25,110	25,983	32,686	35,774	32,499	27,954	21,859	22,850	24,697	27,873	23,099	24,049
Other immigrants	460	206	3,782	9,196	7,115	6,779	10,375	11,312	10,733	10,623	8,845	8,305	8,960	7,039
Category not stated	0	1	0	1	0	2	2	1	2	1	7	3	5	0
Gender not stated	10	12	4	3	4	1	1	2	1	0	0	1	0	0
Grand total	227,456	250,637	229,049	221,349	235,823	262,243	251,640	236,753	247,245	252,172	280,688	248,749	257,895	258,953

Percentage distribution

Category	1989	1990	1991	1992	1993	1994	1995	1996	1997	1998	1999
Males											
Family class	27.8	30.8	33.1	34.4	39.5	37.9	31.7	25.5	22.7	23.4	23.1
Economic immigrants	47.7	45.7	36.8	37.9	42.6	47.9	52.7	58.4	62.9	60.5	62.2
Refugees	22.7	22.0	28.4	25.5	14.7	10.7	15.1	14.0	12.7	14.5	14.2
Other immigrants	1.7	1.6	1.7	2.2	3.2	3.5	0.5	2.1	1.8	1.6	0.6
Category not stated	0.0	0.0	0.0	0.0	0.0	0.0	0.0	0.0	0.0	0.0	0.0
Total - Males	100.0	100.0	100.0	100.0	100.0	100.0	100.0	100.0	100.0	100.0	100.0
Females											
Family class	35.8	38.3	42.6	44.8	47.7	45.6	40.7	34.8	32.7	34.7	34.9
Economic immigrants	46.4	44.8	37.5	37.3	39.9	43.5	47.7	52.6	56.1	52.1	53.1
Refugees	15.8	15.1	18.0	15.7	9.5	7.7	11.4	11.3	9.9	11.8	11.6
Other immigrants	2.0	1.7	1.9	2.2	2.8	3.2	0.3	1.3	1.4	1.3	0.5
Category not stated	0.0	0.0	0.0	0.0	0.0	0.0	0.0	0.0	0.0	0.0	0.0
Total - Females	100.0	100.0	100.0	100.0	100.0	100.0	100.0	100.0	100.0	100.0	100.0
Total males and females											
Family class	31.8	34.5	37.8	39.7	43.9	42.0	36.4	30.2	27.7	29.2	29.1
Economic immigrants	47.1	45.2	37.2	37.6	41.2	45.6	50.1	55.5	59.4	56.2	57.5
Refugees	19.2	18.6	23.2	20.5	11.9	9.1	13.2	12.6	11.3	13.1	12.8
Other immigrants	1.9	1.7	1.8	2.2	3.0	3.3	0.4	1.7	1.6	1.5	0.5
Category not stated	0.0	0.0	0.0	0.0	0.0	0.0	0.0	0.0	0.0	0.0	0.0
Gender not stated	0.0	0.0	0.0	0.0	0.0	0.0	0.0	0.0	0.0	0.0	0.0
Grand total	100.0	100.0	100.0	100.0	100.0	100.0	100.0	100.0	100.0	100.0	100.0

Percentage distribution

Category	2000	2001	2002	2003	2004	2005	2006	2007	2008	2009	2010	2011	2012	2013
Males														
Family class	20.7	21.1	21.5	23.4	20.8	19.6	23.4	23.2	22.5	22.1	18.2	19.5	21.8	27.0
Economic immigrants	64.7	66.8	65.3	60.1	61.4	63.3	58.9	50.5	63.9	64.1	69.3	65.7	65.4	60.6
Refugees	14.4	12.1	11.7	12.9	14.9	14.5	13.7	12.5	9.3	9.5	9.2	11.5	9.1	9.7
Other immigrants	0.2	0.1	1.4	3.6	3.0	2.5	4.1	4.7	4.3	4.2	3.3	3.3	3.6	2.7

Percentage distribution

Category	2000	2001	2002	2003	2004	2005	2006	2007	2008	2009	2010	2011	2012	2013
Category not stated	0.0	0.0	0.0	0.0	0.0	0.0	0.0	0.0	0.0	0.0	0.0	0.0	0.0	0.0
Total - Males	100.0	100.0	100.0	100.0	100.0	100.0	100.0	100.0	100.0	100.0	100.0	100.0	100.0	100.0
Females														
Family class	32.4	32.1	32.7	35.0	31.7	28.5	32.4	32.4	30.2	29.4	24.6	25.7	28.5	34.3
Economic immigrants	55.3	57.6	55.2	49.7	52.3	56.1	51.2	51.6	57.0	57.8	64.0	59.9	59.4	54.1
Refugees	12.1	10.2	10.2	10.6	12.9	12.8	12.2	11.1	8.4	8.6	8.4	11.0	8.8	8.9
Other immigrants	0.2	0.1	1.9	4.6	3.1	2.6	4.1	4.8	4.3	4.2	3.0	3.4	3.3	2.7
Category not stated	0.0	0.0	0.0	0.0	0.0	0.0	0.0	0.0	0.0	0.0	0.0	0.0	0.0	0.0
Total - Females	100.0	100.0	100.0	100.0	100.0	100.0	100.0	100.0	100.0	100.0	100.0	100.0	100.0	100.0
Total males and females														
Family class	26.6	26.6	27.2	29.4	26.4	24.2	28.0	28.0	26.5	25.9	21.5	22.7	25.2	30.8
Economic immigrants	59.9	62.1	60.2	54.7	56.7	59.6	54.9	55.4	60.3	60.9	66.6	62.8	62.4	57.2
Refugees	13.2	11.1	11.0	11.7	13.9	13.6	12.9	11.8	8.8	9.1	8.8	11.2	9.0	9.3
Other immigrants	0.2	0.1	1.7	4.2	3.0	2.6	4.1	4.8	4.3	4.2	3.2	3.3	3.5	2.7
Category not stated	0.0	0.0	0.0	0.0	0.0	0.0	0.0	0.0	0.0	0.0	0.0	0.0	0.0	0.0
Gender not stated	0.0	0.0	0.0	0.0	0.0	0.0	0.0	0.0	0.0	0.0	0.0	0.0	0.0	0.0
Grand total	100.0	100.0	100.0	100.0	100.0	100.0	100.0	100.0	100.0	100.0	100.0	100.0	100.0	100.0

Language ability	2004	2005	2006	2007	2008	2009	2010	2011	2012	2013
Family class										
English	32,872	33,399	35,637	35,857	37,691	37,799	34,559	35,216	31,983	31,397
French	2,386	2,535	2,904	2,639	3,002	2,865	4,358	4,207	3,309	3,652
Both French and English	2,510	2,514	2,727	2,908	2,994	3,093	2,866	2,754	2,496	3,087
Neither	24,507	24,926	29,248	24,838	21,896	21,450	18,441	14,273	27,222	41,548
Total - Family class	**62,275**	**63,374**	**70,516**	**66,242**	**65,583**	**65,207**	**60,224**	**56,450**	**65,010**	**79,684**

344

Language ability	2004	2005	2006	2007	2008	2009	2010	2011	2012	2013
Economic immigrants - p.a.										
English	30,737	36,215	34,650	33,200	39,334	39,439	49,159	40,683	43,307	42,725
French	2,392	2,493	2,597	2,721	2,757	3,111	3,817	3,570	3,982	3,542
Both French and English	12,348	12,367	12,423	13,510	13,903	16,172	16,645	14,335	14,784	12,521
Neither	9,704	10,543	6,049	4,391	5,308	5,282	6,939	5,768	6,191	5,977
Total - Economic immigrants - p.a	**55,181**	**61,618**	**55,719**	**53,822**	**61,302**	**64,004**	**76,560**	**64,356**	**68,264**	**64,765**
Economic immigrants - s.d										
English	29,817	38,386	37,965	36,061	44,759	46,472	57,814	46,882	51,126	45,634
French	3,305	3,602	3,609	3,926	4,381	5,184	5,528	5,237	5,987	5,077
Both French and English	5,713	6,143	5,883	6,308	6,688	7,523	8,271	7,121	7,015	5,345
Neither	39,730	46,564	35,072	31,127	31,938	30,308	38,742	32,522	28,429	27,360
Total - Economic immigrants - s.d	**78,565**	**94,695**	**82,529**	**77,422**	**87,766**	**89,487**	**110,355**	**91,762**	**92,557**	**83,416**
Refugees										
English	15,807	19,790	16,968	13,123	9,480	10,330	11,605	14,956	10,859	9,962
French	2,364	2,705	2,634	2,495	1,695	1,626	2,114	2,506	2,525	2,050
Both French and English	1,776	1,622	883	730	609	752	889	1,495	1,207	899
Neither	12,740	11,658	12,014	11,606	10,075	10,142	10,089	8,916	8,508	11,138
Total - Refugees	**32,687**	**35,775**	**32,499**	**27,954**	**21,859**	**22,850**	**24,697**	**27,873**	**23,099**	**24,049**
Other immigrants										
English	5,476	5,248	7,906	8,967	8,786	8,865	7,206	6,817	7,252	5,523
French	855	731	817	1,042	857	911	1,021	902	861	858
Both French and English	261	364	739	649	431	392	278	268	293	272
Neither	523	436	913	654	659	455	340	318	554	386
Total - Other immigrants	**7,115**	**6,779**	**10,375**	**11,312**	**10,733**	**10,623**	**8,845**	**8,305**	**8,960**	**7,039**
All categories										
English	114,709	133,038	133,126	127,208	140,050	142,905	160,343	144,554	144,527	135,241

Language ability

	2004	2005	2006	2007	2008	2009	2010	2011	2012	2013
French	11,302	12,066	12,561	12,823	12,692	13,697	16,838	16,422	16,664	15,179
Both French and English	22,608	23,010	22,655	24,105	24,625	27,932	28,949	25,973	25,795	22,124
Neither	87,204	94,127	83,296	72,616	69,876	67,637	74,551	61,797	70,904	86,409
Category not stated	0	2	2	1	2	1	7	3	5	0
Grand total	235,823	262,243	251,640	236,753	247,245	252,172	280,688	248,749	257,895	258,953

Percentage distribution

Language ability	2004	2005	2006	2007	2008	2009	2010	2011	2012	2013
Family class										
English	52.8	52.7	50.5	54.1	57.5	58.0	57.4	62.4	49.2	39.4
French	3.8	4.0	4.1	4.0	4.6	4.4	7.2	7.5	5.1	4.6
Both French and English	4.0	4.0	3.9	4.4	4.6	4.7	4.8	4.9	3.8	3.9
Neither	39.4	39.3	41.5	37.5	33.4	32.9	30.6	25.3	41.9	52.1
Total - Family class	100.0	100.0	100.0	100.0	100.0	100.0	100.0	100.0	100.0	100.0
Economic immigrants - p.a										
English	55.7	58.8	62.2	61.7	64.2	61.6	64.2	63.2	63.4	66.0
French	4.3	4.0	4.7	5.1	4.5	4.9	5.0	5.5	5.8	5.5
Both French and English	22.4	20.1	22.3	25.1	22.7	25.3	21.7	22.3	21.7	19.3
Neither	17.6	17.1	10.9	8.2	8.7	8.3	9.1	9.0	9.1	9.2
Total - Economic immigrants - p.a.	100.0	100.0	100.0	100.0	100.0	100.0	100.0	100.0	100.0	100.0
Economic immigrants - s.d.										
English	38.0	40.5	46.0	46.6	51.0	51.9	52.4	51.1	55.2	54.7
French	4.2	3.8	4.4	5.1	5.0	5.8	5.0	5.7	6.5	6.1
Both French and English	7.3	6.5	7.1	8.1	7.6	8.4	7.5	7.8	7.6	6.4
Neither	50.6	49.2	42.5	40.2	36.4	33.9	35.1	35.4	30.7	32.8
Total - Economic immigrants - s.d.	100.0	100.0	100.0	100.0	100.0	100.0	100.0	100.0	100.0	100.0
Refuges										

Percentage distribution

Language ability	2004	2005	2006	2007	2008	2009	2010	2011	2012	2013
English	48.4	55.3	52.2	46.9	43.4	45.2	47.0	53.7	47.0	41.4
French	7.2	7.6	8.1	8.9	7.8	7.1	8.6	9.0	10.9	8.5
Both French and English	5.4	4.5	2.7	2.6	2.8	3.3	3.6	5.4	5.2	3.7
Neither	39.0	32.6	37.0	41.5	46.1	44.4	40.9	32.0	36.8	46.3
Total - Refugees	100.0	100.0	100.0	100.0	100.0	100.0	100.0	100.0	100.0	100.0
Other immigrants										
English	77.0	77.4	76.2	79.3	81.9	83.5	81.5	82.1	80.9	78.5
French	12.0	10.8	7.9	9.2	8.0	8.6	11.5	10.9	9.6	12.2
Both French and English	3.7	5.4	7.1	5.7	4.0	3.7	3.1	3.2	3.3	3.9
Neither	7.4	6.4	8.8	5.8	6.1	4.3	3.8	3.8	6.2	5.5
Total - Other immigrants	100.0	100.0	100.0	100.0	100.0	100.0	100.0	100.0	100.0	100.0
All categories										
English	48.6	50.7	52.9	53.7	56.6	56.7	57.1	58.1	56.0	52.2
French	4.8	4.6	5.0	5.4	5.1	5.4	6.0	6.6	6.5	5.9
Both French and English	9.6	8.8	9.0	10.2	10.0	11.1	10.3	10.4	10.0	8.5
Neither	37.0	35.9	33.1	30.7	28.3	26.8	26.6	24.8	27.5	33.4
Category not stated	0.0	0.0	0.0	0.0	0.0	0.0	0.0	0.0	0.0	0.0
Grand total	100.0	100.0	100.0	100.0	100.0	100.0	100.0	100.0	100.0	100.0

Footnote *pa; Principal applicants

Canada – Permanent residents by category and language ability,

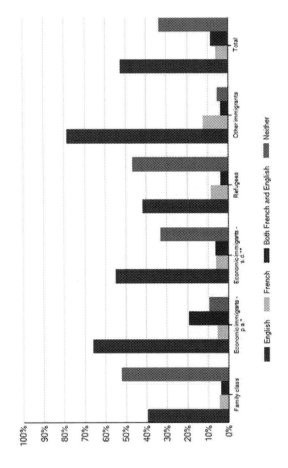

English   French   Both French and English   Neither

348

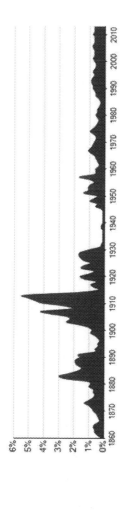

Year	1860	1861	1862	1863	1864	1865	1866	1867	1868	1869
Number	6,276	13,589	18,294	21,000	24,779	18,958	11,427	10,666	12,765	18,630
% of Population	0.2	0.4	0.6	0.6	0.7	0.6	0.3	0.3	0.4	0.5

Year	1870	1871	1872	1873	1874	1875	1876	1877	1878	1879
Number	24,706	27,773	36,578	50,050	39,373	27,382	25,633	27,082	29,807	40,492
% of Population	0.7	0.8	1.0	1.3	1.0	0.7	0.6	0.7	0.7	1.0

Year	1880	1881	1882	1883	1884	1885	1886	1887	1888	1889
Number	38,505	47,991	112,458	133,624	103,824	76,169	69,152	84,526	88,766	91,600
% of Population	0.9	1.1	2.6	3.0	2.3	1.7	1.5	1.8	1.9	1.9

Year	1890	1891	1892	1893	1894	1895	1896	1897	1898	1899
Number	75,067	82,165	30,996	29,633	20,829	18,790	16,835	21,716	31,900	44,543
% of Population	1.6	1.7	0.6	0.6	0.4	0.4	0.3	0.4	0.6	0.9

Year	1900	1901	1902	1903	1904	1905	1906	1907	1908	1909
Number	41,681	55,747	89,102	138,660	131,252	141,465	211,653	272,409	143,326	173,694
% of Population	0.8	1.0	1.6	2.5	2.3	2.4	3.5	4.2	2.2	2.6

Year	1910	1911	1912	1913	1914	1915	1916	1917	1918	1919
Number	286,839	331,288	375,756	400,870	150,484	33,665	55,914	72,910	41,845	107,698
% of Population	4.1	4.6	5.1	5.3	1.9	0.4	0.7	0.9	0.5	1.3

Year	1920	1921	1922	1923	1924	1925	1926	1927	1928	1929
Number	138,824	91,728	64,224	133,729	124,164	84,907	135,982	158,886	166,783	164,993
% of Population	1.6	1.0	0.7	1.5	1.4	0.9	1.4	1.6	1.7	1.6

Year	1930	1931	1932	1933	1934	1935	1936	1937	1938	1939
Number	104,806	27,530	20,591	14,382	12,476	11,277	11,643	15,101	17,244	16,994
% of Population	1.0	0.3	0.2	0.1	0.1	0.1	0.1	0.1	0.2	0.2

Year	1940	1941	1942	1943	1944	1945	1946	1947	1948	1949
Number	11,324	9,329	7,576	8,504	12,801	22,722	71,719	64,127	125,414	95,217
% of Population	0.1	0.1	0.1	0.1	0.1	0.2	0.6	0.5	1.0	0.7

Year	1950	1951	1952	1953	1954	1955	1956	1957	1958	1959
Number	73,912	194,391	164,498	168,868	154,227	109,946	164,857	282,164	124,851	106,928
% of Population	0.5	1.4	1.1	1.1	1.0	0.7	1.0	1.7	0.7	0.6

Year	1960	1961	1962	1963	1964	1965	1966	1967	1968	1969
Number	104,111	71,698	74,856	93,151	112,606	146,758	194,743	222,876	183,974	164,531
% of Population	0.6	0.4	0.4	0.5	0.6	0.7	1.0	1.1	0.9	0.8

Year	1970	1971	1972	1973	1974	1975	1976	1977	1978	1979
Number	147,713	121,900	122,006	184,200	218,465	187,881	149,429	114,914	86,313	112,093
% of Population	0.7	0.6	0.6	0.8	1.0	0.8	0.6	0.5	0.4	0.5

Year	1980	1981	1982	1983	1984	1985	1986	1987	1988	1989
Number	143,137	128,642	121,175	89,186	88,272	84,347	99,355	152,079	161,588	191,556
% of Population	0.6	0.5	0.5	0.4	0.3	0.3	0.4	0.6	0.6	0.7

Year	1990	1991	1992	1993	1994	1995	1996	1997	1998	1999
Number	216,455	232,809	254,789	256,638	224,384	212,866	226,070	216,036	174,195	189,951
% of Population	0.8	0.8	0.9	0.9	0.8	0.7	0.8	0.7	0.6	0.6

Year	2000	2001	2002	2003	2004	2005	2006	2007	2008	2009
Number	227,456	250,637	229,049	221,349	235,823	262,243	251,640	236,753	247,245	252,172
% of Population	0.7	0.8	0.7	0.7	0.7	0.8	0.8	0.7	0.7	0.7

Year	2010	2011	2012	2013
Number	280,688	248,749	257,895	258,953
% of Population	0.8	0.7	0.7	0.7

Facts and figures 2013 – Immigration overview: Permanent residents

Canada – Permanent residents by source country

Source country	2004	2005	2006	2007	2008	2009	2010	2011	2012	2013
People's Republic of China	36,620	42,584	33,518	27,642	30,037	29,622	30,391	28,503	33,024	34,126
India	28,235	36,210	33,847	28,742	28,261	29,457	34,235	27,509	30,932	33,085
Philippines	14,004	18,139	18,400	19,837	24,888	28,573	38,617	36,765	34,314	29,539
Pakistan	13,399	14,314	13,127	10,124	8,994	7,217	6,811	7,468	11,227	12,602
Iran	6,348	5,837	7,480	6,974	6,475	6,580	7,477	7,479	7,533	11,291
United States of America	6,990	8,394	9,613	9,463	10,190	8,995	8,142	7,675	7,891	8,495
United Kingdom and Colonies	7,533	7,258	7,140	8,216	8,979	8,876	8,724	6,204	6,195	5,826
France	4,391	4,429	4,002	4,290	4,532	5,051	4,646	4,080	6,280	5,624
Iraq	1,796	2,226	1,788	2,406	3,543	5,450	5,941	6,196	4,041	4,918
Republic of Korea	5,352	5,832	6,215	5,920	7,294	5,874	5,537	4,589	5,315	4,509
Algeria	3,616	3,626	4,807	3,623	4,005	5,393	4,752	4,325	3,774	4,331
Nigeria	1,518	2,236	2,594	2,375	2,109	3,156	3,906	3,103	3,443	4,173
Egypt	2,393	2,496	2,190	2,356	3,347	3,496	5,982	4,663	5,555	4,164
Haiti	1,652	1,682	1,619	1,598	2,491	2,080	4,744	6,504	5,868	4,143
Mexico	2,259	2,837	2,844	3,239	2,856	3,092	3,865	3,948	4,227	3,996
Bangladesh	2,660	4,171	4,014	2,897	2,939	2,104	4,721	2,694	2,640	3,789
Colombia	4,566	6,424	6,535	5,357	5,452	4,652	5,218	4,366	3,739	3,632
Morocco	3,686	2,939	3,322	4,021	4,226	5,532	6,242	4,399	3,876	3,259

Canada – Permanent residents by source country

Source country	2004	2005	2006	2007	2008	2009	2010	2011	2012	2013
Ukraine	2,431	2,270	1,973	2,218	1,937	2,367	3,159	2,516	2,265	2,487
Jamaica	2,237	1,945	1,722	2,141	2,334	2,456	2,321	2,059	2,182	2,477
Russia	3,989	3,972	3,117	2,983	2,690	2,931	2,288	1,963	2,079	2,466
Federal Republic of Cameroon	436	604	697	1,025	1,279	1,344	1,800	1,638	2,507	2,439
Sri Lanka	4,495	4,930	4,714	4,123	4,756	4,547	4,422	3,309	3,338	2,395
Lebanon	3,293	3,709	3,802	3,467	3,566	3,077	3,432	3,072	1,614	2,172
Socialist Republic of Vietnam	1,816	1,852	3,153	2,574	1,784	2,171	1,942	1,723	1,731	2,112
Democratic Republic of Congo	1,465	1,521	1,623	1,466	1,397	1,581	1,239	1,224	1,714	2,050
Democratic Republic of Somalia	1,364	1,198	1,061	1,166	1,015	1,214	1,528	1,535	1,582	2,028
Afghanistan	2,978	3,436	3,009	2,652	2,111	1,746	1,758	2,203	2,635	2,004
Israel	2,788	2,446	2,625	2,401	2,562	2,316	2,755	1,970	2,134	1,945
Eritrea	414	528	700	699	799	904	931	1,182	1,335	1,718
Brazil	917	969	1,181	1,746	2,138	2,509	2,598	1,508	1,642	1,712
Tunisia	764	756	1,065	869	950	1,195	1,299	1,442	1,503	1,627
Ethiopia	1,535	1,506	1,801	1,512	1,613	1,289	1,865	2,163	1,864	1,605
Romania	5,755	5,048	4,468	3,834	2,837	2,076	1,922	1,776	1,588	1,512
Cuba	866	999	1,064	1,350	1,300	1,433	961	962	1,304	1,402
Nepal	404	607	540	511	581	561	1,392	1,129	1,185	1,308
Jordan	1,733	1,940	1,827	1,421	1,581	1,235	1,831	1,635	1,206	1,255

Canada – Permanent residents by source country

Source country	2004	2005	2006	2007	2008	2009	2010	2011	2012	2013
Republic of South Africa	1,175	988	1,111	1,200	1,123	1,188	1,238	959	1,243	1,240
Moldova	628	655	803	1,099	1,127	1,535	1,988	1,367	1,416	1,231
Federal Republic of Germany	2,020	2,226	2,767	2,449	3,833	3,887	2,956	2,053	1,702	1,217
Mauritius	702	696	512	507	714	872	1,455	1,146	799	1,203
Republic of Ivory Coast	256	294	431	619	646	668	1,066	636	1,024	1,170
Australia	930	909	875	1,033	1,018	1,018	933	851	982	1,121
Venezuela	1,224	1,211	1,192	1,335	1,239	1,353	998	1,452	1,373	1,022
Republic of Ireland	244	224	283	300	412	395	548	525	725	1,015
Syria	1,116	1,458	1,145	1,056	919	917	1,039	1,004	650	1,009
Japan	973	1,067	1,212	1,250	1,284	1,194	1,168	1,265	1,214	982
Poland	1,533	1,405	1,263	1,235	1,267	1,013	795	720	779	851
Senegal	210	278	416	433	555	668	765	740	949	818
Hong Kong	536	729	712	674	897	657	623	591	728	774
Taiwan	2,012	3,097	2,818	2,766	2,993	2,472	2,629	1,704	985	773
Turkey	1,736	2,065	1,638	1,463	1,122	1,238	1,492	1,257	1,068	729
Peru	1,460	1,653	1,473	1,490	1,094	1,884	1,283	886	787	682
Kenya	685	693	622	449	453	489	507	585	725	664
Guyana	1,341	1,215	1,286	1,277	1,137	1,181	953	804	676	656
El Salvador	442	436	430	929	1,115	845	787	690	641	639
Portugal	336	338	424	405	665	623	629	528	560	629

Canada – Permanent residents by source country

Source country	2004	2005	2006	2007	2008	2009	2010	2011	2012	2013
Albania	1,450	1,223	856	702	560	716	561	539	620	603
Dominican Republic	270	303	294	311	438	391	479	739	604	589
Italy	334	344	325	320	370	429	434	374	440	545
St. Vincent and the Grenadines	294	343	383	579	434	511	434	451	523	538
Ghana	738	851	710	688	629	659	802	528	531	517
Bulgaria	2,022	1,738	1,419	1,172	994	784	556	365	451	512
Bhutan	--	5	10	--	36	865	1,464	1,879	1,075	487
Burundi	559	626	468	614	448	566	529	604	684	477
Republic of Guinea	281	256	342	415	327	347	395	352	407	463
Palestinian Authority (Gaza/ West Bank)	376	453	627	441	481	400	654	555	533	462
Stateless	921	842	845	656	622	542	701	563	487	458
Republic of Trinidad & Tobago	730	857	794	975	1,002	1,134	915	588	586	427
Hungary	671	516	520	425	383	312	354	287	300	424
Ecuador	417	491	525	419	437	373	353	348	282	418
New Zealand	350	370	318	350	480	520	490	375	417	414
Rwanda	299	378	360	420	358	415	396	492	562	409
Zimbabwe	1,450	615	454	663	611	508	494	434	437	407
Thailand	392	575	500	487	519	512	499	396	296	400
Peoples Republic of Benin	112	95	116	183	205	238	290	284	391	397

Canada – Permanent residents by source country

Source country	2004	2005	2006	2007	2008	2009	2010	2011	2012	2013
The Netherlands	749	813	837	615	818	786	759	586	504	395
St. Lucia	110	185	190	255	298	257	249	261	382	390
Republic of Indonesia	552	632	613	657	661	504	712	390	395	386
Belgium	411	400	302	363	335	358	363	332	402	379
Honduras	133	166	164	165	187	169	386	538	436	350
Kazakhstan	545	506	408	436	394	431	377	381	462	348
Guatemala	217	190	230	258	263	264	266	288	358	345
Democratic Republic of Sudan	1,823	1,310	1,039	683	622	422	612	531	444	340
Spain	133	126	124	137	169	195	174	179	262	331
Burkina Faso	97	91	147	136	139	162	186	144	269	322
Republic of Togo	163	157	149	235	351	400	354	261	299	315
Greece	120	100	74	110	107	119	101	102	146	298
Republic of Serbia			–	50	259	365	267	299	395	297
Cambodia	348	370	529	460	354	203	200	196	233	288
Argentina	1,591	1,153	847	620	540	467	459	278	263	282
Chile	383	384	427	530	350	375	340	174	291	273
Saudi Arabia	128	198	252	188	249	246	330	278	286	267
Myanmar (Burma)	191	210	953	1,887	975	1,153	556	368	193	262
Libya	196	196	281	198	306	282	384	352	299	255
Belarus	543	558	439	568	524	454	438	357	277	247

357

Canada – Permanent residents by source country

Source country	2004	2005	2006	2007	2008	2009	2010	2011	2012	2013
Madagascar	79	88	96	115	118	169	178	148	165	229
Fiji	495	298	277	304	321	311	398	316	270	228
Republic of Yemen	124	161	140	122	133	128	211	160	174	217
Latvia	94	77	69	88	67	85	70	103	202	213
Armenia	147	224	218	198	205	267	252	236	258	207
Uganda	160	239	201	170	204	185	216	213	222	206
Malaysia	401	593	580	600	658	640	802	409	358	204
Switzerland	337	270	258	308	357	328	285	266	243	201
Republic of Djibouti	67	93	68	50	47	70	123	127	164	194
Republic of Mali	87	87	114	143	154	164	170	155	191	190
United Republic of Tanzania	310	274	291	195	230	136	200	215	224	182
Czech Republic	191	193	146	137	104	159	168	128	173	173
Republic of Kosovo					6	113	233	215	152	171
Grenada	296	283	363	360	284	325	208	173	142	170
Central Africa Republic	13	49	18	30	28	19	26	18	45	169
Uzbekistan	175	330	262	284	215	288	289	162	235	167
Lithuania	220	167	113	108	109	63	57	52	77	145
Singapore	311	392	298	690	734	366	805	219	146	141
Sweden	129	205	139	193	165	167	159	134	140	140
Croatia	151	128	102	102	131	92	91	135	112	125

Canada – Permanent residents by source country

Source country	2004	2005	2006	2007	2008	2009	2010	2011	2012	2013
Georgia	106	114	125	132	112	128	126	139	147	125
Kyrgyzstan	245	173	161	135	168	173	157	159	278	123
Costa Rica	165	188	279	281	246	217	190	149	183	122
Bosnia-Herzegovina	188	211	217	209	182	156	168	140	121	119
People's Republic of the Congo	142	136	143	87	72	70	75	81	91	114
Macedonia	443	285	256	211	191	198	188	130	126	112
Bolivia	85	134	139	107	143	214	180	86	83	107
Republic of the Niger	38	59	57	75	75	82	80	90	95	105
Slovak Republic	597	369	241	215	125	128	135	134	136	105
People's Republic of Mongolia	34	59	64	82	59	118	169	103	68	99
Barbados	90	111	97	130	134	125	121	97	132	97
Nicaragua	67	79	96	76	124	116	94	123	106	96
Austria	118	122	102	98	91	109	124	84	102	90
Gabon Republic	33	67	68	101	86	86	64	63	74	90
Republic of Chad	92	126	96	131	95	87	98	79	97	86
Namibia	9	6	19	13	26	14	16	23	24	82
Denmark	89	62	101	97	108	81	92	93	94	81
Republic of Botswana	9	7	11	8	28	15	42	53	64	76
Finland	54	67	51	62	89	63	63	72	62	76
Iceland	23	10	--	15	13	15	30	38	42	72

Canada – Permanent residents by source country

Source country	2004	2005	2006	2007	2008	2009	2010	2011	2012	2013
Paraguay	74	75	88	98	95	88	89	83	55	66
Sierra Leone	347	191	138	92	103	70	63	96	72	61
Norway	73	57	53	73	66	75	46	49	53	59
Zambia	56	91	77	71	64	60	102	69	46	59
Uruguay	130	217	175	147	160	99	93	81	47	58
Azerbaijan	230	359	236	203	125	165	209	138	161	57
Mauritania	60	86	124	96	112	83	74	54	77	57
The Bahamas Islands	13	14	18	23	30	27	25	40	60	55
Belize	25	37	24	28	48	38	39	36	34	53
Dominica	50	59	72	79	60	59	43	36	43	48
Kuwait	74	66	35	62	53	68	67	58	73	48
United Arab Emirates	41	31	42	37	33	37	86	60	54	46
Angola	268	295	184	106	76	62	61	39	70	45
Estonia	27	26	18	34	34	26	28	15	26	45
Republic of Panama	38	57	73	63	52	73	65	49	34	43
Liberia	409	581	356	153	74	94	162	106	58	39
Tajikistan	14	85	46	44	15	50	52	47	34	39
Serbia and Montenegro	29	441	693	792	456	204	109	39	32	34
Gambia	10	29	38	32	25	10	37	24	18	33
Bahrain	12	12	12	22	9	35	28	21	39	32

Canada – Permanent residents by source country

Source country	2004	2005	2006	2007	2008	2009	2010	2011	2012	2013
Macao	21	21	32	16	12	21	21	13	33	29
Antigua and Barbuda	14	24	32	15	32	38	27	37	51	25
Comoros	--	5	7	11	--	19	22	14	18	22
Slovenia	17	23	11	29	18	27	12	13	36	20
St. Kitts-Nevis	8	11	--	10	25	11	22	12	21	18
People's Democratic Republic of Korea	15	14	10	7	19	11	45	96	66	17
Cyprus	11	7	9	--	7	6	18	6	12	16
Laos	38	42	74	53	32	39	54	22	25	15
Turkmenistan	16	40	26	37	13	20	30	20	20	14
Oman	12	14	18	16	10	7	14	10	13	11
Malawi	17	23	15	13	5	10	28	16	9	10
Republic of Montenegro	0	0	0	7	18	10	14	19	26	9
Luxembourg	9	10	9	9	--	--	8	11	6	7
Yugoslavia	733	329	138	99	95	48	46	17	12	7
Seychelles	15	25	8	9	18	--	10	10	6	5
Country not stated	36	65	80	24	5	0	7	6	13	32
Other countries	104	112	104	92	107	120	120	77	94	112
Total	235,823	262,243	251,640	236,753	247,245	252,172	280,688	248,749	257,895	258,953

Note: Source country is based on Country of Citizenship

Canada – Permanent residents by top source countries, 2011-2013

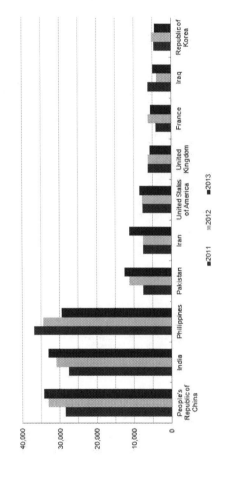

References

1. Barbara A. Crow   Open Boundaries

2. Peter S.L   Race and Ethnic Relations in Canada

3. Cornelius Jaenen, Cecilia Morgan Documents in Confederation History

4. David Matas, Llana Simon   Closing the Doors

5. Mel Hurtig   The Vanishing Country

6. Richard Gwyn   Nationalism without Walls

7. Heather Robertson   Reservations are for Indians

8. Myrna Kostash   The Next Canada

9. Michael Harris   Party of One

10. Raymond Breton, Jeffrey G. Reitz, Victor Valentine   Cultural Boundaries and the Cohesion of Canada

11. Peter Stalker   The Work of Strangers

12. Paul R. Ehrlich Anne H. Ehrlich   The Population Explosion

13. Andre Pratte   Reconquering Canada

14. Alison M. Konrad   Cases in Gender and Diversity in Organizations

15. Valerie Knowles   Strangers at Our Gates

16. Bernard Ostry, Janice Yalden   Visions of Canada

17. Ninette Kelley, Michael Trebilcock   The Making of the Mosaic

18. Joe Clark   A Nation Too Good to lose

19. Janine Brodie, Linda Trimle   Reinventing Canada

20. Robert K. Logan   The Sixth Language

21. Paul Wells   The Longer I'm Prime Minister Stephen Harper and Canada, 2006 William Johnson

22. William Johnson   Stephen Harper and the Future of Canada

23. Jean Chretien   My Years as Prime Minister

24. Justin Trudeau   Common Ground

25. Hilary Rodham Clinton   Hard Choices

26. Michael Welss, Hassan Hassan   ISIS

27. The Arab Spring

28. James Fergusson   Taliban

29. Marc Lynch   The Arab Uprising

30. Elspeth Cameron   Multiculturalism & Immigration in Canada

31. Citizenship and Immigration   Facts and Figure

32. Statistics Canada

33. Samy Appadurai   Canada a Nation in Motion

INDEX

Printed in the United States
By Bookmasters